NATURE'S MESSENGER

ALSO BY PATRICK DEAN

A Window to Heaven

NATURE'S MESSENGER

MARK CATESBY AND HIS
ADVENTURES IN A NEW WORLD

PATRICK DEAN

PEGASUS BOOKS
NEW YORK LONDON

NATURE'S MESSENGER

Pegasus Books, Ltd.
148 West 37th Street, 13th Floor
New York, NY 10018

Copyright © 2023 by Patrick Dean

First Pegasus Books cloth edition June 2023

Interior design by Maria Fernandez

Library of Congress Cataloging-in-Publication Data is available.

ISBN: 978-1-63936-413-8

10 9 8 7 6 5 4 3 2

Printed in the United States of America
Distributed by Simon & Schuster
www.pegasusbooks.com

To

Arthur Edwin Dean (1916–1972)
Concetta Maria Cicero Dean (1918–1972)

and once again,

to

Susan

CONTENTS

AUTHOR'S NOTE

Throughout this book, I have retained the spelling, punctuation, and capitalization used in the primary sources, including Mark Catesby's writings. For the sake of clarity, the eighteenth-century custom of using *f* interchangeably with *s* will not be followed, so the reader will not need "affiftance" in that regard. And although Charles Town did not officially become Charleston until 1783, I will use "Charleston" for consistency except for direct quotations.

Nothing in the following is meant necessarily to excuse or defend the words, actions, or beliefs of the personages therein, including Mark Catesby. To describe someone's interactions with the institution of slavery, or with Native Americans, is not to justify or excuse them.

PROLOGUE

Two weeks of stiff westerly winds had prevented the ship from England from entering Charleston harbor. But finally, on May 3, 1722, a tall Englishman stepped ashore in the British royal colony of South Carolina. Intense but affable, he carried himself like the landed gentleman he was, and the crew of the transatlantic schooner would have unloaded his luggage with deference. A member of Royal Governor Francis Nicholson's household staff met the Englishman, whose name was Mark Catesby, at one of the town's two "bridges," or wharves. Catesby would have stepped onto Bay Street with relief; the voyage, though uneventful, had lasted three months with the two-week delay.

Governor Nicholson was Catesby's sponsor as well as his host. During Catesby's previous trip to North America, traveling in Virginia and the Caribbean between 1712 and 1719, he had made a name for himself by supplying naturalists, collectors, and plantsmen in England with specimens and striking watercolors of American plants and animals. In an age that elevated the collection and classification of the natural world into a fashionable avocation and near-obsession, Nicholson and others in British social and scientific circles knew Catesby to be someone who was knowledgeable about flora and fauna, willing to travel and explore, and skilled at illustrating what he found—in short, perfectly suited, in Catesby's words, "to discribe the Natural productions of the Country."

For that reason, Nicholson and nine other prominent Englishmen had agreed to underwrite Catesby's journey of exploration in South Carolina. To the governor's mind, Catesby was the person they needed to "Observe the Rarities of the Country for the Uses and Purposes of the [Royal] Society."

The Society—formally, The Royal Society of London for Improving Natural Knowledge—was the most eminent gathering of scientifically minded men in Britain, having been granted a charter by King Charles II in 1662. From its very inception, the Royal Society included such giants of the scientific world as the famous architect and astronomer Christopher Wren; Robert Boyle, considered the father of chemistry; and Isaac Newton, who in 1722 was serving as president of the Society. With such powerful and influential "Fellows," as they were called (and still are), the Society gave institutional shape to the quest for knowledge across the English-speaking world. To its members, Britain's colonial settlements, including those along the eastern coast of the vast American continent, were unparalleled frontiers of discovery.

Mark Catesby's obligation, and his obsession, was to explore that American frontier—to seek out and document the flora and fauna of this largely unknown land. He was to collect, draw, and describe as many of the trees, bushes, flowers, birds, mammals, insects, and fish as he could. In England, nobles, nurserymen, and wealthy merchants expected live plantings and seeds from him for their private gardens, herbariums, and businesses. Before his time in America was through, however, Catesby would chafe under those expectations.

◆

Mark Catesby's early life gave him an ideal background from which to enable his ambitions. The Catesbys and his mother's family, the Jekylls, were not only established gentry in eastern England with property in London; they were also intellectually inclined, with careers in law and public service. Mark Catesby grew up surrounded by a network of correspondence about and interest in the natural world. One of England's most renowned clergyman-naturalists, John Ray, lived near and was close friends with Catesby's uncle, Nicholas Jekyll, who kept a botanical garden at his estate in Castle Hedingham, Essex.

The grammar school in Catesby's area was known for its academic rigor. William Byrd II of Virginia, who would play an outsize role at the beginning of Catesby's career as a naturalist and horticulturalist, came to England to attend the school, and two of Catesby's brothers were students. Though details of Mark Catesby's education are lost to history, he was obviously furnished with the tools for his future artistic, scientific, and literary success.

In 1712 Catesby accompanied his sister Elizabeth to Virginia, where she joined her husband; he carried with him not only the intellectual training he had received in natural history and botany, but also the social connections engendered by his family status and education. To this he had added skills and abilities which would make possible his crowning achievement. He taught himself drawing and painting, and later etching; his original eye and independence of style would inspire artists and naturalists such as Audubon and Humboldt a century or more later. His compositions look strikingly modern; his snakes curl and writhe in rhythm with the vines they're paired with, and you can almost hear his "Blew Jay" scream.

Catesby would also show himself capable of "living rough," braving the elements to collect, analyze, and illustrate specimens in the wild. Finally, he had formed a personality which would allow him to interact, throughout his career, with the richest and most powerful people in Britain and the Americas as well as with Native Americans, enslaved Blacks, and his fellow naturalists.

Although there had been English settlements in North America since the founding of Jamestown, Virginia, in 1607, no one in the succeeding century had published images of the birds, mammals, and plants there. Few in Great Britain had seen an image of the immense, boldly colored ivory-billed woodpecker, the creamy petals and red-coated seeds of a southern magnolia tree, or the distinctive features of an American bullfrog. This was the gap that Mark Catesby was determined to fill. While meeting his patrons' demands for plant specimens and "rarities" of the animal and insect world, Catesby also had in mind a masterwork of natural history, a comprehensive book containing startlingly bold and innovative depictions of the world as he saw it, with its complex interactions and its wild beauty.

A modern Catesby scholar has described this masterwork, *The Natural History of Carolina, Florida, and the Bahama Islands,* as "the earliest and most important examination of environmental relationships" of this era and place, extending beyond animals and plants to "the ways in which English colonists, enslaved peoples of African descent, and native Americans were coming together—by choice or by coercion—to forge a new social order." Catesby's observations on the variations in cedar trees due to climate and location even anticipate Charles Darwin's theories of natural selection a century later. From the edge of empire, Catesby would bring back insights into not only the natural world of birds and beasts, but the human world of profit and war, collaboration and conflict.

◆

As anyone familiar with the lives of the American Founding Fathers knows, the eighteenth century, often called the Age of Reason, had its shameful shadow, cast by a practice that was anything but reasonable. George Washington and Thomas Jefferson may have read Paine, Locke, and Hume, but their political and intellectual preoccupations existed side by side with their legal possession of other human beings. In the same way, Britain's reach toward dominance of the seas and of the world economy cannot be separated from its colonial and imperial project. The Royal Society's desire for knowledge of the far corners of the globe was inextricably linked to the larger movement toward commercial and political dominance which, a century later, would lead to the British Empire at its most extensive.

They had no way of knowing it, but the British of Catesby's day were on the edge of a kind of historical liftoff. Two effects of the Treaty of Utrecht, which ended the War of Spanish Succession nine years before his arrival in Charleston, would reshape the world. First, the general European peace created calm and stability, especially in flashpoints of conflict such as the Caribbean, where France, Spain, and England had furiously squabbled for over a century. Second, Spain gave Britain the *Asiento de Negros*—the commercial license to ship enslaved Africans to the New World. The rise of Britain as the dominant maritime and commercial power in the world was now fully underway, abetted by this new ability to traffic legally in human beings. Only fifty years later, the phrase "this vast empire on which the sun never sets" would be used in print for the first time to describe Great Britain's global reach.

The same ships that brought settlers and visitors like Catesby to the American colonies also brought enslaved people from Africa and the West Indies. At a time when Barbados and Jamaica were the richest colonies of the Crown, South Carolina in the 1720s was just settling on rice as its main cash crop. That fateful decision would turn the colony, as it had the islands of the Caribbean, into a single-crop, labor-intensive, slavery-dependent economy and culture. Nor would Catesby be immune to the prevailing European view of slavery; he would seek to purchase an enslaved African boy to assist him on his journeys of exploration into the American interior.

Importantly, however, Catesby also sought out enslaved Africans on South Carolina Lowcountry plantations, curious to learn about the plants they grew for food and for medicinal purposes. Though never expressing opposition to the institution of slavery, Catesby could be an acerbic critic of what he saw as mistreatment of enslaved Africans—even that of his friend William Byrd. For Catesby's curious and probing mind, the interesting question was the relationships created when two new cultures, white European and African, were introduced into the native landscape of America. What would result from this dynamic and powerful process; what beneficial and harmful outcomes could be observed in this blending of influences?

◆

Catesby's explorations likewise brought him into close contact with another culture that was doomed to fall victim to Western colonialism and imperialism. The narrow strip of Lowcountry along the coast which contained Charleston may have been genteel, with English furniture and harpsichord lessons for planters' children, but sixty miles inland began a territory that was contested and uncertain. Decades of white-Native interaction, ranging from mutually profitable trade to Native enslavement, had created a complex matrix of alliances, hatreds, and uncertainty.

An earlier English naturalist and explorer of the Carolinas, John Lawson, had been captured and murdered by a group of Natives, which had ignited the Tuscarora War less than a decade earlier. His writings, including detailed studies of Native customs and "manners" in *A New Voyage to Carolina*, would be essential to Catesby's work. In fact, his sponsors hoped that Catesby would finish the work that Lawson had begun.

The tensions exacerbated by the Tuscarora War had exploded once again in the Yamasee War between South Carolina's whites and the Tuscarora on one side and a coalition of different Native tribes including the Yamasee on the other. This conflict had largely concluded in 1718, four years before Catesby's arrival, though the underlying issues remained. The inevitable downward trajectory of settler-Native relations had continued since. Rising tensions, all-out war, and eventual forced relocation (most infamously along the Trail of Tears) were on the horizon.

Catesby, however, perhaps because of his acceptance of and admiration for some aspects of Native culture, was able to work with and among the Natives on what was then the frontier, near present-day Augusta, Georgia. Not only did Catesby ride with them on hunts for buffalo and other game; he also "employ'd an Indian to carry my Box, in which, besides Paper and Materials for Painting, I put dry'd Speciments of Plants, Seeds, &c.—as I gathered them. To the Hospitality and Assistance of these Friendly Indians," Catesby would write, "I am much indebted."

Mark Catesby displayed a willingness to seek out Black and Native knowledge of South Carolina's plants and animals, and to treat that knowledge as something of value, which was unusual for white men of his class and time, who typically dismissed such knowledge out of hand. His experiences among enslaved Black people and Native Americans would profoundly shape his *Natural History*.

◆

For now, though, Catesby's travels lay in the future. Standing at the Bay Street wharf on this warm May day, the thirty-nine-year-old Catesby could look ahead with relish to his travels of discovery in what Europeans considered the New World. Over the next three years, he would visit the neoclassical plantation homes of the Lowcountry, explore the inland forests of the frontier, and sail to the subtropical islands of the Bahamas to the south. He had been to America once before, had seen and documented some of what he found in Virginia and the Caribbean, but he had done so without a systematic plan. Now, a decade later, having acquired paying patrons as well as a reputation as a skilled practitioner of natural history, Catesby would launch what would become his life's work, eventually creating an artistic and scientific masterpiece for the ages.

I

THE AUGUSTAN AGE

The half-century before Catesby's birth in 1683 was as tumultuous and shattering as any in English history. In 1642, friction between the Stuart monarch Charles I (who believed that kings were answerable only to God) and the Puritan Parliament (which, unfortunately for Charles, controlled the country's finances) had exploded into the country's Civil War. Parliament's victory over the king's forces resulted in the beheading of Charles in 1649, leading to the formation of the Protectorate of Oliver Cromwell—a quasi-monarchy headed by Parliament's military commander—four years later. After Cromwell's death (of natural causes, as it happens), widespread fatigue with the restrictions of life under Puritan rule eventually led to the restoration of the Stuart monarchy under the beheaded king's son, Charles II, in 1660. So, after two decades, England had ended where it began, but at horrendous cost: of England's wars, only World War I killed a larger percentage of its population than its Civil War.

Among those families divided by the Civil War were the Jekylls, Mark Catesby's mother's family. Great-uncle John Jekyll, his grandfather Nicholas's brother, fought for Parliament and was captured in 1643. But John's brother, the Oxford-educated Rev. William Jekyll, "is said to have died in 1642 at the siege of Abingdon while in the King's service," according to genealogies.

The record is murkier concerning the Catesbys during the Civil War. Captain Richard Catesby served in a small Royalist regiment of dragoons with the Oxford Army in 1643; a John Catesby was quartermaster of a Royalist cavalry regiment based at Newark. A Captain Catesby, perhaps one of these two, appears in the Parliamentary proceedings of December 16, 1642, as a prisoner of war "in the Castle at Oxon . . . who [has] been indicted upon Treason." And in 1666, the hearth-tax rolls for the City of London list "Marke Catesby" as having seven hearths in his stand-alone dwelling—an average number of hearths in that part of the city, indicating for its owner financial solidity if not immense wealth.

Soon after the Restoration, England and its capital city would endure catastrophes just as elemental as war. The Great Plague of 1665 to 1666, the last vast outbreak of bubonic plague in the British Isles, killed an estimated 100,000 Londoners—a quarter of the city's populace. Bites by fleas hosted by rats and by lice hosted by humans spread the *Yersinia pestis* bacterium, causing flu-like symptoms, grossly enlarged lymph nodes known as buboes, organ failure, and death.

"Lord! How empty the streets are and how melancholy," the diarist Samuel Pepys wrote on October 16, 1665. Rules issued by the king stipulated that "if any House be Infected . . . such house (though none be dead therein) be shut up for fourty days, and have a Red Cross, and Lord have mercy upon us, in Capital Letters affixed on the door." By February 1666, it was felt safe for King Charles to return from his exile in Oxford. London, however, was not done with catastrophe.

Seven months later, at a little after midnight on September 2, a fire began in Thomas Farriner's bakery in Pudding Lane, a tenth of a mile from London Bridge. Hot, dry weather and the timber-and-pitch construction of almost all of London's buildings caused the flames to spread quickly, aided by a strong wind from the east. The Great Fire of 1666 lasted five days, gutting the medieval center of London, the square mile known to this day as the City, within the ancient Roman walls. Among those losing their homes and businesses in the fire was Mark Catesby's great-uncle John Jekyll, who had survived the Civil War only to lose his haberdasher's shop to the inferno.

The diarist John Evelyn noted on September 4 that "the burning still rages . . . All Fleet street, the Old Bailey, Ludgate hill, Warwick lane, Newgate, Paul's chain, Watling street, now flaming, and most of it reduced to ashes; the stones of [St.] Paul's flew like grenados, the melting lead running down the streets in a stream, and the very pavements glowing with fiery redness, so as no horse, nor man, was able to tread on them." He could see "the eastern wind still more impetuously driving the flames forward. Nothing but the Almighty power of God was able to stop them; for vain was the help of man." The flames destroyed 13,200 houses, eighty-seven parish churches, and St. Paul's Cathedral. Modern scholars estimate a death toll perhaps in the thousands, though records are sketchy, especially for London's largely undocumented poor.

London would rebuild. Led by the brilliant Christopher Wren, who designed fifty-one new churches as well as the new St. Paul's, the city's leaders restored its heart, as well as its financial center, to what would be even greater heights of wealth and power. Parliament declared the rebuilding of St. Paul's complete in 1711, forty-five years after its destruction in the Great Fire.

Less successful was the restoration of the Stuart monarchy. In 1688, when Mark Catesby was five, six prominent politicians from England's two parties, the Whigs and the Tories, and a bishop of the Church of England led the peaceful overthrow of Charles II's brother, King James II. The Catholic James had been appointing Catholics to government positions, in defiance of the Test Acts, and otherwise defying Parliament in the tradition of his deceased brother. When James produced a likely-Catholic heir, the "immortal seven" published a public letter inviting James's Protestant daughter Mary and her husband Prince William of Orange to the throne. The Glorious Revolution, as the winners and subsequent histories have named it, was intended not only to make the English throne Protestant once and for all, but also to assure a relatively calm stretch of royal dynastic stability. The first goal was and has been successfully met, to the present day; as for the second, England's development as a parliamentary democracy, led by prime ministers, soon made the monarchy less influential.

◈

It is not surprising that out of this blood and tumult would come the English Enlightenment, obsessed with rationalism, order, and science. Even more than on the Continent or abroad in Britain's colonies, the thinkers, writers, and artists of the British Isles must have yearned for an intellectual structure which could cauterize the social, political, and religious wounds of the previous century. Classifying, sorting, and naming, Enlightenment thinkers and scientists strove to put every piece of the cosmos in its place. Architecture, art, and music were classical, symmetrical, balanced. The music of George Frideric Handel fit the age perfectly; his *Water Music* was composed in 1717 for George I, and he composed a coronation anthem for George II, *Zadok the Priest*, which has been performed at every British coronation since 1727. Isaac Newton, seeking the rules underlying the universe, personified this period. Even the medieval sport of cricket had its rules codified.

The poet Alexander Pope's dictum, "Order is heaven's first law," was the byword of what was called the Augustan Age in England. The Hanoverian kings, beginning with George I in 1714, were written and spoken of as temperate, poised rulers in the classic Roman mold of Caesar Augustus, hence the name given to the era. The intellectual and cultural touchstone of the time was *The Spectator,* a daily publication begun by Joseph Addison and Richard Steele in 1711. Addison's *Spectator* essays—a form gaining new popularity—with their balanced clauses, stately cadence, and calm assurance, set the tone. To the modern historian Roy Porter, *The Spectator* "represented the temperate and tolerant society, the virtuous commonwealth, that was considered to be the proper and appropriate consequence of the revolution of 1688," and served an important social function: "By blending entertainment and instruction, the *Spectator* taught ease and affability to squireens and tradesmen with time on their hands, money in their pockets but little breeding."

This sort of social and cultural education was necessary in a rapidly changing society. On the one hand, England in 1700 "was still a second-rate rustic nation of hamlets and villages," in Roy Porter's words. What industry there was "still fed off the soil: timber, hides, hops, flax, madder, saffron," and it was mainly cottage industry. Spinning, lacemaking, and tanning were done in people's homes, and scheduled around the farm calendar. Family life and work in places such as Mark Catesby's native Suffolk "danced in step to the phases of nature," and social life, "with its feasts, fasts and fairs, its post-harvest bonfires and forced winter unemployment," was "syncopated with the rural rhythms of toil and tribulation, abundance and idleness."

But this rural and rustic culture was on the threshold of phenomenal change and growth. The decades of Catesby's youth coincided with the beginnings of Britain's transformation into a modern economic power. Even with the twin catastrophes of civil war and the Great Fire, despite the bloodshed and social and economic dislocation, the English economy grew more rapidly between 1650 and 1700 than in any other half-century between 1270 and 1870. As a result, at the end of the seventeenth century people found themselves newly in possession of discretionary income. Between 1570 and 1770, rural life in England had transformed. For those not condemned to be tenant farmers or waged laborers, prosperity offered breathing room to think, to play, to enjoy leisure. By Catesby's time, certain classes of the English countryman "reached for a book in the evenings, rather than for the axe or mattock of his forebears."

What was the source of this growth? The answer can be found in the burgeoning overseas trade, which would eventually coalesce into the British Empire. By 1700, in India, in Africa, in the Caribbean, English merchants and business interests, backed by the steadily growing English naval fleet, elbowed their way into the raw materials and developing markets found there. India in particular had become a source of substantial wealth, driven by the machinations of the East India Company. As early as the 1620s, Company member and economist Thomas Mun had written that the Company's trade was "the very touchstone of the Kingdom's prosperity." The Company's reach and power had only increased in the century since.

Trade had come to be considered the most important activity of the nation; as a career, it became more prestigious than ever in this always class-conscious nation. Men of business weren't yet considered candidates for the aristocracy, but more and more they successfully ascended to the ranks of gentlemen. As Daniel Defoe wrote in *The Complete English Tradesman* (1726), "Some of the greatest and best, and most flourishing family among not the gentry only, but even the nobility, have been rais'd from trade, owe their beginning, their wealth, and their estates to trade." Trade, wrote Defoe, "is the readiest way for men to raise their fortunes and families; and therefore it is a field for men of figure and good families to enter upon."

In a complex interweaving of events and influences, the Royal Society, the Addisons and Steeles of the literary world, and the seafaring merchants of London, Bristol, and Liverpool all fed into the development of the British Empire. Expansion—economic, geographical, and intellectual—was the theme of this age. And men like Mark Catesby, following their curiosity to the edges of empire, would be both the beneficiaries of this expansion and players in its continuation.

◆

The country's growing prosperity created new opportunities for learning as leisure time became available for greater numbers of Englishmen. At the same time, expanding communication networks—newspapers, letters, formal societies, and informal clubs—created connections and multiplied shared knowledge. Modern historian Richard Drayton points out how "an informal empire of gentlemanly amateurs emerged to span Britain's eighteenth-century world. Observations, information, specimens, and argument journeyed from physicians in Edinburgh to absentee planters in London, parsons in New England, and merchants in Calcutta and Canton."

Widespread as this network was, it was only one part of a community that had supported European intellectual life since the Renaissance. In 1417, a Venetian humanist had written a letter to a scholar of early Roman authors, thanking him for "bringing enrichment to the republic of letters." By the early sixteenth century, Erasmus was being called the monarch of The Republic of Letters.

This virtual community of scholars arose organically from humanists' need to circulate information across vast distances.

The networks of correspondence they created allowed them to exchange books, announce discoveries, sustain structures of patronage, and develop a sense of shared values. Mark Catesby happened to be born in the heart of the community's golden age, the years between 1650 and 1750. Even on the eve of the French Revolution, this community of scholars was still vibrant, with an estimated thirty thousand members.

Sir Hans Sloane, who acceded to the presidency of the Royal Society in 1727, was one of Catesby's most influential patrons and friends; his surviving private correspondence consists of over five thousand letters. Benjamin Franklin, part of the Republic of Letters, sent and received three times that many during his life; his network included Philadelphia, London, and Paris. Missives such as Sloane's and Franklin's were designed to be more public than we are accustomed to; they were written with the understanding that they would be shared among friends and colleagues. Letters were also published in scholarly journals (such as the letters to and from Mark Catesby which found their way into the *Philosophical Transactions of the Royal Society*) and were read aloud in both organized and more casual groups.

The Republic of Letters, especially in England, was integral to Catesby's success as naturalist, artist, and author. As we shall see, letters shared among collectors, botanists, nurserymen, and merchants were the vehicles by which Catesby's specimens and artwork became widely known. This exposure would make him an attractive candidate to send to America to explore its natural wonders.

The ideal among British gentlemen-amateurs was the *virtuoso*— "the courtly man of parts, conversant in all branches of learning, expert in 'the excellencie' of all manner of objects and adept at conversational performance." Increasing wealth and leisure combined with enthusiasm for all the new discoveries of the day meant that a virtuoso should ideally be a man of property who stayed abreast of scientific news, collected specimens, and could make informed conversation about both.

Above all, the virtuoso was expected to be curious. More than the modern use of the word to mean a casual interest, "curious" to the Georgians implied an active, engaged intellect, as well as referring to the new, the novel, the unusual. It was not only "one of the keywords of Georgian taste"; it also described "a conversation piece designed to raise the wonder, admiration and comment of visitors." To be truly curious was to have a range of intellectual interests so broad as to be considered a polymath. As one social historian has put it, "A telescope in the library was the counterpart of the tea table in the parlour." The Georgians were fascinated by objects of all kinds: exotic plants in botanical gardens, machinery in factories, artworks, and curios collected during their travels.

Fashionable gentlemen of the age were expected to display an interest in science, culture, and nature. It was the time of the Grand Tour, when young men of means were expected to follow well-defined itineraries to view the Renaissance art of Italy, the chateaux of France, and cabinets of curiosities across Europe. "Taste was an important concept in eighteenth-century Britain, though a slippery one," a modern historian has written. "Young aristocrats were expected to return home [from the Grand Tour]

with . . . above all, an appreciation of art and architecture, literature and poetry that would equip them with what was needed to
demonstrate sensibility and taste in their houses and gardens."
For Alexander Pope and the Augustan social and intellectual
elite, "a display of taste in gardening, like that in the other arts,
[was] central to their place in polite society."

The study of the world's plants and animals—part of what
the age meant by the term "natural history"—flourished in this
intellectual atmosphere. Merchants, sailors, and traveling private
citizens shipped seeds and plantings of flowers, trees, and shrubs
from around the world back to London, and specimens never
seen before flowed through nurserymen's stocks and into the
gardens of England. On the scene in London, visiting from his
native Sweden, would be the most important classifier of them
all, Carl Linnaeus, who was devising the system used today for
naming and classifying all living things. It is because of Linnaean taxonomy that we describe ourselves as *Homo sapiens*.

Those botanical finds from overseas would be key compo-
nents of a gentleman's *wunderkammer*, or cabinet of curiosities,
in which he might display animal skeletons, fossils and other
notable rocks, gems, insects, as well as plants—especially rare or
exotic plants. What began in medieval times as pilgrimage sites,
with relics of saints and other sacred objects, became during
the Renaissance the productions of aristocrats or royalty whose
museums were considered to be a *theatrum mundi*, or theater
of the world.

In this pre-scientific era, though, before classification, no one
knew how to organize these collections; there was no agreed-
upon format. Some of them were literal cabinets, with hinged

doors and compartmented drawers holding insects and fossils. Other "cabinets" were whole rooms or series of spaces, lavishly decorated and displaying fine art as well as specimens. Rembrandt had a cabinet including Indian javelins, a bust of Seneca, a conch shell, and a bird of paradise—the last two of which he sketched. We have these details because Rembrandt's creditors listed the items when he went bankrupt—at least partly due to his passion for acquisition.

By Catesby's time, the craze for amassing collections of the unusual, or "curious," had led to gentlemen's collections of massive size. The most famous of these collections held so huge a trove of paintings, books, and natural history specimens that it would become the foundation for the first of the great national museums.

Sir Hans Sloane served as a court physician, was made a baronet—the first physician to be given that honor—and also was president of the Royal College of Physicians. In 1727 he succeeded Isaac Newton as president of the Royal Society. Sloane had revived the society's journal, *Philosophical Transactions*, thereby putting himself squarely in the flow of current scientific information. He embodied the virtuoso and the member of the Republic of Letters, with his extensive contacts in Britain and around the world, expanded by his correspondence across Asia, the Americas, and Europe.

Among Sloane's many initiatives was the endowment of the Chelsea Physic Garden, under the leadership of Philip Miller. Along with the botanical garden at Oxford, Chelsea was among the most important herbal gardens in England. Sloane arranged to connect Chelsea with the herbarium at the Royal Society and charged Miller with adding fifty new plants to the Society's catalogue of specimens each year. The list of additions would be published in *Philosophical Transactions*.

Sloane became the preeminent collector of his time, amassing many thousands of books, manuscripts, specimens, and other objects, gathered by numerous hands from around the world. "You cannot err," he told his agent, "in buying [me] any books of voyages . . . or old physick books." Sloane would leave this immense, unparalleled collection to his country; combined with King George II's library, the bequest became in 1753 the foundation of the British Museum.

In addition to its herbarium, the Royal Society had its own cabinet of curiosities, which included fossils, animal skeletons, and oddities such as "the giant's thighbone." As the eighteenth century wore on, conflict arose, even in the Royal Society, concerning the distinction between useful items of scientific study and those which were merely monstrous or bizarre. Thus the state of the Society's repository of specimens varied tremendously throughout the first half of the eighteenth century, devolving by 1710, before being restored to good order by 1736. Finally, in 1781, the Society gave all its artifacts to the British Museum.

One in particular of Sloane's many and diverse personal connections, James Petiver, would be important to Mark Catesby's career. In a time of fairly rigid class structure, Petiver traveled across social boundaries in service of his passion for plants. The son of a haberdasher, Petiver became an apothecary, which is how he met Sloane. He cultivated one of the most extensive correspondence networks of his day, exchanging letters with naturalists, explorers, colonists, and sea travelers of all classes and occupations. He wrote his "Directions for the Gathering of Plants" to systematize (that very Augustan idea) how specimens were collected. In 1690 he instructed his correspondents to "gather yr speciments as compleat and intire as you can," and "take with you a small Spudd or Trowell, a knife, Pen & Ink . . . also a long pasteboard box [to] put your Roots Seeds Berries & such Plants in."

Around that same time, John Woodward, naturalist, physician, and member of the Royal Society, would disseminate his "Directions for the Collecting, Preserving, and Sending over Natural Things, from Foreign Countries," admonishing his sources not to focus solely on rarities: "In the Choice of these Things, neglect not any, tho' the most ordinary and trivial; the Commonest Peble or Flint, Cockle or Oyster-shell, Grass, Moss, Fern, or Thistle, will be as useful, and as proper to be gathered, as any the rarest production of the Country."

Petiver's sources were so fruitful—John Ray described Petiver's correspondence as "the greatest both in East and West Indies of any man in Europe"—and his reports from overseas so fresh that Sloane rewarded Petiver with a fellowship in the Royal Society in 1695. At this point in the Society's history, it was rare indeed for a tradesman like Petiver to be admitted, and he was not shy about splashing the fact of his fellowship across the covers of his printed works.

Like Petiver, Peter Collinson was important to the world of natural history and to Mark Catesby's career. Collinson, a Quaker merchant and botanist, had more than a hundred correspondents in America and Europe. Using his trade connections, he accumulated exotic specimens for his gardens, especially American varieties.

Catesby thought so much of Collinson that he would send him extensive numbers of specimens of "Seeds and Acorns" from America even though Collinson was not a sponsor of Catesby's journey. Catesby even wrote Collinson, "I earnestly intreat you will burn or concell this Letter and the purport of it for reasons you easily conceive." Catesby feared incurring the wrath of his prominent subscribers by sending specimens to someone with no stake in his project. Collinson, for his part, would more than repay Catesby as a major supporter of the *Natural History*.

Peter Collinson was also a patron of Pennsylvania's John Bartram, botanist, nurseryman, and father of William Bartram, who would retrace some of Catesby's journeys in South Carolina a half-century later. Collinson connected John Bartram with Catesby, writing to Bartram with requests from Catesby when the latter was too busy working on the *Natural History*. Catesby and Bartram had a friendly and direct, if spotty, correspondence from 1740 until Catesby's death in 1749.

In all, it was a time when someone like Mark Catesby—curious but not scientifically trained; well-born though neither titled nor particularly well-off; ambitious and adventurous as well as well-connected—could parlay his interest in natural history into a living. The prosperous, expanding, expansive British society of which he was a part had room for unconventional career paths for ambitious and talented men like Catesby. It also provided a ready audience for the fruits of his curiosity: the gentleman-amateur collectors, botanists, and gardeners of Augustan England.

2

SUDBURY AND CASTLE HEDINGHAM 1683–1712

Sixty miles northeast of London sits the town of Castle Hedingham in northeast Essex. Logically enough, at least by English convention, it takes its name from and clusters around Hedingham Castle, ancient seat of the earls of Oxford, and straddles the Colne River. (The seventeenth earl in this now-dormant line, Edward de Vere, is the man who is most often proposed to have *actually* written the plays of William Shakespeare.) The castle's keep, built around 1140 after the Norman conquest of England, still stands, as do many medieval timber-framed buildings in the town.

St. Nicholas Church is on Falcon Square, barely a quarter-mile southwest of the castle. It, too, is late Norman and Gothic, begun around 1180. In its parish register is this entry: "Mark Catesby, son of John Catesby, gent [gentleman] and Elizabeth, his wife, Baptize March 30, 1683." Another hand later added, "Nate [born] March 24, 1682"; it is generally supposed that

Catesby's later fame led someone to add this detail. March 24 would have been the last day of 1682 according to the Julian calendar, then in use in England. Because of the change by Britain in 1752 to the Gregorian calendar we use today with January 1 as the first day of the year, Catesby's birth date is now considered to be March 24, 1683.

The short interval between birth and baptism indicates that he was probably born at the home of his mother's brother, Nicholas Jekyll, in this town on the ancient Colchester-Cambridge road. Seven miles separated Castle Hedingham from the Catesby family home in Sudbury, just inside the western border of Suffolk; perhaps Mark's mother, Elizabeth, needed to be near her family—she had lost several children in their infancy before this. Five of those she delivered, however, did manage to survive until 1700, when John Catesby made his will. Mark was the fourth; the eldest was John (1670–1690), followed by his brother Jekyll (1672), then sister Elizabeth (1680 or 1681), who would be directly responsible for Mark's first travels to North America. His sister, Ann, was born in Sudbury in 1688, and the youngest, another John, in 1697.

Sudbury, an ancient market town, also sat on a river, the Stour. "I know nothing for which [Sudbury] is remarkable, except for being very populous and very poor," wrote Daniel Defoe in 1724. The author of *Robinson Crusoe* also said of Mark Catesby's hometown, "they have a great manufacture of says and perpetuanas [two types of wool fabrics], and multitudes of poor people are employed in working them; but the number of the poor is almost ready to eat up the rich." Then again, Defoe has been described in modern times as a "rackety, cross-grained, indomitable writer" who was "mildly obsessed" with the decline of Old England, so perhaps he is not the most reliable narrator—at least on this subject.

The region's undulating farmland would have carried sheep in great numbers, with hedgerows and copses of woods scattered about. Its clay soil lent itself to forest and pasture rather than cropland; the great Epping Forest, a six-thousand-acre remnant of which still remains, stood between Catesby's home and London. His was an open landscape, with large empty spaces between the villages, linked by straight roads.

Thus rivers flowed through both of the main towns of Mark Catesby's youth on their way to the North Sea. The agricultural lands just outside of Sudbury and Castle Hedingham would have had plenty of verge land, hedgerows, uncultivated copses, even remnants of mighty forests not far away. They would have sheltered nightingales, warblers, and turtle doves, as well as butterflies: pearl-bordered fritillaries, silver-washed fritillaries, wood white, and purple emperor butterflies.

In this preindustrial time, the biodiversity of this corner of England would have been profuse, and undoubtedly alluring to someone of young Mark Catesby's disposition. Given what he called his "early Inclination . . . to search after Plants, and other Productions in Nature," it's highly likely he spent time botanizing in the gentle folds of the countryside, collecting specimens along the Stour, and examining his uncle's botanical garden. His first forays into fieldwork—studying the plants, birds, animals, and fish around him—would be as simple as taking a walk, perhaps from the building still standing on North Street in Sudbury, described on a 1714 map as "Mr. Catesby's House."

◆

Catesby's father, John Catesby, was a man of position, owning property in Suffolk as well as in London. Mark Catesby's biographers Frick and Stearns described John as "a member of a tight little group which governed this cloth-manufacturing town up to the loss of its charter in 1684, and possibly afterward." He served as Sudbury's town clerk and clerk of the peace, as well as mayor for at least four one-year terms.

John Catesby was a lawyer—a solicitor, who in the British system would work mainly on routine legal matters, while barristers represented clients in court. It was a time in England when, in a modern historian's words, "The professions flourished, creating an entirely new class of middling society . . . [including] clergymen, the attorneys of common law courts and the solicitors of Equity and Chancery; the physicians and even the surgeon-apothecaries were also acquiring new status." In most cases, that status included being dignified with the title of "Mr.," or "gent." These new professions tended to cluster in towns which were "homes for such professional agents of gentlefolk as attorneys, surveyors and doctors." Sudbury was such a town, and such "professional agents" were Mark Catesby's people.

Catesby's father was a person of status in London as well as in Sudbury. In 1673 he was elected warden of the Worshipful Company of Skinners, the ancient trade guild of the fur industry. Known as the Skinners' Company, it was incorporated by royal charter in 1327 as one of the seven oldest of the medieval guilds which enforced monopolies in their trades, along with regulating wages, labor conditions, and industry standards. By the seventeenth century the company, like many of the guilds, was moving away from its involvement in trade toward a more civic, ceremonial, and philanthropic role; its wardens were by this time men of importance in the City, from a variety of occupations. As warden, John Catesby, in his satin-trimmed gown and hood, could have accompanied the master of the guild on his official visits around the City of London, and participated in elaborate guild pageants honoring London's lord mayor.

One incident reveals John Catesby as someone willing to litigate a dispute in the political arena. On February 27, 1699, the House of Commons received a petition from "John Catesby and William Cook Gentlemen, and others, free Burgesses of the Borough of Sudbury." The petition concerned a Mr. Gourdon, who had stood for election to Parliament from Sudbury. The petition asserted that "by Bribery, and other undue Practices," Gourdon "procured himself to be returned" (elected). The petition was referred to a committee, where presumably it died; nothing more is known about the case.

Such a man would also be interested in educating his children, or at least his sons. Mark Catesby may have attended Felsted Grammar School, in the town of Felsted, about fifteen miles from Castle Hedingham and about twenty miles from Sudbury. The school was founded in 1564 by the 1st Baron Rich, a former Lord Chancellor who made a fortune overseeing the dissolution of the monasteries under Henry VIII. According to the *Oxford Dictionary of National Biography*, "Since the mid-16th century Rich has had a reputation for immorality, financial dishonesty, double-dealing, perjury and treachery rarely matched in English history."

Two of Oliver Cromwell's sons had been educated at Felsted decades before; more directly related to Catesby's life, his two older brothers studied there, as did William Byrd II of Virginia, who would figure prominently in Mark Catesby's future, and William Cocke, who would become Catesby's brother-in-law and would furnish the reason for his first visit to America. The school's reputation can be seen in yet another passage from our man Daniel Defoe, this time in his *The Compleat English Gentleman* of 1728, where he writes of "the great schools of Eton, Winchester, Westminster, Felsted, Bishop Stortford, Canterbury and others, where the children—nay, the eldest sons—of some of the best families in England have been educated."

After Felsted, the eldest Catesby son, John, was admitted to Clifford's Inn, one of the four Inns of Chancery that provided training for becoming a barrister, in 1686; he enrolled at Queens' College, Cambridge, a year later, and in 1690 entered the Inner Temple, one of the four Inns of Court to which all barristers belonged. The next brother, Jekyll, was admitted to the Inner Temple two years later.

If John Catesby was disappointed that his youngest son had not followed his brothers into the law, he did not allow it to affect the generous bequests in his will: Mark inherited houses in Sudbury as well as in the Parish of St. Bride's in the City of London, and lands in Chilton and Great Cornard in Suffolk. It is thought that Mark Catesby, who was twenty years old at his father's death, went periodically thereafter to London to oversee his inherited holdings. He would eventually sell some of them in 1710, probably to fund his upcoming seven-year stay in Virginia.

With John Catesby's passing in 1703, Nicholas Jekyll, who would have been in his mid-fifties, became the head of the family. In a letter to a friend decades later, Nicholas would describe himself as being like "a Father to [Mark], and to his sister." This may well have pushed young Mark Catesby away from Sudbury, and toward Castle Hedingham and his future.

◆

The Jekylls, like the Catesbys, were a family of lawyers. But their pedigree and status were a bit loftier than that of the Catesbys, tracing back to Bartholomew Jekyll, during the reign of Henry VI in the mid-1400s. Among Mark Catesby's Jekyll forebears were royal functionaries, antiquarians, and authors of sermons and religious works. His uncle Nicholas continued in the family line of lawyers, and was also a prominent historian. Most importantly for his nephew's future, Nicholas, like many gentlemen of his time, cultivated a botanical garden.

It is easy to imagine young Mark being drawn to the more intellectual Jekyll side of his relations, though given the scarcity of records, this may be an unfair judgment on the Catesbys. Still, it was Nicholas Jekyll, not John Catesby, who was caught up in the contemporary fashion for botanizing, and whose correspondence with one of the greatest botanists of the age has survived.

Jekyll's intellectual interests brought him into contact with John Ray, who lived in Black Nutley, ten miles from Castle Hedingham and sixteen from Sudbury. Ray, who has been called "the father of natural history in Britain," was the son of a blacksmith and an "herb-woman" or collector of medicinal plants. He attended Braintree Grammar School and Trinity College, Cambridge. After receiving his degree in 1648, Ray lectured in Greek, mathematics, and humanities at Trinity; he published his first book, the *Catalogue of Cambridge Plants*, in 1660, the same year he took holy orders in the Church of England. He and Francis Willughby, a brilliant Cambridge student eight years younger than Ray, collaborated on two landmark books of British natural history, *Ornithology* and *History of Fishes*.

Unfortunately for Ray, the Restoration Parliament that year passed the Act of Uniformity, requiring all ministers to sign an act of loyalty to the Church of England and mandating the use of the Book of Common Prayer in services. Ray refused to submit to the act and lost not only his priestship but also his fellowship at Trinity College, after which he depended on the generosity of his well-heeled friend Willughby. Scholars even today are unsure exactly why Ray refused to sign, as his writings place him squarely in the orthodox Anglican camp, and he should have had no philosophical quarrel with its demands. Upon Willughby's death in 1672 at age thirty-eight, Ray continued the work they had begun, editing and publishing the *Ornithology* in 1676 and the *History of Fishes* in 1686. (The Royal Society spent so much on a gorgeous, full-color printing of the *History of Fishes*, and it flopped so badly, that the Society almost could not afford to print Newton's landmark work, the *Principia*.)

In their *Ornithology*, Ray and Willughby had invented a new method of classification using physical features such as beaks, feet, and size. As a result, the book was, in the words of

Willughby's biographer, "a blockbuster, a massive compendium of ornithological knowledge," and "spectacular in its scope," as well as "the most 'scientific' book on natural history so far." After Willughby's death, Ray continued to be a major figure in the development of scientific classification of plants and animals. His last book based on the research and notes of Willughby, the *History of Insects,* was published in 1710, five years after Ray's own death. The *History of Insects* broke scientific ground by grouping its subjects based on the presence or absence of metamorphosis, rather than on categories such as aquatic versus terrestrial specimens, or the presence or absence of wings. Ray's development of these systems of biological classification, based on his work alongside Willughby, made his reputation as one of the foremost naturalists of his day. The *History of Insects,* in particular, was key to the genesis of Linnaeus's binomial system of scientific nomenclature in the mid-1700s.

John Ray achieved eminence in another area, as well. He may have lost his position in the Church of England, but Ray nevertheless followed in the English tradition of the parson-naturalist. The Church had historically been the career choice for younger sons of noble families, many of them classically educated, in an era when the typical vicar or rector of a rural church had fewer demands on his time than in succeeding centuries. As a result, letters, articles, and books poured from parsonages and rectories throughout the English countryside in the eighteenth and nineteenth centuries, many of them on natural history. The most famous of these is the *Natural History and Antiquities of Selborne,* by Gilbert White (1720–1793). Charles Darwin was avidly reading the parson-naturalists while at Christ's College,

Cambridge in the 1830s, with the Church as his career path, before his fateful voyage aboard the *Beagle*. Given these men's training and biases, it was logical that the study of nature would go hand in hand with Christian theology.

John Ray published *The Wisdom of God Manifested in the Works of the Creation* in 1691, when Mark Catesby was eight. Natural theology, with its primary belief that nature holds abundant evidence of the wisdom and beauty of God's creation, became what the historian Richard Drayton calls "the most important organizing idea in British science, shaping a tradition of missionary and vicarage naturalism which stretches into the Victorian era." And in the realm of natural theology, "No work was more important in its propagation than Ray's *Wisdom of God Manifested in the Creation*."

There was little to no conflict between science and religion in the late sixteenth and early seventeenth centuries, before the nineteenth-century discoveries and assertions of Darwin and geologist Charles Lyell upset long-held beliefs about Noah, the biblical flood, and the timeframe of geologic change. Naturalists saw creation as evidence of God's infinitely wise design for Earth and its inhabitants. This applied especially to humans, who since the Middle Ages had been thought of as existing at the top of what was called the Chain of Being, below the angels but above all other creatures on Earth. Ray's *Wisdom of God* cemented his double status as a preeminent theologian as well as botanist.

For Mark Catesby, though we have no theological writings as such, passages in the *Natural History* offer insight into his views. While comparing American and European birds, Catesby begins, "Admitting the World to have been universally replenished with all Animals from Noah's Ark after the general Deluge, and that those European Birds which are in America found their Way thither at first from the old World . . . ," assuming the biblical story to be fact. Catesby also refers to the insects in Carolina being "protected from the Cold by such various and wonderful Methods, that nothing excites more Admiration of the Wisdom of our great Creator," a clear example of the natural theology of which John Ray was so prominent an advocate.

During his time in Black Nutley, Ray was in constant communication with Sir Hans Sloane, the collector. In the 1690s, when Mark Catesby would have been a teenager, Sloane sent Ray books, pictures, and specimens, which Ray used in his writings, including his *Historia Plantarum*, his attempt at a botanical compendium. When Sloane was compiling his book about the natural history of Jamaica and wondered whether it "should be thought worthy of Publication," he decided that "the greatest Judge I could advise with, in these Circumstances, was Mr. Ray," for "his Probity, Learning, Language, &c."

Catesby's uncle Nicholas Jekyll also furnished Ray with scholarly materials. In Ray's work on language, *A Collection of English Words Not Generally Used*, Dale credited "my ingenious friend Nicholas Jekyll" for his philological contributions. Catesby would come of age amid this intellectual and botanical network, stretching from Castle Hedingham and Sudbury to Black Nutley and London.

The Finnish naturalist Peter Kalm, who met with Catesby toward the end of the latter's life, would later write that "when he was a small boy, Mr Catesby had often visited Ray." Catesby's friend George Edwards also wrote, twelve years after Catesby's death, that Catesby "hapned to fall into the acquaintance of the great naturalist Mr. Ray, who then lived in Essex not far from him. This acquaintance inspir'd Catesby with a gen[i]us for natural history."

We know that Catesby took Willughby's *Ornithology* to America. He used it to identify one of the first birds he saw in 1722, even before he landed in Charleston: "On the Coasts of America we had several other Birds came on Board us which gave me an opertunity of discribing some of them . . . Amongst the Birds the Turn stone or Sea plover of Mr Willoughby was one which by comparison of it agrees exactly." Mark Catesby's groundbreaking work in natural history would spring from his youthful association through his uncle Nicholas with Ray and indirectly through Ray with Willughby.

◆

Another important local connection for young Mark Catesby was Samuel Dale, physician and apothecary who lived in Braintree, three miles from Ray's Black Nutley. He was Ray's assistant during Ray's declining years and an acclaimed author in his own right. Dale in 1711 collected botanical specimens from Nicholas Jekyll's garden. As this was the year before Catesby's first journey to North America, "in all probability, arrangements were made at this time for the younger man to send specimens of the Virginian flora to the Essex botanist." It is Samuel Dale who most probably gave Catesby, by then in his late twenties, his apprenticeship in natural history.

Today a common reference point for an apothecary is Shakespeare's *Romeo and Juliet,* in which an apothecary provides Romeo with poison with which to join Juliet by killing himself. But in Catesby's time, they played a less dramatic, though at least as important, role. Before the development of modern medicine and the pharmacy, it was apothecaries who researched and developed herbal remedies and medicines for physicians; this led naturally to apothecaries' becoming students of botany and other natural sciences. James Petiver, whom we met in chapter 1, was an eminent example of an apothecary's inclinations toward the study of plants and herbs. Dale contributed papers to the *Philosophical Transactions of the Royal Society* on a variety of topics, including the first account of the strata of Harwich cliff, a stretch of Essex beach revealing fifty-million-year-old fossils from the Eocene rainforest.

Thus Catesby grew up surrounded by an interconnected web of correspondence and influence, not only in Essex but also reaching to London and influential collectors there such as Sloane. In this time when face-to-face personal contact and correspondence were the most important, and practically the only, ways of sharing botanical news, gossip, and specimens, the Republic of Letters was making regular deliveries in his neighborhood. Between his uncle Nicholas Jekyll, John Ray, and Samuel Dale, Catesby had a repository of expertise in natural history perhaps as good as any outside of London and the cities of the Continent.

In light of this, it is a little difficult to understand Catesby's statement that "The early Inclination I had to search after Plants, and other Productions in Nature, being much suppressed by my residing too remote from London, the Center of all Science, *I was deprived of all Opportunities and Examples* to excite me to a stronger Pursuit after those Things to which I was naturally bent" [emphasis added]. Perhaps writing this in the 1730s in London, looking back from his late forties on his youth, gave him an exaggerated sense of the deprivations of Essex and Suffolk. Or perhaps he was indulging in a bit of self-promotion in the first few pages of the *Natural History*: Look, he may be saying, at what this country bumpkin was able to do in spite of his lamentable lack of opportunity.

◆

There are no known images of Mark Catesby, his parents, or the Jekylls. The earliest letter we have from Catesby was written on May 5, 1722, from Charleston, when he was thirty-nine. We are forced to extrapolate backward from the "tall, meagre," and "sullen" man with "a silent disposition" of Catesby's later years.

We may imagine the young Catesby, of Sudbury and Castle Hedingham circa 1710, dressed like one of those young squires in a Thomas Gainsborough portrait such as *Mr. and Mrs. Andrews*, painted around 1750. Gainsborough was born in 1727, the year after Catesby returned from America; like Catesby, he was from Sudbury. He attended Sudbury Grammar School, as indeed did Robert Andrews, the subject of his portrait. Gainsborough was only twenty-two when Catesby died, putting him a generation after the naturalist; however, Englishmen's fashions changed only slightly during the early eighteenth century, making the painting a valid source for comparison.

So, picture young Mark Catesby in a tricorne, buff knee breeches, white silk stockings, and black shoes with large buckles; he would wear a blousy overshirt, with a vest or waistcoat. He probably sported a white scarf tied neatly around his neck. This was thought of as casual attire in this time and place, such as an outdoorsy young member of the landed gentry might feel comfortable wearing. From what we know of Catesby, he probably would not have had quite the self-satisfied expression of the young husband as depicted by Gainsborough.

Whatever his appearance, Mark Catesby did not follow in his brothers' paths; his preference for natural history over the law, already so obvious, made such career trajectories less than defensible. Instead, he probably took the solid grounding from Felsted School, with its Greek and Latin, rhetoric, mathematics, geometry, and natural philosophy, and added to it experiential learning at the hands of someone like John Ray or Samuel Dale. It was a time when credentials and formal training were nonexistent for most livelihoods; apprenticeships and self-education were the routes to developing in a career, not college and exams. His uncle's botanical garden and library, along with his interactions with Ray and Dale, may well have furnished young Mark Catesby with everything he needed to make his way as a naturalist.

About his artistic training, as about so much of Catesby's youth, we know little besides his statement in the preface to the *Natural History* that he was "not bred a Painter." Both Ray and Dale possessed illustrated books of flora and fauna, as did ostensibly his uncle Nicholas; he could well have accessed these for artistic models. Manuals of drawing and painting, aimed at well-rounded gentlemen of Catesby's status, were increasingly plentiful during this time. By the time he departed for South Carolina in 1722, Catesby would own several books which provided standard models of illustrations, including Francis Barlow's *Aesop's Fables*. His exposure to Hans Sloane's vast collection of natural-history books and artwork at around this same time, added to the rest of his informal and self-directed education as an artist, would provide Catesby with the knowledge and technical expertise needed to create his distinctive portrayals of the New World's plants and animals.

In this transitional period in British history, when a new middle and upper-middle class was burgeoning in rural towns as well as in London, Mark Catesby's education and family ties to the intellectual botanical community—the Rays and Dales, and indirectly, the Sloanes of the British botanical community—would serve him well. By engaging with that network, he would turn his passion for plants and animals into a career.

3

THE TEMPLE COFFEE HOUSE CLUB AND THE ROYAL SOCIETY

Nicholas Jekyll, John Ray, and Samuel Dale brought the Republic of Letters, that intricate interchange of scientific news, discoveries, and other information, to the part of rural England where Mark Catesby came of age. Collecting specimens, writing books and articles and letters, and planting gardens in Castle Hedingham and Black Nutley and Braintree, they participated fully in the ongoing eighteenth-century British fascination with the natural world. The three men were perfectly situated to give Catesby a thorough grounding in natural history. Nevertheless, Catesby had it right when he called the ancient city which lay a day's horseback ride to the southwest "the centre of all Science."

And in London, two special developments, beginning in the seventeenth century and reaching new heights in the eighteenth, added to the city's status as the nation's intellectual center. One was a widespread social phenomenon; the other, a developing institution. Together, they were driving forces during this unique time in the history of natural history.

◆

Sometime in early 1652, an immigrant to London, Pasqua Rosée, opened London's first coffeehouse in St. Michael's Alley, in Cornhill, the city's business district. "House" is a bit of a misnomer though: his establishment was an open-air stall in an alley. In an indication of the cosmopolitan nature of this new beverage, the Greek Rosée had worked for an English merchant who dealt in Turkish products, including coffee. Today you can view Rosée's 1652 handbill in the British Museum; titled "The Vertue of the COFFEE Drink," it claims that coffee "is excellent to prevent and cure the Dropsy, Gout, and Scurvy," not to mention "very good to prevent Mis-carrying in Child-bearing Women" and "a most excellent Remedy against the Spleen, Hypocondriack Winds, or the like." More truthfully, the handbill states that coffee "will prevent Drowsiness, and make one fit for business," and warns that "you are not to Drink of it after Supper, unless you intend to be watchful, for it will hinder sleep for 3 or 4 hours." The coffee was advertised as "Made and Sold in St. Michael's Alley in Cornhill, by Pasqua Rosee, at the Signe of his own Head." Whatever the true benefits of the drink, it caught on. At their peak in the eighteenth century, there were probably thousands of coffeehouses in Britain.

Even more than today, in the eighteenth century London was the social, commercial, and scientific hub of Britain. And its coffeehouses were the social, commercial, and scientific news and information centers of London. A modern writer describes them as "an eighteenth-century business internet, as well as social centres. Men interested in the same things, whether business, politics or pleasure, tended to converge on the same establishment." In this era of sociability, coffeehouses provided a unique and popular service; there, in Peter Ackroyd's words, "a roaring fire guaranteed warmth and hot water; a penny on the counter brought you a dish of coffee or chocolate; the newspapers, hanging on the wall, were all that were needed for entertainment and conversation." These amenities were not offered in elegant surroundings; most of London's coffeehouses offered only bare wooden floors and stiff Windsor chairs for their décor.

Because that dish of coffee cost so little, and because information was plentiful and free, coffeehouses came to be called "penny universities." A visitor to a London coffeehouse could take lessons in French, Italian, or Latin; listen to lectures on poetry, mathematics, or astronomy; or even sign up for lessons in dancing or fencing. Coffeehouses were so effective in spreading knowledge and learning that some British aristocrats feared their leveling effect on education—and feared what a newly educated rising class of merchants might start to think.

The coffeehouses were clustered in Cornhill, near the Royal Exchange and the offices of the Virginia Company, the East India Company, and the Royal Africa Company. Lloyd's Coffeehouse—which eventually became the global powerhouse Lloyd's of London—attracted shipping insurers who met there to learn all the latest nautical news. Jonathan's was convenient for stockbrokers; traders to the Baltic met at the Baltic coffeehouse in Threadneedle Street; the Grecian in Devereux Court was the place for Fellows of the Royal Society. And between 1689 and about 1706, the coffeehouse for naturalists was the Temple Coffee House near Fleet Street.

There Sir Hans Sloane, James Petiver, and others from across Britain and abroad gathered "to pore over plant specimens and discuss the latest botanical discoveries from the New World and beyond." Samuel Dale, apothecary-botanist and Mark Catesby's neighbor, also attended gatherings at the Temple. By the late seventeenth century, natural history had become a respectable enterprise for men like these; at the Temple you might encounter Anglican bishops, apothecaries like Petiver, American settlers, East India merchants, and sea captains who were between voyages. It was a democratic place, where "tradesmen mingled easily with gentlemen, apothecaries shared intelligence with noble lords, and simple carpenters contributed as much as highly placed baronets." And it was overwhelmingly a fraternity; though there were in fact coffeehouses for women, they were such a novelty as to reinforce the idea that the coffeehouse was a masculine preserve.

Details about the Temple House Coffee Club's activities and membership are sketchy, but they suggest that the club was "both a significant focal point for scientific virtuosi and a fertile environment for the proliferation of botanical knowledge in the late seventeenth and early eighteenth centuries." The proceedings were probably like that of another "Botanical Society" begun in 1721 as weekly meetings in the Rainbow Coffee House, before it was moved to a private house. At this group's Rainbow meetings, "every member was obliged to exhibit a certain number of plants, to make observation upon their characters, and to set forth their various uses." Augustan coffeehouses were an integral part of that network of botanical and natural-history aficionados that Mark Catesby would access.

◆

Less than a decade after Rosée's coffeehouse opening in St. Michael's Alley, a group of keen scientific experts, enthusiasts, and experimenters decided that a more formal venue was needed to discuss and examine the phenomena which it seemed were being discovered and described almost daily. The organization they created would become one of the most esteemed of its kind in the world.

On November 28, 1660, Christopher Wren, the twenty-eight-year-old architect, astronomer, and physicist who in less than a decade would become famous for leading London's rebuilding after the Great Fire, delivered a lecture at Gresham College in central London. Later that evening, a group of intellectuals gathered with the idea of forming a "learned society." Their regular meetings soon attracted other leading polymaths of the age, including Robert Boyle, considered the first modern chemist, and John Wilkins, Anglican clergyman, philosopher, and author. In 1662 the society received royal approval and the formal name it bears to this day. In 1703 Sir Isaac Newton became president of the Society, and in 1710 it moved into its first permanent headquarters on Crane Court, Fleet Street, where a lamp would be hung over the entrance to the court on meeting nights.

The Royal Society served as the nexus for Englishmen and visitors from the Continent who were interested in science and natural history. Its presidents included Wren and Samuel Pepys, as well as Newton; its motto, "Nullius in verba," usually translated as "take nobody's word for it," embodied the fellows' determination to find truth through scientific experiment, and not, as had been the custom since medieval times, by consulting ancient authority. The Society's founding and programs helped to make science a mainstream activity in a way that had not been common before. No longer hidden in university or theological settings, science was being promulgated by curious amateurs, who conducted their own experiments, debated the results with their friends, and communicated their findings in letters, pamphlets, and books.

From the beginning, the Society had two important functions. The fellows were intent on performing their own experiments, and on hearing firsthand from those who had seen or experienced natural phenomena. The Society published Hooke's *Micrographia*, with groundbreaking illustrations using a microscope, and Newton's *Principia Mathematica*, featuring his elaboration of the laws of gravity. They began to record the proceedings in their journal, the *Philosophical Transactions*.

The Society's second main purpose was to encourage and solicit the gathering of artifacts and specimens from the growing number of travelers from Britain to the widespread lands, and markets, of the Middle East, Africa, Asia, and America. The Society's repository of objects grew as private collections were added, particularly that of Robert Hubert, whose collections, described in his *Catalog of Many Natural Rarities*, were a famous attraction in London. The Hubert "rarities" included an Egyptian mummy, exotic birds (dead), and a two-headed calf. Although the lists of items in collections such as Hubert's have a bit of a freak-show air, the Society was careful to stress the opportunities for scientific experiment, and the enlargement of general knowledge, that such specimens offered.

It was Boyle who in the first volume of the *Transactions of the Royal Society* in 1666 gave detailed instructions on the collection of specimens "for the use of travellers and navigators." These "General Heads for a Natural History of a Countrey, Great or Small," were almost all-inclusive, concerning "those things that respect the Heavens, or concern the Air, the Water, or the Earth." The Society wanted its correspondents to find out "what Grasses, Grains, Herbs, (Garden and Wild) Flowers, Fruit-trees, Timber-trees (especially any Trees, whose wood is considerable) Coppices, Groves, Woods, Forrests, &c. the Country has or wants." In addition, these amateur volunteers were kindly requested to learn "What Animals the Country has . . . both as to wild Beasts, Hawks, and other Birds of Prey; and as to Poultrey, and Cattle of all sorts, and particularly, whether it have any Animals, that are not common, or any thing, that is peculiar in those, that are so."

As the phrase "timber-trees" suggests, there was always a commercial angle to the Society's proceedings. From its very beginnings, the Society looked outward to the horizons where British ships in pursuit of trade pushed into Asia, Africa, and America. In Richard Drayton's nice turn of phrase, the Royal Society "harnessed national commerce to the chariot of natural history." Merchants were recruited, and their voyages co-opted into the grand game of collecting specimens.

One intrepid voyager of the time paid close attention to these instructions. Daniel Defoe's fictional Robinson Crusoe, whose tale of shipwrecks, pirates, and life as a castaway was published in 1719, was among other things a naturalist. His detailed journal, with what a modern scholar calls its "array of Caribbean specimens and artifacts (including melons, limes, tobacco plants, and earthenware pots)," seems to have been planned according to Boyle's collecting instructions.

◆

The Royal Society, like the coffeehouses, was firmly a fraternity. It took almost three centuries from its founding, until 1945, for the first two women, Kathleen Lonsdale and Marjory Stephenson, to be elected Fellows of the Royal Society. This was, sadly, typical of an age in which eighteenth-century women were prohibited from voting and from owning property; the universities, the professions, and the Church were denied to them as well, though there were those exceptions who wielded power behind the scenes due to their social standing or personal magnetism.

Modern scholarship, however, has pointed out the debt owed by the experimenters and the virtuosi of the time to the women of the house. Many experiments in chemistry, biology, and medicine were carried out in the homes of the fairly wealthy and the landed and titled of Britain. The technology and knowledge needed for these experiments had been developed in the kitchen, traditionally the domain of women. It was they who were expected to have the surgical and pharmaceutical knowledge to maintain the family's health; popular cookbooks of the day included remedies for a number of illnesses. In the process, women acquired skills such as grinding, weighing, distilling, drying, purifying, heating, and cooling. This experience had obvious applications to the scientific field, and made women instrumental in carrying out the private projects' of the amateur scientific enthusiasts of Augustan England.

The age also saw individual women who were noted for their interest in chemistry, mathematics, and astronomy. Margaret Cavendish (1623–1673) thought and wrote with such brilliance in such varied fields as poetry, fiction, drama, and science that she dared to publish works in her own name in an era when most women writers remained anonymous. Margaret Flamsteed (1670–1730) married John Flamsteed, the first Astronomer Royal, in 1692; after his death she oversaw the publication of his two most important books, and his research notes display her intricate knowledge of astronomy. Women such as these, however, like the existence of women's coffeehouses, were the exceptions that proved the rule; they were considered novelties, and not evidence of any need to include women as a whole in the intellectual life of the nation.

There were, however, acceptable outlets for women's interest in natural history and scientific knowledge. Augustan sociability made it increasingly fashionable for women to attend public lectures and even use scientific instruments. A book published in 1719, *Astronomical Dialogues between a Gentleman and a Lady*, "emphasized the conversational benefits that attended a lady who knew just enough natural philosophy to converse with males but not so much as to embarass them."

◆

We don't know whether Mark Catesby ever visited a London coffeehouse. Perhaps a teenaged Catesby and his father had a customary coffeehouse stop in the City while in town to see to John's businesses; later Mark might even have visited the Temple with his uncle Nicholas. Before his first overseas voyage Catesby could have dropped in at the Virginia Coffee House in Cornhill for news and intelligence about Williamsburg and the Virginia colony, to add to what his brother-in-law William Cocke could supply. A few years later, while back in London gathering sponsors for his research trip to South Carolina, Catesby probably would have known to stop in at the Carolina Coffeehouse, on Birchin Lane, "the epicenter for conversations about the colony, its business opportunities, and its residents," where "thousands of prospective emigrants first learned about the Carolina Colony and booked passage to that distant land." And of course it is easy to imagine the young naturalist at the Temple, overhearing the latest botanical news, or perhaps even discussing it with Dale, Petiver, or Sloane.

But we can't be sure. Nor are there any records connecting Catesby to the Royal Society before 1729, when he presented the first section of his *Natural History* to the fellows. With his access to his uncle's library and his connections to Ray and especially to Dale, he could have been quite familiar with the Society and the accounts of its proceedings in the *Philosophical*

Transactions. He may well have attended meetings before 1712 as a guest, and heard the French François Xavier Bon's "Discourse upon the usefulness of silk of spiders," or even James Petiver's "farther account of divers rare plants" in "several curious gardens about London," particularly "in the Company of Apothecaries physick-garden at Chelsey." In the 1730s and 1740s, back in London after his two trips to the New World, the Society would be Mark Catesby's intellectual home base. He would read the successive chapters of the *Natural History* there; he would attend meetings, sit on committees, and send articles to the *Philosophical Transactions.*

What we do know is that by taking the network he knew in the countryside of his youth and extending it to the virtuosi, to the collectors and enthusiasts in the Temple Coffee House and the Royal Society, Catesby created a market for the plants and seeds he would send back while on his first trip to the colonies in the New World. He never showed any hesitation about connecting with the powerful scientific elite of London, understanding that the route to America, to the frontier of natural history, went through the ancient city on the Thames. He had moved in overlapping circles of society: the corresponding botanist-naturalists, from country parsons to the rich and powerful; the virtuosi, with their elaborate cabinets of curiosities; the Royal Society, mainly well-born and of a scientific bent. Leveraging his connections in this way, he would begin to establish himself as an artist and explorer on the edge of empire.

4

WILLIAMSBURG, WILLIAM BYRD, AND THE FRONTIER 1712–1717

"Not being content with contemplating the Products of our own Country, I soon imbibed a passionate Desire of viewing as well the Animal as well as Vegetable Productions in their Native Countries," Catesby wrote in the *Natural History* of his coming of age. Fortunately, he found a way to fulfill that desire. Virginia, he wrote, would be "the Place (I having Relations there) suited most with my Convenience to go to; where I arriv'd the 23d. of April 1712."

Those relations were his sister Elizabeth, who had married William Cocke, and their children. Cocke had sailed to Virginia in 1710, established a medical practice, and become a leading citizen of the colony's capital, Williamsburg. When Elizabeth left for America with their children two years later, Catesby accompanied her.

Elizabeth had married William against her father's wishes. In his will John Catesby provided a grudging amount for her in case her "supposed Husband" was "imprisoned for debt or other cause or . . . goe beyond sea or otherwise absent and abscond himself from her." Her father, however, would be mistaken about William Cocke, who would bring Elizabeth to the New World and who would thrive there, personally, professionally, and politically. After Felsted Grammar School, Cocke had received his M.B. at Queens' College, Cambridge. In Virginia, he became an ally of Lieutenant Governor Alexander Spotswood, was made secretary to the colony, and in 1713 became one of Her Majesty's councilors.

When the twenty-nine-year-old Catesby arrived in Virginia accompanying his sister and her children, he might have felt something like culture shock. Suffolk and Essex, like most of England, had had a homogeneous culture for centuries: one language, one religion (although with sectarian issues), one worldview. Now he found himself in a frontier colony with at least three distinct cultures: a shallow British one (dating in Virginia only to 1632, when Catesby's grandfather was still a teenager), a transplanted African one (though in fact comprised of a number of African cultures and languages, most English eyes saw it as only one), and that of the indigenous Americans. The rural countryside of eastern England was homogenous indeed to compared to this New World.

Williamsburg was then the only town in Virginia, its twenty-two buildings barely making a mark upon the landscape. Tobacco farmers were scattered throughout the surrounding area, clearing fields and planting around the charred stumps of trees. Too poor for oxen, they used hoes for the backbreaking work of turning wilderness into farmland. Far from the brick neoclassical edifices we consider to be Colonial Williamsburg's trademark today, the farmers' houses were covered with rough clapboards and had wooden chimneys.

In Williamsburg, however, stood several fine brick buildings: the statehouse and governor's mansion, built after the town's selection as Virginia's capital in 1699, and William and Mary College, also begun in the 1690s and named in honor of England's king and queen. Residents of Williamsburg, wrote one contemporary observer, "live in the same neat manner, dress after the same modes, and behave themselves exactly as the gentry in London"—though a modern writer has warned that that observer "was not an impartial observer," but "a proud Englishman who wrote with patriotic zeal." His readers, "if they believed him at all, would have read his statement to mean only that Virginia colonists had not adopted Indian ways."

Cocke's connections allowed Catesby to befriend the most powerful landowners and merchants in the Virginia colony. The most prominent of these was William Byrd II, scion of one of the great families of colonial Virginia, whom Catesby met within a week of his arrival in Williamsburg. A fellow of the Royal Society, Byrd had served as Virginia's official agent in London and as a representative to the House of Burgesses and had attended Felsted with Cocke. He "criss-crossed the Atlantic as the agent of the Virginia Assembly," and knew Sir Hans Sloane personally, regularly sending him botanical specimens from America.

At Westover, his country seat on the James River, Byrd amassed the largest library in the colonies, with over three thousand volumes; in his journal he would record that Catesby "directed how I should mend my garden and put it into better fashion than it is at present." Catesby now had the chance to show Byrd and the Virginians what he had learned of plantsmanship. His pattern of cultivating patrons along with plants, which would prove so useful in London and in South Carolina, began with William Byrd in Williamsburg.

Within weeks of his first visit to Westover, Catesby again made the thirty-two-mile trip there with William and Elizabeth Cocke, which typically took between four and nine hours depending on the pace of the traveler's horse. Catesby lingered for three weeks after his sister and brother-in-law departed, making forays in search of hummingbirds' nests and learning from his host about the flora and fauna of the New World. It was a sociable time, with cakes and wine and strolls around the grounds of Westover. On one notable occasion, according to Byrd's journal, he and Catesby enjoyed themselves so much aboard a ship on the James River that on the way home, they "were so merry that Mr. Catesby sang." This rare glimpse into Catesby's behavior hints that though he could abandon his customary reserve, it was a rare occurrence for him.

This idyllic existence at Westover and Williamsburg relied on what for Catesby would have been an entirely new domestic construct: households operating by the labor of enslaved Black people. Byrd, who read Greek and Hebrew in his immense library of classical and Enlightenment literature, not only owned enslaved people, but was perhaps even more than typically cruel to them. In the same journal in which Byrd recorded that Catesby "directed how I should mend my garden and put it into better fashion than it is at present," he wrote, "I beat Jenny for throwing water on the couch." On September 18, Byrd wrote, "Mr. Catesby and I took a walk and I found Eugene asleep instead of being at work, for which I beat him severely."

Catesby gives us something of an opinion of Byrd's behavior in the *Natural History*; discussing the widespread consumption of "Indian corn," both by whites and enslaved Black people, Catesby adds, "its strong Nourishment . . . adapts it . . . as the properest Food for Negro Slaves." When forced to eat wheat instead, the enslaved Blacks became so weak "that they begged of their Master to allow them Indian Corn again, or they could not work." This was related to him by Byrd, who, according to Catesby, then "found it in *his* Interest to comply with their Request" (emphasis added)— but not, rather pointedly, out of any concern by Byrd for their personal welfare or comfort.

On September 22, 1712, Catesby accompanied Byrd to the Pamunkey Native American town on the Pamunkey River, where the Virginia officials settled a dispute between the Chickahominy and the Pamunkey tribes. This was probably Catesby's first contact with Indigenous Americans, besides those he saw in the town of Williamsburg. The Pamunkey were the largest and one of the most powerful tribes of the Powhatan confederacy; Powhatan himself, the noted chief, and his daughter Matoaka (better known today as Pocahontas) were Pamunkey, living almost a century before Catesby's time. It had been the Pamunkey who captured Captain John Smith at Jamestown, and who gave the settlers provisions without which they would not have survived their first winter in the New World.

Byrd recorded in his diary on September 23, "There is an Indian called P-t W-l who has now his 20 wives. There was also an Indian who was ill of a bite of a rattlesnake but was on the recovery having taken some snakeroot." Byrd believed in snakeroot's curative powers and regularly made a drink with it, sometimes mixed with sage. Catesby never disputed Byrd's beliefs, at least in print, though his skepticism in the *Natural History* as to the efficacy of snakeroot as a snakebite antidote is fairly obvious.

◆

"In the Year 1714," Catesby wrote, "I travelled from the lower part of St. James's River in Virginia to that part of the Apalatchian Mountains where the Sources of that River rise." It is possible that it was Byrd who invited Catesby to join him on this journey to western Virginia, where Catesby performed his initial fieldwork in America, making drawings of plants and animals which he thought native to the country. He also took extensive notes on the topography and geology of the area, writing a detailed description which he included in the *Natural History*. "Here we kill'd plenty of a particular Kind of wild Geese," Catesby wrote; "they were very fat by feeding on fresh Water Snails, which were in great plenty, sticking to the Tops and Sides of the Rocks." Ascending a ridge, Catesby's party "could discern some of the nearer Mountains, and beheld most delightful Prospects, but the Country being an entire Forest, the Meanders of the Rivers, with other Beauties, were much obscured by the Trees."

For perhaps the first time, Catesby was in a land that had not been completely transformed according to Western practices, that had not been settled and planted according to European custom. On this trip up the James he would encounter the Native American landscape: the woodlands and grasslands as they had been lived in, and often altered, by the cultural practices of the Indigenous people who had been on the land for centuries.

The early explorers had noted the Indigenous practice of setting fires in all areas of North America, from New England to Florida and west over the Allegheny Mountains. The forests that resulted, open and majestic, reminded the first European observers of their great parks. The fires set by Native Americans also created large glades and meadows, made the grass thicker and more lush, and spurred fruits and berries to grow thick and ripe. One modern writer has referred to the resulting eastern broadleaf forests as "in effect, one vast Indian orchard."

In the *Natural History* Catesby refers to "an annual custom of the Indians in their Huntings, of setting the Woods on Fire many Miles in Extent." What he called "their annual Custom of Fire-Hunting" usually took place in October when "some Hundreds of Indians . . . spreading themselves in Length thro' a great Extent of Country, set the Woods on Fire." The wind then drives the fire "to some Peninsula, or Neck of Land, into which Deers, Bears, and other Animals are drove by the raging Fire and Smoak," where "being hemm'd in" the animals are "destroy'd in great Numbers by their Guns." This October burning, in addition to aiding Natives' hunting, might also have been done to cause the effects on the forest as stated above, making it more open and its grass lusher. William Bartram, who described the wide vistas and huge trees of the Southeastern woods that he saw during his travels across the South in the 1770s, never mentions fire. Neither Catesby nor Bartram seem to have understood how the landscape they witnessed was affected by Indigenous practices, but rather accepted it as "natural," or "unspoiled," or "primeval."

◆

When it came to his activities as a naturalist, Catesby downplayed his time in Virginia, writing, "I chiefly gratified my Inclination in observing and admiring the various Productions of those Countries." He seemed to reproach himself about his first visit to America: "I thought then . . . little of prosecuting a Design of the Nature of this Work [the *Natural History*]."

But Catesby was not exactly idle for those seven years. Sometime during this first visit to America, Catesby visited the Eastern Shore, the peninsula of land extending south across the Chesapeake Bay from Williamsburg. It is now often called the Delmarva peninsula, as it contains parts of Delaware, Maryland, and Virginia. "*Accomack* is a narrow slip of Land in *Virginia*," wrote Catesby in his *Natural History*, "having the Sea on one side, and the Bay of *Chesapeck* on the other, here I saw Fig-trees, with Trunks of a large Size, and of many Years standing, without any Injury received by hard Weather." He observed that "on the opposite Shore were only Fig-trees of a very Small size, occasioned by their being often killed to the Ground."

Back in Williamsburg he also cultivated what he referred to as "my garden," probably on his brother-in-law William Cocke's property. He carried out experimentation and transplanting of trees, shrubs, and flowers there and in the gardens of William Byrd II and of Thomas Jones, a prosperous merchant and planter who would marry Catesby's niece Elizabeth.

Nor did Catesby merely "observe and admire" the "various Productions" he found in Virginia. When Lieutenant Governor Spotswood sent a packet of seeds to Henry Compton, the Bishop of London, in the spring of 1713 he wrote, "These are collected by a Gentleman now in this Country, a nephew of Mr. Jekyll's of Castle [Hedingham] and one very curious in such things." Importantly for his future as a naturalist, Catesby also sent specimens to Samuel Dale, as well as to Thomas Fairchild, perhaps the most famous nurseryman in England. In addition, Catesby would later write of "Sweet flowering Acacia" trees he saw growing at Castle Hedingham; he is thought to have sent these to his uncle Nicholas Jekyll from Virginia.

Catesby asserted that he "only [sent] from thence some dried Specious of them in Tubs of Earth, at the request of some curious friends." His choice of dried plants was an astute one, especially for someone who was new to the practice of sending fragile specimens long distances in uncertain conditions. Those conditions made the *hortus siccus* (literally, dried garden) the mainstay of serious eighteenth-century botanists.

In the twenty-first century, live plants can be shipped practically overnight from the United States to Great Britain via such companies as UPS or Federal Express. Other companies specialize in purpose-made corrugated plant-shipping boxes;

and just as Petiver and Woodward provided eighteenth-century instructions for sending plants from faraway places to England, such companies now provide, on their Internet websites, a "Checklist of Essential Material for Safely Shipping Plants," including corrugated boxes, sterilized potting soil, bubble wrap, flea collars, ties or rubber bands, and paper towels.

In the 1720s, however, the difficulty of sending live plants, or even seeds, safely and securely across vast distances and over oceans led explorers and collectors to depend on the botanical method which had prevailed since the mid-sixteenth century: the *hortus siccus*. As a modern historian has noted, "a well-labeled herbarium specimen is the link between a plant's identity and the evidence of its occurrence at a particular point in time and space."

Preserved, pressed specimens were easier to ship, and more likely to arrive at their destinations intact. Done properly, dried plants could be studied and compared with other specimens back in England. In fact, around two thousand dried specimens sent by Catesby during his two trips to America still exist today in the herbaria of Oxford and Cambridge Universities, the Natural History Museum, London, the Linnean Society, and Royal Botanic Garden Edinburgh.

Collectors who were willing to take the gamble also sent live plants in barrels of soil and seeds, which could become part of an English botanical garden, or *hortus vivus* (living garden). The owners of these gardens were sometimes motivated by the desire to study rare and exotic plants—and, presumably, to show them to others. Others were more interested in growing medicinal plants.

During his time in Virginia, then, Catesby sent mainly dried plant specimens, as well as seeds and a few live plants, back to England, mainly to Samuel Dale. Dale reported to the botanist and patron William Sherard that Catesby had brought back seventy specimens, half of them new to England. Although not nearly on the scale of his time in South Carolina, his shipments of botanical specimens foreshadowed the sizable number of live plants, seeds, and dried plants he would send to the sponsors of his second exploration of America.

Catesby remained in Virginia for seven years; little record remains of the last several years of his time there, though in all likelihood he tended to his brother-in-law William Cocke's business affairs and his family while Cocke was in England from 1716 to 1718. Despite his low opinion of his time spent there, Catesby saw and recorded much. His masterwork, though titled *Natural History of Carolina*, would abound with references to plants and animals which existed in Virginia as well as the Carolinas; some of its etched and painted plates came directly from preliminary sketches and paintings done during this first stay in America.

It is not known exactly why Catesby chose to return to Britain. The oldest Catesby brother, Jekyll, who could be presumed to have acted as head of the family, died in September 1717. This made Mark at least the titular head of the family, as his brother John was only twenty and still a minor. Mark may therefore have thought it necessary to return to England after Jekyll's death, both to see to the family property and finances and to look after John.

Nevertheless, his first visit to the New World portended more intensive explorations to come. He had befriended important people in America, seen a good bit of its topography, and its flora and fauna, and had had his first interactions with enslaved Africans and Native Americans. He had also established himself in the minds of prominent figures in London as a talented and dependable naturalist who could bring back meaningful knowledge from British America. Within two years of his return to London, he would sail once again for North America, this time with a more definite plan for achieving his goals as plantsman, naturalist, artist, and author.

5

JAMAICA AND THE CARIBBEAN
1717–1718

During his first foray to the New World, Mark Catesby's curiosity was enough to send him from Virginia to the Caribbean. In 1717 he took passage to Jamaica on a cargo boat carrying sheep; according to Catesby, the animals "as they approached the South, gradually dropt their Fleeces, which by the Time they arrived at the Island, was all fallen off, and was succeeded by Hair, like that of Goats." To him this was proof of "the wise Designs of Providence," for "bestowing on these Creatures extraordinary Cloathing so neccssary to human Life in cold Countries," while also "easing them of that Load which otherwise might be insupportable to them in sultry Countries, and of little use to Man."

Sailing around the eastern end first of Cuba, then of Jamaica, and catching sight of Jamaica's capital and main port, Kingston, he could have agreed with James Knight, one of Jamaica's first historians, who wrote,

At some leagues distance, this Island makes a very Solemn and surprising Figure, the Mountains, being preposterously modelled and appearing one above Another to a Stupendous height, with such strange Irregularity and Seeming Confusion, as if they had been thrown together by Chance . . . A Range of Clouds commonly hang about the Summit of those Mountains, the heads or tops of which sometimes appear above the Clouds.

As with his time in Virginia, no letters from Catesby's first visit to the Caribbean survive. But his entries in the *Natural History*, as well as later letters written after his return to England, give us something of an account of Catesby's exploration of the natural history of these islands—and, to a lesser extent, his view of Jamaican society and its economy.

◆

When North Americans think of the colonial period, we have been trained to think mainly of Massachusetts and Virginia, of John and Samuel Adams, of Benjamin Franklin, of Jefferson and Washington. Our mental images of Colonial America date largely from the later 1700s, when those places and men were the center of the action. The national mythology seems to jump directly from Jamestown and the Pilgrims to Paul Revere, Bunker Hill, and Concord.

But in the early 1700s, the center of gravity in the Western Hemisphere lay to the south of Boston, Philadelphia, and

Williamsburg. It was in the West Indies and South Carolina, the mainland colony which was in many ways an outpost of the Caribbean, where Continental powers, pirates, and planters focused their ambitions, their firepower, their manpower. It was there that the wealthiest colonies—first Barbados, then Jamaica, then South Carolina—flourished, thanks to the international trade in sugar and rice. And, not coincidentally, it was there that the slave economy first reached its fullest and most complete domination of life, industry, and government.

Catesby in 1717 was visiting the richest colony in the nascent British Empire, thanks to sugar and the enslaved labor force that made its cultivation possible. Jamaica was just then claiming this distinction over Barbados, which for a century had been the leading producer of colonial wealth before soil exhaustion took its toll on sugar production. Kingston, in turn, was at that point the richest and most important town in British America.

Christopher Columbus had spotted the island on his 1494 second voyage to the New World—or the West Indies, as he would call them to the day he died. Columbus, Hans Sloane wrote in his book about Jamaica, "was extremely pleased with this Island, thinking it surpassed any he had yet seen, for Verdure, Fertility, Victuals, &c." After the Indigenous Taino people were nearly exterminated by disease and mistreatment, the Spanish had begun bringing slaves from Africa to work the sugar fields of the colony they called Santiago. By the 1660s, the English were casting an envious eye on the island and its wealth; during the interregnum under Oliver Cromwell, an English fleet seized Jamaica from Spanish control. When Sloane came to the island two decades later, the lush subtropical environment had reclaimed "the Settlements and Plantations of, not only the Indians, but even the Spaniards . . . so that there were no Footsteps of such a thing left, were it not for old Palisadoes, Buildings, Orange Walks, &c. which shew plainly the formerly clear'd places where Plantations have been."

As with Barbados beforehand and South Carolina later, Jamaica by 1680 had a larger Black population than white; sugar already was its largest export by value. By that same year, its capital Port Royal was the second most populous town in the British Americas, behind only Boston. It was also one of the rowdiest, known for the drinking and carousing of its planter's sons and its buccaneers such as Henry Morgan. In fact, the sugar economy might have developed even faster except that almost half of the male white population of Jamaica was involved not in agriculture, but in buccaneering. Not content with waylaying heavy-laden Spanish ships returning to Europe, Morgan successfully laid siege to the Panamanian town of Porto Bello in 1668. Then, in a feat seldom attempted even today, Morgan and his men fought their way through the thick jungle of Panama's isthmus, across what's now called the Darien Gap, and sacked the city of Panama in 1671.

The "pirate economy" was based simultaneously on plunder of the Spanish and on illicit trade with them. It made Port Royal one of the wealthiest communities in English North America and a haven of privateers (privately owned ships sailing and fighting ostensibly under the commission of the Crown), buccaneers (an umbrella term for both privateers and pirates, from a French word *boucane*, referring to the frame on which early French pirates on Hispaniola smoked meat), and occasionally outright pirates (formally distinguished by acts of theft at sea, committed under no nation's flag). Morgan himself eventually became a plantation owner, and later lieutenant governor of Jamaica; the former pirate occasionally filled in as governor, and died on his Jamaican estates in 1688.

A 1692 earthquake destroyed Port Royal, dislodging the buccaneers from Jamaica and moving the capital to Kingston. Two-thirds of the town had disappeared into the harbor, including the cemetery containing Henry Morgan's grave. Sloane wrote of the quake, "When the Sand tumbled upon the shaking of the Earth, into the Sea, it covered the Anchors of Ships riding by the Wharfs . . . the greatest part of the Town fell, great numbers of people were lost, and a good part of the Neck of Land where the Town stood was three Fathoms covered with water."

A yellow fever epidemic followed soon after, reducing Jamaica's population from ten thousand to seven thousand people by 1700. This string of catastrophes for the island's people finally subsided, however, and the end of the War of Spanish Succession in 1713 led to a generation of relative peace in the Caribbean, allowing Jamaica to become Britain's largest and richest colony, thanks to sugar.

For the British in Jamaica, though, the peace was only relative. In the interior of Jamaica, in the folds and ravines of the Blue Mountains, the Maroons—fiercely independent people who had escaped Spanish enslavement, as well as free Blacks and a smattering of the remnant Taino—defended their *palenques*, stockaded mountain farms. First against the Spanish, then the English, the Maroons—from the Spanish *cimarron*, "wild" or "untamed"—raided plantations and welcomed runaway slaves into their communities. Clashes between the Maroons and British authorities intermingled with periods of collaboration, when Maroons, as the price of their autonomy, helped the British recapture other enslaved people attempting to escape their bondage. This dynamic continued, provoking periodic conflicts including the Maroon Wars of the 1730s and 1790s, until the mid-1860s. Today, Maroon communities still exist in Jamaica, somewhat autonomous and separate from the dominant Jamaican culture. Self-governing and free from taxation, they strive to retain their culture and traditions.

The other threat to the Jamaican peace was a phenomenon that has provided romantic myths, stories, books, and movies to a fascinated public for centuries. It is a quirk of history that like the cowboy-and-Indian period of the American Wild West, which spanned only a couple of decades, the historical Golden Age of Piracy—the age of Blackbeard and the Jolly Roger—lasted only from about 1716 to 1726. Mark Catesby happened to land in Jamaica just as this phenomenon was making itself felt across the Gulf of Mexico and the Caribbean, not to mention in Madrid and London.

Piracy in the region was nothing new. Since the early 1500s, the amount of Spanish wealth being shipped through the Caribbean, and the lack of any enforceable authority, made it the theater of constant conflict. Fierce Elizabethan sea dogs, most famously Sir Francis Drake, roamed the seas with the tacit approval of the Crown, seeking, as pirate historian Marcus Rediker has written, "in one deft move both to singe the Spaniard's beard and to line their own pockets with gold and silver."

The end of the War of Spanish Succession in 1713 indirectly created the Golden Age of Piracy. Ironically, the cessation of hostilities caused the British Navy to reduce its ranks, leaving a number of able-bodied seamen without livelihoods. At the same time, with the *Asiento* it had acquired from Spain, Britain now had the right to import up to 4,800 slaves a year legally—it imported many, many more illegally—to Spanish America via the South Sea Company. The resulting boom in the slave trade would be matched with an increase in piracy, and the lowest years of the trade in human slaves came in 1720–1722, the years of greatest pirate activity. Pirates were not just targeting Spanish ships; they considered British vessels as fair game, too.

The pirates were not all British: some were from America and the Caribbean, and from Holland, France, Spain, Africa, even parts of Asia. One seventeenth-century English merchant seaman and privateersman was known to speak English, Spanish, French, Dutch, and the Mediterranean *lingua franca*, a kind of pidgin common language spoken across the Mediterranean region between the eleventh to nineteenth centuries.

They were not all men, either, at least according to our main source about this era, *A General History of the Robberies and Murders of the Most Notorious Pyrates*, written in 1724 by Captain Charles Johnson. Johnson is almost certainly a synonym for a London journalist named Nathaniel Mist; however, there is some foundation to believe that at least one other writer contributed to the book: none other than Daniel Defoe. The author relates the stories of Anne Bonney and Mary Read. He knows that some readers "may be tempted to think the whole Story no better than a Novel or Romance," but as "it is supported by many thousand Witnesses" who were present at the women's trials for piracy, "the Truth of it can be no more contested, than that there such Men in the World as Roberts and Black-beard, who were Pyrates."

Anne Bonney had been born in Ireland around 1700, but moved to Charleston with her father, who disowned her after she married a small-time pirate named James Bonney in 1718. Anne and James moved to the Bahamas, where she fell in with "Calico Jack" Rackham, a pirate captain. Leaving her husband, she sailed dressed as a man with Rackham and his crew, which also included one of the few other pirate women, Mary Read, who also disguised herself as a man. Rackham's ship and crew were captured in 1720 in Jamaica, and sentenced to hang for piracy. Rackham was executed, but the two women pled pregnancy. Mary died of fever in prison; no one knows what became of Anne Bonny.

This was the era of Edward Teach or Thatch, alias Black-beard, who "consciously cultivated an image of himself as Satan, tying up his long black hair and beard in pigtails and inserting sparklers around his face to create an eerie, fiery glow when capturing prize vessels." The Jolly Roger pirate flag was not an invention of the mythologizers. It was flown by at least 2,500 pirate crews, and possibly many more. The flag was generally black, with white figures, most commonly a human skull, though sometimes with an entire skeleton. Other recurring Jolly Roger symbols were the cutlass and the hourglass.

Pirate society was surprisingly democratic. Captains could be replaced by a vote of the crew at any time. All who were aboard pirate ships signed contracts specifying the proportions of captured goods to be awarded each seaman; typically the captain and first mate received double shares, the rest single.

As is often the case in the Caribbean, the south coast of Jamaica is surrounded by numerous smaller islands, a topography perfect for piracy. There are inlets, lagoons, and shallow bays for hiding and escaping from bigger ships, and for stashing provisions (and, perhaps, buried treasure). The islets also provide water, and plentiful food from the sea: fish, shellfish, and turtles. Willing buyers and sellers of the pirates' booty were never very far away.

In an interesting parallel to the web of correspondence and coffeehouse meetings that provided naturalists in Britain with the latest news, gossip, and discoveries, pirates made use of the informal network which flourished among seamen in and around the varied places of the seagoing life. Information flowed constantly between ship, dock, brothel, jail, and tavern, alerting the pirate crews to the latest shipwreck of a Spanish silver fleet or the imminent arrival of the Royal Navy looking to crack down on the buccaneers' illegal activities.

Mark Catesby may or may not have had the experience of walking past pirates' corpses hanging from the gibbet in Kingston Harbor as a warning to others, as would be done with Calico Jack's body a few years after Catesby's time in Jamaica. But he would have met Kingstonians who had first- or secondhand experience of pirates and piracy. On his next visit to America, the fates of the specimens he attempted to ship to England and the success of his efforts as a naturalist would for a time be tied to the world of transatlantic piracy.

◆

In spite of the difficulties caused by Maroons and pirates, the British in Jamaica and their other holdings in the Caribbean created a dynamic and revolutionary agricultural economy, though it was one built on the exploitation of enslaved human labor. Turning cane into sugar on a large scale required skills, techniques, and technology which were on the leading edge of industrial innovation. The process was more like modern assembly lines than any agriculture of the time in Europe. The sugar industry in the Caribbean was one of the first spheres of activity producing highly regimented, quality-controlled, mass-produced agricultural products. To do this, Jamaica's planters had to stay abreast of the most current scientific and labor management strategies.

Unfortunately for the island's enslaved people, sugar and slavery turned out to be a perfect fit. The mindless, soul-numbing drudgery of sugarcane processing matched the need of slaveowners for work which would crush the spirits of the enslaved, minimizing the prospect of rebellion or any other kind of independent action. James Knight wrote, "When they begin to work or grind their Canes, they Continue at it night and day, Sundays excepted, relieving their Servants, Negroes and Beasts every four hours." There were slaves in the Caribbean before sugar, on tobacco and cotton plantations. But the ascendance of sugar, and its demands for cheap labor, meant a boom in imports of enslaved Africans.

By 1717 green tea was overtaking coffee as the English drink of choice, and sugar consumption rose in step with tea imports.

The resulting development of a very sweet tooth in Britain and North America fueled the demand for Jamaican sugar. In Jamaica and the rest of the British West Indies, the boom in commodities like sugar, as well as the hot markets for gold, pearls, and mahogany, created a get-rich-quick mentality, made keener by short life expectancies of the tropics. Between 1650 and 1800, nearly one-third of all white people arriving in the Caribbean died within three years; whites born on the islands perished at the same rate. "The risk of early death dominated everything, contributing to the settlers' fatalism, fast living and callousness," historian Matthew Parker has written. "The West Indies had none of the things that sustained and nourished the northern colonies: a stable and rising population, family long lives, and even religion. Instead there was money, alcohol, sex and death."

Colonists in this outpost of Englishness were determined to keep their native customs, especially when it came to diet, dress, and housing. They insisted on their astoundingly inappropriate English beef and beer, English waistcoats and periwigs, and English brick houses in the tropical heat and humidity. But unlike the stolid country gentry typified back home by Catesby's father John Catesby and uncle Nicholas Jekyll, the English planters acted like typical *nouveaux-riches*, indulging in displays of conspicuous consumption and ostentatious living. One planter's main hall was big enough to hold sixty chairs and seven tables; eighteenth-century Jamaican estate inventories list extensive collections of silver services, chariots, and horses—but relatively few books.

They did not exactly live above the store, either. The constant fear of revolt was one reason; for another, as Hans Sloane put it,

"The Houses of considerable Planters are usually removed from their Sugar, or other Works, that they may be free from the noise and smells of them, which are very offensive."

◆

The sugar boom of the eighteenth century was bound inextricably with the slave trade. So, too, was the involvement of the era's British botanists and collectors in transatlantic natural history.

Sir Hans Sloane married a wealthy heiress of a Jamaica sugar plantation. His collections were funded by the profits from slave labor on Jamaican plantations, estimated to have totaled $4 million in today's money. For his theory of gravity, Isaac Newton studied the gravitational tug of the moon on ocean tides; one set of tide readings which Newton depended on came from French slave ports in Martinique. The Royal Society itself invested in slaving companies.

More directly, the triangular trade—slaves from Africa to the Caribbean, raw materials from the Americas to Europe, guns and textiles sent from Europe to Africa—was practically the only way to sail across the Atlantic. Explorers in the New World like Catesby often had little choice but to be guest passengers on slave ships. After their arrival in the colonies, the naturalists often also had to rely on slavers for food, shelter, mail, equipment, and local transport.

But explorer-naturalists were not allowed everywhere in the New World. Even after the end of the War of Spanish Succession, all of Spanish America remained officially off-limits to

British citizens. The *Asiento,* however, made an important exception to this policy: British ship captains, surgeons, and others who were part of the slave trade. Collectors back in London relied heavily on these participants in the *Asiento* to collect specimens and intelligence for them, as they were "among the few Britons who could investigate reports of cochineal, cinchona, and other natural rarities firsthand."

This created a mutuality of interest between the Sloanes and Petivers of the world and those in charge of the brutal, dehumanizing, and deadly—to seamen as well as to enslaved African people—trade in slaves. As a modern historian writes,

> We do not often think of the wretched, miserable, and inhuman spaces of slave ships as simultaneously being spaces of natural history. Yet Petiver's museum suggests that this is exactly what they were. Among the thousands of specimens housed within the Sloane collection in London's Natural History Museum today can be found West African and American specimens transported alongside enslaved Africans or gathered by men employed in the British slave trade. Petiver was not alone in exploiting the routes of the trade to gather specimens and observations of distant regions. Sloane himself acquired natural curiosities from people involved in the slave trade.

Ships' surgeons, in particular, were important allies of the naturalist-collectors. They were typically well-educated, with a basic knowledge of botany as well as anatomy and surgery.

Like apothecaries, they were interested in the medicinal value of plants. The surgeons' scientific training and education made them perfect allies in seeking out rare, unusual, interesting, and commercial botanical finds around the globe.

This reliance on the crews of slave ships tended to dictate and define the very scope of the specimens collected. Plants and animals, insects and reptiles, tended to be gathered where enslaved humans were loaded onto ships, or led from the decks of those ships to be sold. The origins of James Petiver's specimens attest to this connection:

> Slave ship surgeon Richard Planer, for example, sent Petiver a yellow butterfly from Mount Serrado in West Africa, a "Pompom" lizard from "Guinea," an insect from "the *Guinea* Coast," and a finely toothed moss from Mount Serrado, as well as a black butterfly and "very *curious Insects*" from the coast of Cartagena. Similarly, ship surgeon James Skeen gave Petiver a butterfly and African grass from Cape Three Points on the Gold Coast, a butterfly from Ouidah in the Bight of Benin, a shell from Jamaica, and "three or four Books of *Plants*, with . . . *Shells* and *Insects*" from Ouidah and Cape Three Points.

The trade which brought Africans against their will to the Caribbean served naturalists and botanical collectors in another way. The enslaved people themselves contributed to the scientific endeavors in the colonies. "Informants ranged from field slaves familiar with the habits, traits, and location of unusual species to West African 'magi' who combined, roughly, the roles of European physician and priest." These "Negro Doctors" were respected for their knowledge of herbal medicines, at a time when "the authority of white male physicians remained highly disputed, both in Europe and the Americas." While in South Carolina, Catesby referred in a letter to William Sherard to "a famous Negro Dr who I have been credibly informed have done great good."

Mark Catesby certainly knew that some of the specimens he sent to Dale and others back in England were carried aboard ships which transported enslaved people. The staggering scale of the transatlantic slave trade, involving thousands of sailors and millions of Africans and dominating the seas, would have made that truth hard to ignore. It is likely that neither Catesby nor any of his natural-history connections mentioned it because it was so commonplace to them. It would be like present-day writers mentioning that the cars they drive run on gasoline.

Later in the century, the British government would sponsor voyages of exploration by the likes of Captain James Cook and Joseph Banks which were not tied to commercial routes. These expeditions roamed regardless of the demands of the merchant economy, and broadened British knowledge of the world. In Catesby's time, however, natural history still rode on the coat-tails of slave profits.

◆

In Jamaica, Catesby examined plants and animals not only as a naturalist thirsty to satisfy his curiosity, but also as one seeking interesting commercial possibilities for his sponsors back in England. He was fascinated by the cacao tree, with its fruit which "when ripe, has a shell of a purple colour, in substance somewhat like a pomegranite." He wrote, "At Jamaica, in the year 1714, I saw the remains of extensive Cacao-walks, planted by the Spaniards." Recalling how "the Spaniards, and of late the French, [supplied] not only us, and our northern Colonies, but all Europe with this valuable commodity," Catesby speculated about a time in the future when "our Sugar-islands . . . might not only supply our home-consumption, but come in for a share of exportation to foreign markets."

He was also sending plants from Jamaica back to England. Samuel Dale in January 1719 referred to Jamaican plants in his possession, probably received from Catesby; more definitively documented were "two [quires] of Jamaica plants sent me by Mr. Catesby" which Dale mentioned in April of that same year.

Catesby included seven species from Jamaica in the *Natural History,* including some from outside the professed geographical range of the book. Catesby wrote of the "Yellow and Black Pye" (the Venezuelan troupial, *Icterus icterus*), "They are called in Jamaica, Bonano Birds, that fruit being a part of their Food. They are very sprightly and active Birds, and are often kept in cages for the docility and antique gestures." He also illustrated a centipede, "Scolopendra" (the Florida Keys centipede, *Scolopendra alternans*), whose bite "in Jamaica is said to be as pernicious as that of a *scorption.*"

In his description of "The Alligator," Catesby pointed out that "in Jamaica . . . [they] are found above twenty Foot in Length." He also described "The Green Lizard of Jamaica" (the

Jamaican turquoise anole, *Anolis grahami*) as "usually six Inches long, of a shining grass green Colour . . . frequenting Hedges and Trees," but "not seen in Houses that I observed." The lizard is notable for its behavior when approached: "they by filling their Throat with Wind swell it into a globular Form, and a scarlet Colour, which when contracted the red disappears, and returns to the Colour of the rest of the Body." Catesby thought the lizards' behavior "seems to proceed from menacing, or deterring one from coming near him, tho' they are inoffensive." Catesby painted the lizard perched in the Logwood tree, *Haematoxylum campechianum,* which was an important source of dyes. In fact, its value made it a target of pirates, including Blackbeard, who turned vessels hauling logwood into pirate ships.

There is ample evidence that during this time Catesby also visited Bermuda, Hispaniola, Barbados, and Puerto Rico. The British Natural History Museum today holds a pressed specimen of the Bermudan blue-eyed grass (*Sisyrinchium bermudiana*) sent by Catesby to Dale in 1715. He wrote that he could not "when in Bermudas distinguish any difference between the Cedars of that Island and those on the Continent except that their Leaves are generally thicker and more succulent." He then refers to plants in Bermuda, "many of which altered so much from those I had lately seen in Jamaica & Hispaniola that it was some time before I could determine them to be the same kind." He wrote of the "Tropick Bird" that "they breed also in great numbers on some little Islands at the east-end of Porto-Rico." Of the flying fish, Catesby wrote, "They are good eating Fish, and are caught plentifully on the Coasts of Barbados, where at certain Seasons of the Year the Markets are supplyed with them."

◆

From the Caribbean Mark Catesby returned to Virginia; whether or not he did so on a slaver's ship is not known. Finally in 1719, after seven years in America, he returned to England. He had established himself as a knowledgeable purveyor of plants and seeds to England, and proved that he could safely and competently explore the mountains, rivers, and forests of the (to Europeans) "wild" North American backcountry. He had also executed watercolors of several birds of Virginia, including the "Baltimore Bird" (Baltimore Oriole, *Icterus galbula*), the "Red-Start" (American Redstart, *Setophaga ruticilla*), and the "Soree" (sora, *Porzana carolina*) to show to his mentors such as Samuel Dale. After this first journey overseas, Catesby would be unabashed, once back in London, about making the best use of his newfound reputation as an explorer, naturalist, and artist.

6

LONDON 1719–1722

By the fall of 1719, Mark Catesby was back in England, but he had already decided not to remain there any longer than was necessary. On October 15, Samuel Dale would report to William Sherard not only that "Catesby is come from Virginia," but also that he "intends againe to returne" to the American colonies.

Since the death of John Ray nine years before, Sherard had come to be considered the foremost English botanist of the day. He had been born in Leicestershire, in the East Midlands of England, in 1659. After studying law at St. John's College, Oxford, then turning his attention to the study of botany in Paris and Leyden, Sherard in 1703 became the British consul at Smyrna, the ancient Greek City which was then part of the Ottoman Empire. Sherard returned to England in 1717 a wealthy man and became a patron of botanists. On his death in 1734 he would endow the Sherardian Chair of Botany at Oxford, stipulating that the first holder of the post would be

Linnaeus. Catesby could not hope for a better patron for his plan to continue his natural-history work in America.

Dale assured Sherard that Catesby "will take an opportunity to waite upon you with some paintings of Birds etc., which he hath done," and pointedly added, "It's [a] pitty some incouragement can't be found for him; he may be very useful for the perfecting of Natural History." In May 1720, Dale arranged for Catesby to be introduced to Sherard in London. The thirty-seven-year-old Catesby must have impressed the sixty-one-year-old Sherard; afterward, Sherard wrote his friend Dr. Richard Richardson that Catesby was "a Gentleman of a small fortune [and] pretty well skilled in Natural History who designs and paints in water colours to perfection." For his part, Catesby would describe in the *Natural History* how he "sent some observations on the Country, which [Dale] communicated to the late William Sherard, L.L.D. one of the most celebrated Botanists of this Age, who favoured me with his Friendship on my Return to England in the Year 1719; and by his Advice, (tho conscious of my own Inability) I first resolved on this Undertaking, so agreeable to my Inclination."

Having resolution and inclination was one thing. Carrying out such a costly plan for another extended stay in North America—this time, without nearby family to lean on—was another. Catesby had seemingly gone through a good bit of his "very small fortune" during his first seven-year stint as a naturalist in the New World. He would have to find significant funding to spend even a few years in continuance of his work in British America. Fortunately, he was in the right city, at an opportune time.

In the eight years since Catesby had left England, the craze for all things botanical had only intensified. Britain's growing prosperity translated into a frenzy of renovation and refurbishment, led, as in most things, by London. The intervening years had only reinforced the British capital's preeminence in politics, law, fashion, art, and science. The towering literary figure of the age, Dr. Samuel Johnson, famously wrote that "When a man is tired of London, he is tired of life; for there is in London all that life can afford." As London went, in architecture and leisure as in all things, the rest of the country followed.

To the Georgians, the Jacobean and Stuart reigns had left them a London that was cramped, dark, unattractive, and smelly. The city needed spaciousness, with wide streets and neoclassical buildings based on the Greek and Roman pattern as exemplified in the works of the sixteenth-century Italian Renaissance architect Andrea Palladio. In reaction to the ornate Baroque style of the previous era, Georgians wanted plain unadorned brickwork, geometrical harmony and restrained classically inspired ornament. With its newfound wealth, London sprawled in all directions, its terraced rowhouses, grand townhouses, and imposing commercial headquarters all obeying the same Augustan rules of order and classical form that would inspire the construction of Thomas Jefferson's Monticello and George Washington's Mount Vernon in America.

And, of course, there had to be gardens. "Almost every Body, whose Business requires them to be constantly in Town, will have something of a Garden at any rate," Thomas Fairchild wrote in *The City Gardener*, published in 1722. He penned the book, he wrote, so that "every one in London, or other Cities . . . may delight themselves in Gardening, tho' they have never so little Room, and prepare their Understanding to enjoy the Country, when their Trade and Industry has given them Riches enough to retire from Business."

Fairchild's book advised on the planting of city squares with hedges and groves of trees, intermixed with flowers and shrubs: "The common green Holly will grow very well . . . [and] the Lilac . . . will thrive very well, and blossom very freely in London, especially in open Places." Among the varieties he listed were several from the American colonies. "The Virginian Accacia makes a good Figure, and a large Tree," Fairchild wrote. "There was one of them growing in the close passage between the New and Old Palace yard [of] Westminster, about two or three years ago, and I suppose it may be still growing there." Fairchild also praised the Virginia aster, "a fair Flower, and makes a fine Show." Another Virginia transplant seemed to have firmly established itself: "The Creeper of Virginia is a Plant well known to grow in the closest Places in the City, even where there is no sun at all . . . there is hardly a Street, Court, or Alley in London, without some examples of what I relate of it."

Catesby had sent specimens to Fairchild while in Virginia, as he had to Samuel Dale. Given that Fairchild published his book a full decade after Catesby went to Virginia, there is every possibility that the acacia, aster, and Virginia creeper Fairchild describes in *The City Gardener* could have been growing in his nursery from seeds and plants sent to him from America by Mark Catesby.

The rise of commercial nurserymen such as Fairchild meant that the fad for gardening could begin to spread more widely across the social classes of London and the rest of Britain. For the first time, gardeners could acquire flowers, shrubs, and trees at more affordable prices and in greater variety. And much of that variety was coming from America, where similar climate and growing seasons meant that the seeds and plants sent by Catesby and others could be left to fend for themselves outside. No expensive greenhouses or hothouses, which might be needed for exotic plants from Asia and Africa, were necessary.

As a result, more and more private houses—even very modest ones—had gardens. The Finnish botanist Peter Kalm noticed how "at nearly every house in the town there was either in front toward the street, or inside [behind] the house and building, or in both, a little yard," where the owners had planted "in these yards and round about them, partly in the earth and partly in pots and boxes, several of the trees, plants and flowers that can stand the coal-smoke in London."

Augustan order and symmetry ruled in these gardens. Typically the garden paths and plots were laid out to echo the windows and doors of the house, in proportions pleasing to the eighteenth-century eye. The gardens were made to be walked in, displaying the newly available varieties of blooms and foliage—some of them even, perhaps, from the American colonies.

In the garden, Londoners and all of Britain's botanical enthusiasts could indulge many of the interests of the age. They could collect and classify specimens, sometimes neatly labeling them to impress and edify their visitors. They could learn the characteristics and distinguishing features of flowers, vines, shrubs, and trees. They could feel the thrill of the exotic by planting a specimen from faraway Virginia or Carolina. And they could indulge the Georgian taste for sociability, hosting tours of their gardens and formal garden parties.

The fashion for things botanical extended beyond gardens and flowerpots. In England and her colonies, flowered designs could be found on men's and women's clothes and on the chinaware laid on their tables. Chintz, imported from India until British mills learned the secret of its production in 1759, covered walls and upholstered furniture, and framed windows, as did flowered silk damask and calico. Women's silk dresses and brocaded silk shoes were festooned with flowers, as were men's waistcoats. Georgians used cuttings of actual flowers, often extravagantly, to decorate the indoors, as well. This was a convenient way to demonstrate one's taste, as well as one's skill with gardening.

In short, it was the perfect time for an enterprising naturalist to make his mark, and Mark Catesby could foresee two avenues for doing so. First, he would become even more skilled at collecting, preserving, and safely sending botanical specimens to the nurserymen, botanists, and wealthy gardeners whose acquaintance he had been steadily cultivating. To that end he would spend time with Fairchild in Hoxton and at the Chelsea Physic Garden, and visit Sir Hans Sloane in order to access his enormous trove of natural history drawings and paintings. Then, after another journey of exploration in America, he would produce an illustrated guide to the plants, as well as the birds, mammals, insects, and fishes of the New World, which would impress his patrons and the wider public. Fortunately for Catesby, those collectors were now actively looking for naturalists to send to the corners of the newly expanding British trade zone, from Africa and Asia to North America and the Caribbean.

◆

The Temple House Coffee Club had supplied the funds for John Lawson's earlier voyage to Carolina; now Sherard and his network of botanical enthusiasts took on the role of patrons to Catesby, offering "some incouragement" to him "for the perfecting of Natural History." By October 1720, Catesby had received a proposal for his journey back to the New World. Colonel Francis Nicholson, preparing to leave for South Carolina as its first royal governor, offered Catesby a yearly pension of £20 to follow Nicholson to the colony "to Observe the Rarities of the Country for the Uses and Purposes of the [Royal] Society." With the prestige of the Royal Society (although without any of its funds) behind the project, Sherard found nine additional sponsors of Catesby's trip, including Sherard himself, Sloane, the Duke of Chandos, and the Earl of Oxford. As Catesby would write in his preface to the *Natural History*, "But as Expences were necessary for carrying the Design, I here most gratefully acknowledge the Assistance and Encouragement I received from several Noble Persons and Gentlemen."

James Brydges, the Duke of Chandos, briefly upended the plan when he decided that Catesby should instead be sent to the Royal Africa Company where, Sherard wrote, "he will do our business as well if not better than in Carolina, which is better known to us." The Company had begun with a royal charter in 1672 and been given the monopoly over the purchase of enslaved Africans and their transportation to America. By 1717, though, that monopoly had ended, and Chandos, who had acquired a controlling interest in 1720, determined to move the Company away from the slave trade and toward exploring the continent for medicinal plants, spices, and other products of possible commercial value. Chandos considered Catesby to be someone "whose capacity and knowledge may be usefull" to go out to Africa on behalf of the company "to make such discoveries as they can of ye Products of those Parts of ye World." Eventually the duke lost his enthusiasm for the Africa plan. On January 27, 1722, Sherard wrote Richardson, "Mr Catesby goes next week for Carolina. He has put off going until the last ship . . . I hope he'll make me suitable returns that I may furnish all my friends." Finally, in February, Catesby began his voyage to Charleston, on the American coast.

Catesby's second foray to the Americas was planned at an altogether different level than his first. This time, his goals would be clearly defined—and they would be commercial as well as scientific. Knowledge would be sought after; so would business opportunities. The results of Catesby's explorations would find their homes not only in gentlemen's cabinets of curiosities, but also in the stocks of Thomas Fairchild's and Christopher Gray's nurseries in greater London. Above all, Catesby would also parlay what he found across the Atlantic into his singular masterpiece, a book of art and science which would assure his legacy.

7

CHARLESTON 1722-1724

Standing on the ship's deck midway through his voyage across the Atlantic Ocean, Mark Catesby was amazed by the sudden appearance of an owl. The bird, which was generally thought incapable of long distances on the wing, hovered over the ship and then "after some attempts to rest" it flew on. "That an Owl should be able to hold out so long a Flight, is to me most amazing," he would write. Other than that incident, during what Catesby described as a "pleasant tho' not a short Passage" the passengers and crew had sought "Diversions not uncommon in crossing the Atlantick Ocean" such as fishing for porpoises, dolphins, bonito, and albacore. The last three were especially savored, though Catesby noted that "even the Flesh of Sharks and Porpuses would digest well with the Sailors" considering their usual steady diet of salted meat. Those aboard also watched dolphins pursue flying fish to exhaustion. Impatience, mixed with relief, would have been Catesby's feelings as he stepped onto the wharf in Charleston Harbor.

He wrote to William Sherard on May 5, 1722, two days later—the earliest letter of Catesby's that has survived. Catesby relayed the owl story then added, "On the Coasts of America we had several other Birds came on Board," including the first one he classified, a "Turn stone or Sea plover" (ruddy turnstone, *Arenaria interpres*). Mindful of his patron's expectations for this trip to America, Catesby wrote, "I am told up the rivers there are abundance of fossils and petrifactions and that those parts have not been searched for plants, which gives me hopes in some measure of effecting what you perticularly desire," namely, being the first to cultivate these plants in Britain. Catesby had a second goal: to be the first to bring illustrated descriptions of those plants, and of animals, back to his native country.

The thirty-nine-year-old Catesby of 1722 was vastly more informed and experienced than the one who had landed in Williamsburg a decade before. He had in the interval met and interacted with Native Americans and enslaved Africans; seen the workings of the Virginia colony; and had seen, sketched, and collected the flora and fauna of North America from the Tidewater to the Shenandoah. He also knew that he could examine, describe, and illustrate what he saw to the satisfaction of the most discriminating botanists, plantsmen, and collectors in England. After all, had he not been called "brilliant" by William Sherard?

◆

The Charleston that Catesby found that May boasted about three thousand residents, about half of whom were European and half enslaved Africans, with no more than a dozen free Black people. John Lawson, in his 1709 account *A New Voyage to Carolina*, had described the town's "very commodious Harbour . . . seated between two pleasant and navigable Rivers," the Ashley and the Cooper. He noted its "very regular and fair Streets" and inhabitants who "by their wise Management and Industry, have much improv'd the Country."

A slightly different opinion of the town at that time comes from Margaret Kennett, who wrote from Charleston to her friend in 1725, "As to the Buildings in Charles Town they are of Brick Lime, and Hair, and Some Very fine Timber Houses and are generally Glazed with Shash Window after the English Fashion." She was much less approving of those houses' inhabitants, however: "The Greatest Misfortune that attends [Charleston] is the Hypocrisie and Knavery of its Inhabitants for they are to the Last Degree Ignorant and Opiniated and there is not a tenth part of the inhabitants that can give a Rational Account of any thing." In short, Kennett concluded, "They are Trained up in Luxery and are the Greatest Debauchees in Nature."

As the only real port in the American South, Charleston was already becoming one of the richest towns in America. At the wharves, rice, naval stores, and deerskins were loaded onto ships bound for London while dugout canoes from the interior brought Native Americans and settlers to the metropolis for brightly colored English woolens, blankets, brass kettles, knives, and flints. Catesby might have been dazzled by the variety of languages to be overheard in the town as Protestant French Huguenot and Dutch immigrants—to say nothing of the dozens of languages spoken by enslaved Africans—made Charleston more linguistically diversified than any other place on the American mainland.

Governor Nicholson in June 1722 would rename the port Charles City, as part of his plan "For the Better Government of Charles Town," but the Crown disallowed the change—fortunately for the town, the proposed name not being nearly as pleasant to the ear. Mark Catesby headed nine of his letters in 1722–1723 "Charles City" before reverting to "Charles Town" in November 1723.

A 1711 map shows a well-fortified town on the east bank of a peninsula of land between the Ashley and Cooper Rivers. Inside its walls, built by the forced labor of enslaved Africans, were depicted ten neat blocks of homes, shops, churches, and warehouses. Outside the fortifications the map showed a "Minister's House" and "Quaker Meeting House," a handful of farms labeled with their owners' names, and on the southern point of the peninsula, a "Watch House," ostensibly to warn against French and Spanish warships, not to mention pirates. The town's walls were not only protection from sea-borne threats, however; during the Yamasee War of 1715–1717, inland settlers had fled to the city's enclosure to escape the violence between Europeans and Native Americans.

War with the Yamasee and their allies was only one of the reasons that Charleston circa 1722 could be described as a city in recovery. Smallpox epidemics, a 1720 drought followed by two years of heavy rains which destroyed about half of the rice crop, and even a 1713 hurricane which damaged the town's fortifications had all delayed the growth of the port city.

Historian George C. Rogers Jr. vividly described Charleston's prime location in this era of wind-powered ships:

> Charleston's golden age coincided with the last century of the age of sailing vessels. As long as the age of sail lasted, Charleston was on the main Atlantic highway, which circumnavigated the Bermuda High. Vessels leaving England . . . generally sailed southwesterly to the Azores to catch the trade winds and then with full sail made for the West Indies, Barbados standing out front like a doorman to welcome all to the New World. They next made their way through the West Indies to the Gulf Stream. From the Florida Keys to Cape Hatteras they hugged the American coast before veering off to England and northern Europe. It was a great circle, and Charleston was on its western edge.

◈

Being on "the main Atlantic highway," of course, meant having to deal with those highwaymen of the sea, Blackbeard and his brother (and, as we've seen, sister) pirates. In addition to their other revenue streams, South Carolinians prospered as willing providers of pirates' supplies, their colony's marshy inlets offering safe hiding places for ships such as Blackbeard's *Queen Anne's Revenge*. Charleston also served as a recruiting ground for sailors willing to attack the Spanish fleets riding the Gulf Stream on their way to Cádiz.

All of which did not ensure Charleston's safety from their buccaneering customers. Four years before Catesby's arrival, Blackbeard had blockaded the port for a week, stopping and ransacking nine vessels over the next five or six days. Nine prizes and over £1,500 in cash later, Blackbeard hove to just outside the harbor and sent a message to Governor Robert Johnson, Nicholson's predecessor: if he were not given medical supplies for his crew, he would kill his three dozen hostages and attack the town. As usually happened, Blackbeard's threats got him what he wanted—£400 worth of medicine—without bloodshed.

Blackbeard would not have long to live. After sailing north and living briefly as the law-abiding son-in-law of a prominent planter in Bath, North Carolina, Blackbeard returned to pirating after only a few months. He and his men were attacked just off Ocracoke Island by Lieutenant Robert Maynard of the HMS *Pearl* on November 22, 1718. Blackbeard and most of his crew were killed, Blackbeard being shot five times and cut about twenty before succumbing. After the battle Maynard hung Blackbeard's head on the bowsprit of the *Pearl* as the vessel sailed from North Carolina back to Virginia; the pirate's head then was displayed on a pole at the entrance to the Chesapeake Bay for several years. In Boston, an enterprising thirteen-year-old named Ben Franklin composed, printed, and hawked on the city's streets his poem "The Taking of Teach the Pirate."

Though Blackbeard had been gone for more than three years when Mark Catesby arrived in Charleston, other pirates carried on looting and raiding. Catesby's letters to Sherard included several mentions of pirates. "I suppose ere this You would have received my Spring Collection p[er] Capt Robinson after having been I fear much deminished and injured by pirats," he reported, adding, "I shall be glad to hear of their being better than I expect." Upon learning that another ship with his specimens had been attacked, he wrote Sherard, "I dread the mischief the Pirates have done to the things I sent." The pirate threat in North America and the Caribbean would not abate for the duration of Catesby's time in America.

◆

Pirates would not have been on Catesby's mind as he stepped ashore in Charleston that May, except perhaps for fleeting gratitude that they had not harassed his ship. His immediate duty was to report to Governor Nicholson, who "received me with much kindness," he wrote to Sherard, "to which I am satisfyed your Letter contributed not a Little." Nicholson's good graces were important to Catesby, and not just because the governor was his major sponsor. As had happened in Virginia, Nicholson's patronage in South Carolina could give Catesby entrée to the plantations of rich, powerful planters—and gain him their support for his explorations.

Catesby was eager to leave Charleston for the interior Lowcountry, the coastal plain of marshes, inlets, and fertile lowlands. He described the area in the *Natural History*: "The inhabited Parts of Carolina extend West from the Sea about 60 Miles, and almost the whole length of the Coast, being a level, low Country." Arriving at the onset of summer, Catesby was surprised to find the Lowcountry abounding "not only with all the Animals and Vegetables of Virginia," but containing "even a greater Variety."

He threw himself into his fieldwork, writing Sherard six months after his arrival, "I am but now returned from 40 miles up the Country . . . and in a few days am going a greater distance another way." With the letter Catesby sent the first of about twenty shipments of plants to Sherard; in it he referred to three types of magnolias, two "Trumpet or Sidesaddle flowers" (pitcher plants, *Sarracenia*), and "4 or 5 different kinds of Lillys including the Attamasco" (*Zephyranthes atamasca*), which Catesby illustrated with an "American Partridge" or northern bobwhite stooping to feed at its base. He also described the southern magnolia, *Magnolia grandiflora*: "It grows here generally near Rivers and Bays to ye bigness of a large and tall Tree," its flower very large with "thick and white leaves" while the tree's leaves are "very large and thick of a shining Green," the undersides "being of a reddish or fulvous color which lessens much the beauty of the tree by giving it a rusty hew." The magnolia's flowers, Catesby wrote, "are very sweet and perfumes the Air."

In the same letter Catesby showed his knack for ingratiating himself with South Carolina's planters. He asked Sherard to send him "a few common Roots such as Lillys (except the White Lilly) Martagons Daffodils or any bulbous root" which he wanted "to gratify some gentlemen at whose houses I frequent," who were "desirous of such improvements," as there were few of such plantings available, "tho' the Country is productive of every thing."

◆

To deliver his gifts to those "gentlemen at whose houses I frequent," Catesby would have taken advantage of the two main arteries for travel in the Lowcountry. Appearing on a map like the symmetrical curving antlers of an African antelope, the Ashley River bounded the western edge of Charleston's peninsula, while the Cooper River defined the eastern. On the upper reaches of the Ashley Mark Catesby could visit Pine Hill, plantation of Thomas Waring; about the "Acacia" tree (water locust, *Gleditsia aquatica*) he noted, "This Tree I never saw but at the Plantation of Mr Waring on Ashley River, growing in shallow water." Another Ashley River planter who hosted Catesby was William Bull, of one of the oldest and most prominent families in South Carolina. At Bull's Ashley Hall Catesby found the "Dahoon Holly," which he called "a very uncommon Plant in Carolina, I having never seen it but at Col. Bull's Plantation on Ashley River, where it grows in a Bog." Probably Catesby's closest friend among the planters, Alexander Skene, lived at New Skene plantation near Dorchester. In the *Natural History* Catesby described "The Umbrella-Tree" (*Magnolia tripetala*) as plentiful, "particularly in the path leading from Mr. Skene's house to his Savanna." Catesby sent letters in January 1723 from "Mr Skeyns" at New Skene.

Going up the Cooper River on the other side of Charleston, he might visit Boochawee, home of former governor James Moore. Moore derived the estate's name from the Native American term for the land between Charleston's two rivers. Colonel Joseph Blake's Newington plantation on the upper Cooper River was known for its splendor, including fine gardens, and an allée of live oaks lining its entrance drive.

Robert Johnson of Silk Hope in St. George's Parish was another former governor of the colony. Johnson accompanied Catesby on collecting journeys, and gifted the naturalist recipes for caviar and pickled sturgeon. He would later be an "Encourager," or subscriber, to Catesby's book. Catesby wrote in the *Natural History* that "Concealing useful things" deprives "the Publick of a Benefit designed them by the Donor of all Things." For that reason, "I here insert a Receipt for pickling Sturgeon and Caviair, which . . . is not known to many, especially in America, where it can be of most Use. These Receipts I was favoured with by his Excellency Mr. Johnson, late Governor of South Carolina," who had them "translated from the original in High Dutch, which was wrote in Gold Letters, and fixed in the Town Hall at Hambourg."

The Lowcountry boat of choice for traveling the Ashley and Cooper Rivers and their many tributaries was the periagua, its name a Spanish term derived from the Carib word for dugout canoe. Explorers in Carolina described immense cypress trees with trunks thirty-six feet in circumference, which could yield a boat almost twelve feet wide. A variation of the periagua was formed by splitting a hollowed-out log into which the makers inserted a flat board for a bottom, widening the craft to allow for more passengers and cargo. Many periaguas had removable masts for sailing in open water.

The planters whom Catesby knew likely owned personal periaguas equipped with sails and oars; as well as small cabins, awnings, and comfortable seating, and even liveried servants as oarsmen. With very few roads beyond Charleston, planters

typically used periaguas on the waterways between their plantations and the port town.

Periaguas were also used by the less affluent, though without
the luxury options of the planters. Slaves fished from them;
merchants and Native Americans hauled goods from the backcountry to the markets and wharves of Charleston. With their
versatility and the ability to carry anywhere from thirty up to
hundreds of barrels of rice, the craft were indispensable to the
early economy of South Carolina.

Catesby accepted the planters' hospitality, and reciprocated
by advising on their plantings and even planting alleés of trees.
But he was not above criticizing their ways. John Lawson had
written that Europeans were not sufficiently attentive to the
soil, the climate, or conditions under which crops grew (or
did not grow): "I must confess, I never saw one Acre of Land
manag'd as it ought to be in *Carolina*, since I knew it; and
were they as negligent in their Husbandry in *Europe*, as they
are in *Carolina*, their Land would produce nothing but Weeds
and Straw."

Similarly, in a letter to John Bartram, Catesby seemed
stunned that the planters in South Carolina would not attempt
to produce oil from the jasmine plant. Red jasmine (*Plumeria
rubra*) was considered an aid to digestion and respiration. "I
distributed this seed to many not doubting but my intention
of introducing so usefull and benefical a thing would succeed,"
he wrote. "But so little inclination have they to any thing out
of the common rode that except my friend Mr Skene none of
them I gave it to gave themselves any trouble about it. Yet some
of these very negligent persons with all others that eat Mr Skenes

Oyl commended it and desired to know where to buy some of the same."

◆

When he returned to England and wrote the *Natural History*, Catesby would explain his priorities and focuses as he collected and documented North America's plants and animals during his journeys of exploration throughout South Carolina and the Bahamas. First, he "had principally a Regard to Forest-Trees and Shrubs, shewing their several Mechanical and other Uses, as in Building, Joynery, Agriculture, and others used for Food and Medicine." In addition, "I have likewise taken notice of those Plants, that will bear our English Climate." As for the fauna of the New World, he felt compelled to focus on birds, "There being a greater Variety of the feather'd Kind than of any other Animals . . . and excelling in the Beauty of their Colors, besides having oftenest relation to the Plants on which they feed and frequent." In fact, he intended "(so far as I could) to compleat an Account of them," rather than trying to thoroughly cover "Insects and other Animals; by which I must have omitted many of the Birds, for I had not Time to do all." As a result, "I believe very few Birds have escaped my knowledge, except some Water Fowl and some of those which frequent the Sea."

When it came to mammals, Catesby reasoned that since "Of Beasts there are not many Species different from those in the old World," he would focus on those which were different than those in Europe. "Of Serpents," he claimed, "very few I believe have escaped me, for upon shewing my Designs of them to several of the most intelligent Persons, many of them confes'd not to have seen them all, and none of them pretended to have seen any other kinds." (Catesby was overly optimistic there: though there are about forty species of snakes in Carolina, he described no more than sixteen.) He described only five or six fish from North America, sensibly "deferring that Work till my Arrival at the Bahama Islands."

Catesby was quite specific and intentional when it came to how he drew and painted them. For the plants, "I always did them while fresh and just gather'd." Significantly, unlike many naturalists, most famously John James Audubon, Catesby painted the animals, reptiles, and "particularly the Birds . . . while alive (except a very few) and gave them their Gestures peculiar to every kind of Bird."

As with South Carolina's snakes, Catesby's claims for his North American bird count were too optimistic. Although he was aiming for a "compleat account," Catesby's total of 110 different birds cited is less than a third of those now tallied in the colonies where he lived.

It's hard for modern readers to imagine the scope of Mark Catesby's work as a naturalist in a new country: not only describing and sketching the plants and animals of North America, many of them for the first time, but also classifying them according to the rules of science. Were those two different species of birds he had observed, or male and female of the same species, or adult and juvenile? What Latin terms should be used in the name? Was the animal the same as similar species Catesby knew in England?

He described one practice in his illustrations that would make his work groundbreaking: "where it would admit of," he wrote, "I have adapted the Birds to those Plants on which they fed, or have any Relation to." This choice of Catesby's would make the *Natural History* one of the first works of its kind to illustrate the interplay of different species in a holistic way—a foretaste of the scientific discipline that we now call ecology.

◆

Catesby would encounter two major challenges in his work in America: how to safely deliver what he had collected to his patrons in England, and how to satisfy their demands while following his own program of natural history exploration.

The live plants, seeds, and dried specimens had to be carefully treated in this place of heat and humidity, and in this time before air conditioning or vacuum sealing. Placing specimens between sheets of paper kept them safe while preventing decomposition. The collector James Petiver in his "Directions for the Gathering of Plants" described this process: "Wherever you go ashoar, or into the Fields or Woods, carry with you the Collecting-Book (to gather the Samples or Specimens in, which you must shift into this Book the same Day, or within two or three at farthest after you have gathered them)." Catesby apparently followed this practice; he wrote Sherard, "I thought of deferring sending these 2 books of plants til I made a larger Collection but I concluded you'd approve of my sending the first opertunity what I had got."

Catesby also dried birds by baking them and covering them with tobacco dust. His preferred vessels for seeds were gourds, which would have been easier to come by than the paper and boxes needed to protect plants. He wrote Sloane requesting large-mouthed bottles for his birds and bugs. In these, specimens would be preserved using brine or spirits. Catesby placed snakes and other small animals in jars filled with rum.

Given his meticulous nature, it's no surprise that some of the best advice from that era about shipping live plants came from Catesby himself. At some point prior to 1724 he felt the need to write to Thomas Fairchild, the prominent nurseryman in Hoxton, about shipping methods: "Sir, I desire when you send Plants by Shipping to remote Parts, to send them in Tubs, and not in Baskets; for Baskets contribute much to the miscarriage." As to the seasons, "Winter is the best time; October if it could be, and to put the Tubs in the Ballast [the bottom of the boat, below decks], which keeps them moist and moderately warm." If left above deck, "They are often wetted with Salt Water, and require the greatest Tendance from bad Weather, and even with the greatest Care they miscarry, as they did with me." Summer, wrote Catesby, was the worst: "It is so hot in the Hold in Summer, that they spend their Sap at once, and dye, so that is not a Time to send any Thing." At least one British botanist, Richard Bradley, in his book on horticulture published in the mid 1720s, cited Catesby as the best known authority for shipping plants overseas.

Catesby was right to urge that plants be left below. The open deck subjected delicate specimens, however well packed, not only to salt, but also to wind and weather. The ubiquitous mice and rats were a severe hazard—as were the sailors who were known to drink the water or even the rum used to preserve the fruits of naturalists' efforts. And since no one on board was liable to face the consequences, plant boxes were often sacrificed overboard in the event of storms or attacks by pirates.

Nor were the ships' captains and masters dependable or trustworthy. William Byrd II's brother-in-law John Custis, like Byrd an avid gardener, complained in a letter to Peter Collinson, "I very much believe Capt Harding had strict orders from his Master to take care of the plants sent," but "not only he but most if not all the Masters take little notice of such orders when they are out of sight." The tenuous and hazardous connection by sea between Britain and America threatened not only the specimens themselves, but also the relationships between collectors and providers of specimens on both sides of the ocean.

But despite all the drawbacks, naturalists and collectors were forced in the end to rely on ships' crews. Captains and ships' doctors and surgeons not only carried specimens collected by others, such as Catesby; they also performed natural history themselves, urged on by Petiver and other eminent botanists and patrons. Roaming from London to Calcutta, from Kingston to Ouidah, British mariners were perfectly situated to provide the Sloanes of the world with their prizes.

Given his dependency on seamen, Catesby quickly realized the importance of good relationships with the ships' captains. Delivering specimens into the care of passengers, surgeons, or captains with whom he had a personal connection was his best chance of successful delivery. He complained in a letter to Sherard, "My much absence from Charles Town prevents my acquaintance with Masters of Ships . . . which often puts me in some difficulty how to send by one who I can rely on that what I send may be put in a dry place." As for the masters themselves, "They are many of them surly fellows that they are not to be prevailed on."

The difficulties did not end once specimens reached the dock in Bristol or London. There was no government mail service at this time; packages and letters had to be sent through friends, or left in prearranged places, such as coffeehouses or taverns. A typically convoluted arrangement is described in a letter from Catesby to Sherard, asking him to pass along specimens to Catesby's uncle Nicholas Jekyll in Castle Hedington: "A packet of [letters] I have put into the Middle Book of Plants which [you] will be pleased Sir to send to Mr Collinson who will give them to some Hedington Man at the Spread Eagle or Cross Keys in Grace Church Street."

◆

After a month in South Carolina, Catesby could sense a conflict between his two main goals—to satisfy his benefactors back in England while carrying out the program of research he felt necessary to produce the book he had in mind. "The more specimens I collect," he wrote Sherard, "the more time it takes and consequently prevents my collecting as many kinds as I should. Especially when I am several hundred miles off, it will increase their bulk." Did his patrons—especially Hans Sloane and Charles Du Bois, treasurer of the East India Company—insist on having their own separate specimens, he wondered? That would be quite a burden as he tried to make his way across the colony, carrying everything necessary with him. He evidently feared sending specimens only to Sherard for him to distribute: "If you doe not impart any of these to Sr Hans and he knows I have sent I fear he will resent it. I leave it Sr to your discretion what to doe."

The possibility of duplicate shipments meant not only lost time for Catesby, but an increase of all the problems associated with transatlantic shipping. In December of 1722 he returned to the topic, writing Sherard, "I hope it is not expected that what I send should be to every one separately," as "'tis almost impracticable without half my time lost." Many separate shipments would further try the patience of those shipmasters Catesby was trying so hard to cultivate, already so grudging with the space onboard their ships. In addition, he wrote, "Makannicks ['mechanics,' or carpenters] here are intolerably imposing and dear in their work," charging exorbitant rates for the boxes needed to send plants across the ocean.

For their part, the collectors didn't seem to understand any aspects of their naturalists' plight. Sir Hans Sloane was especially greedy for specimens from anyone and everywhere; in the words of his biographer, "Sloane supported Catesby's work but the great collector also threatened to swallow it whole."

◆

Though Catesby would eventually have a base in Charleston at the home of his friend, Oxford-educated physician Thomas Cooper, he spent as much time as he could in the field. He had plans to travel inland to the other bioregions. "My method," he wrote Sherard, "is never to be twice at . . . one place in the same season." He explored the Lowcountry one summer and "the heads of the Rivers" the next, "so alternately that in 2 years [I visit] the two different parts of the Country."

His schedule was disrupted that September, however, when he was "seized with a swelling" in his cheek, "possibly due to an abscess . . . and by the ignorance of the surgeon," he had been confined indoors for three months "in great misery having my fface twice cut and laid open with lents and injections every day." He hoped to make up this lost time the following summer, "if God gives me life and hea[l]th." One can only imagine what those treatments felt like in that period in medical history when the only anesthetics or pain medicine were opium or laudanum.

While Catesby was convalescing, Charleston experienced "the greatest Floud attended with a Hurricane that has been known since the country was settled." The storm left deer lodged in trees and drowned cattle, hogs, horses, and people. Of course it disrupted any gathering of botanical specimens; "it dispersed all the Laurels, Umbrella, and many other things I sent out for, but nothing to be found," Catesby wrote Sherard.

Catesby's illness in the fall of 1722 probably provoked his next plan of action. He wrote to Sherard, recounting his difficulties in collecting: "I can plainly perceive that I cant make a general collection without help for in Summer the heats are so excessive." In addition, although fall, "the time for seed and roots," is more favorable for collecting, "Yet they [occur] in such different parts of the country and at such distances one from the other that the fatigue is too great," and as a result "I got my late illness by over heating my self." Catesby decided to prevent another such episode by acquiring the help he needed: he wrote to ask Sherard whether he might draw twenty pounds against his credit to buy a "Negro Boy."

8

SLAVE GARDENS
AND MEDICINES

Mark Catesby had encountered enslaved Africans in Virginia, notably at William Byrd II's Westover. His comments on Byrd's treatment of his slaves are evidence that Catesby's continual attention to the natural world also included a keen perception of relationships and attitudes around him.

In South Carolina, though, Catesby encountered an entirely different type of slave economy and slave culture. John Lawson in *A New Voyage* had noted that in 1709 the number of "Christian Inhabitants" of both North and South Carolina was pretty equal, "but the Slaves of South Carolina are far more in Number than those in the North." In fact, free and enslaved Black people had been in the majority in South Carolina for more than a decade before Mark Catesby's arrival.

Most of the colony's traffic in humans had taken place between Charleston and the West Indies, though a few slave ships had traveled from Charleston to Africa and back. Beginning around 1710, however, while the shipment of enslaved Africans from the West Indies remained constant, the number of slaves brought directly from Africa to Charleston had steadily risen. Eventually, forty percent of all Africans forcibly brought to America would first set foot in Charleston Harbor.

South Carolina in 1722 was just beginning to commit to rice as its dominant crop, and just beginning to see an explosion in the number of enslaved Africans brought in from the West Indies and later directly from Africa. Naval stores—tar, pitch, rosin, and turpentine—were just as important as rice to the colony's economy, as both Britain's Royal Navy and merchant shipping increased demand for naval supplies. Even so, by the early 1720s South Carolina was exporting six million pounds of rice a year; the colony's exports accounted for 15 percent of all exports by value from the colonies to Britain.

From that time on, rice and slavery rose in tandem. Younger sons of the Barbadian planters who had made their tiny Caribbean island the largest source of colonial wealth for the nascent British Empire, thanks to the economy of sugar production, would eventually make South Carolina the wealthiest of the North American colonies. Though the main crop would be different, the required slave labor to make it profitable would be the same. In the 1720s alone, almost nine thousand slaves were imported into South Carolina, the great majority of them after 1724.

The Barbadian influence in South Carolina made it more akin to the islands of the Caribbean than to the rest of North America. Those scions of sugar brought with them the showy, hedonistic society of the white planters' West Indies, along with its speech patterns, architectural styles, and cultural norms. Seven of the early Carolina governors had Barbadian backgrounds.

Rice changed things. Though certainly not free, enslaved people in South Carolina had previously had more liberty of movement and action than we are accustomed to assuming. Slaves had been entrusted with delivering mail between white settlers, typically as boatmen and runners. They also had been guides; John Lawson had been sent a slave "to guide us over the Head of a large Swamp" through the marshes between the Ashley and Santee rivers. Africans who had formerly lived and fished along Africa's Gold Coast were put to work fishing along the Carolina coast, deftly tossing nets from their dugout canoes. And under the task system, once slaves completed a specific job they were through for the day, allowing time for hunting, fishing, or socializing.

This unusual degree of "freedom" was possible because whites' attitudes toward enslaved Africans in the early eighteenth century differed from that of the decades to come. The racially specific beliefs that Black people were suitable only as slaves due to their supposed passivity, lack of ambition and intelligence, and inability to handle or even appreciate freedom had not yet become widespread. Alexander Skene, who seems to have been one of Catesby's closest friends among the Lowcountry planter class, offered education to his enslaved Black people, and encouraged them to attend services at his Anglican church, St. George's in Dorchester.

But change was coming to this colony that imperial officials were beginning to refer to as "Carolina in the West Indies."

As the rice economy increasingly dominated the economic and political life of South Carolina, and as the planters depended on unprecedented numbers of enslaved Africans, imported both from the Caribbean and from Africa, slaves' actions and activities became more circumscribed. Inexorably, they were being thought of less as unfree laborers, not much different than indentured servants, and more as slaves by virtue of their racial characteristics. Planters weren't as keen on offering education or religion to "their" enslaved black people. Behind all these changes in attitude was the specter of revolt.

The "Act for the Better Ordering and Governing of Negroes," passed in 1661 in Barbados, had been the white Barbadian elite's way of dealing with the growing fear of slave insurrection arising from the overwhelming numerical advantage of enslaved Black people. The Act had codified a new system of better legal treatment for white servants than for Blacks, with the aim of allying the poorer whites with the planter class. This act would be copied by South Carolina in 1740, and for similar reasons: the year before, the Stono Rebellion had taken the lives of twenty-five colonists and between thirty-five and fifty enslaved Africans. The 1740 act would deny slaves the right to keep boats or canoes, horses, cows, or hogs. More importantly, it would solidify enslaved peoples' status as nonhuman in the eyes of state law, and stipulated the slave status of slaves' children, extending slavery into perpetuity.

South Carolina's planters did not merely depend on the muscles of the Africans they enslaved. The planters had tried to grow rice by plowing the soil, sowing seeds in rows, and counting on rainfall and floods to water the crop. But South Carolina was not England. The semitropical climate created burgeoning plant growth that smothered the crops, while roots and stumps made plowing difficult to impossible. Other methods of growing rice had to be learned.

The planters found their solution in the knowledge of the humans they had bought and brought across the Atlantic. Many of the enslaved came from rice-growing regions in Africa and knew more about the cultivation of the crop than any Englishman. Slaves from the Windward Coast and Senegambia came to be highly coveted by Carolina planters for their knowledge of rice farming; they commanded premium prices in the slave markets in downtown Charleston. The Carolina method of rice farming, with its dikes and flooded fields, was a blend of English engineering with skills which were brought over from the west coast of Africa.

"Charleston's planters," in one scholar's words, "knew that they owed their wealth to the agricultural know-how of their slaves."

◆

Catesby's willingness to purchase a young enslaved African male has to be paired with his other interactions with the enslaved people he found on Lowcountry plantations. As a visitor to these estates and a guest in the mansions of their owners, Catesby catalogued native and introduced plants, ornamentals as well as crop varieties, and lent his nurseryman's expertise to the farm managers. But Catesby did something else, something almost unheard of in his day. He left the precisely planted and ordered main grounds of the plantation mansions, and followed the dirt paths out to their slave quarters.

Catesby wanted to learn about the enslaved people who were cultivating wild and domestic plants in their own gardens. There was plenty for him to absorb. The task system, with its time off when specific work was completed, allowed enslaved Africans time to cultivate their own personal gardens; this was an echo of conditions in West Africa, where enslaved or indentured people traditionally had the right to raise their own food on their own ground. After tasks were done, on Sundays, or after sundown, they used light from animal-fat flames in old cooking pots to light their work in the gardens. Sometimes they cultivated their precious food and medicine plots by moonlight.

These gardens Catesby visited were more than sources of food. Modern culinary historian of the African Diaspora Jessica B. Harris described them this way:

> These spaces were little landscapes of resistance: Resistance against a culture of dehumanizing poverty and want, resistance against the erasure of African cultural practices, resistance against the destruction of African religions, and resistance against slavery itself.

Resistance, and cultural interchange. Enslaved cooks working in the plantations' Big Houses introduced Europeans to African vegetables and ways of cooking. Native Americans adopted both European and African fruits and vegetables. The dish of Carolina peas and rice known as Hoppin' John, the custom of eating greens with black-eyed peas for good luck, the cultivation of peanuts and okra: all these were brought to America by Africans from their home traditions.

Mark Catesby wanted to know about these traditions and their roles in the lives of enslaved Africans. The naturalist is one of our earliest witnesses to the creation of this cultural gumbo—another dish originating in Africa—from disparate people, places, and customs that would in time come to be considered Southern cooking.

In his entry in the *Natural History* on "Snake-Root," Catesby described slaves' knowledge about the plant, which was thought to be an antidote to snakebite, and which "the Negro Slaves (who only dig it) employ much of the little time allowed them" to search for. Catesby learned that snakeroot "was used to calm stomach ailments, induce perspiration, alleviate the pain of childbirth, or affect the menstrual cycle." Catesby also made a more definitive statement as to the efficacy of snakeroot: "Where a vein or Artery is pricked by the bite of a Rattle Snake no antidote will avail any thing, but Death certainly and suddainly ensues sometimes in 2 or 3 minutes which I have more than once seen."

Catesby himself almost became one of those cases, according to a tale he related to Sherard. He was visiting Colonel Joseph Blake at Newington plantation on the Cooper River: "I being at the house of Coll Blake a Negro woman making my Bed a few minutes after I was out of it cried out a Rattle Snake." Surprised by "ye performance of the wenches bawling," Catesby and Blake left their tea and went to see the cause. They found that "the wench had laid a Rattle Snake actually between the sheets in ye very place where I lay, vigorous and full of ire biting at . . . every thing that approach'd him." Catesby wryly added, "Probably It crept in for warmth in the night, but how long I had the company of [this] charming bedfellow I am not able to say."

Catesby demonstrated his respect for the botanical knowledge of enslaved Africans in another of his letters to Sherard. He enclosed a sample of a root (which has never been identified), "so called by way Eminence by a famous Negro Dr who I have been credibly informed have done great good with the juice of the root boyled or infusion." In a time when Black literacy was suspect in planter circles, and would before long be illegal in South Carolina and the rest of the American South, Catesby's conferring of the title "Dr" is notable. He described the root as "an excellent stomacick and highly cryed up for its other vertues."

In addition to documenting their medicines Catesby sought knowledge of enslaved Africans' food practices. In the *Natural History* he described what he called *Arum maximum Aegypticum* (*Xanthosoma sagittifolium*, arrowleaf elephant's ear); its corm is known as taro and is the basis of many dishes including Hawaiian poi. The arum, he wrote, was "a Tropick Plant, not caring to encrease much in Carolina . . . yet the Negro's there (who are very fond of them) by annually taking up the Roots to prevent rotting, get a small Encrease." Noting that eight or ten hours of boiling were required to make them edible, Catesby notes the introduction, just before he left the colony, of a "new Kind, wholly without that bad quality," which was "a welcome Improvement among the Negros" and "a Blessing," as they were "delighted with all their African Food, particularly this, which a great part of Africa subsists on." William Bartram would echo

Catesby forty years later while traveling along the Savannah River: "They have likewise another species of the esculent Arum, called Tannier, which is a large and beautiful plant, and much cultivated and esteemed for food, particularly by the Negroes."

Describing what he called the "Anona" tree (*Asimina triloba*, the pawpaw), Catesby wrote that "all Parts of the Tree have a rank, if not a foetid Smell; nor is the Fruit relished but by very few, except Negros." Once again the naturalist had been paying attention and taking notes.

In addition to taro root and the pawpaw, Catesby described how enslaved Africans ate a preparation of "Indian Corn" which "is called Mush, and is made of the Meal, in the Manner of Hasty-Pudding." He added, "This is eat by the Negroes with Cider, Hog's-lard, or Molasses." As for enslaved Blacks in the Caribbean, Catesby noted that "The Land Crab" was crucial to their diets: "The light-coloured [crabs] are reckoned best, and when full in Flesh are very well tasted." These crabs "In some of the Sugar Islands . . . are no small help to the Negro Slaves, who on many of the Islands would fare very hard without them."

Interestingly, Catesby makes no mention in the *Natural History* of three important African imports during this time: okra, watermelon, and black-eyed peas. Okra probably was first introduced into the continental United States in the early 1700s, most likely from the Caribbean, where it has a long history. The mucilaginous pod was mentioned in a Virginia cookbook in 1724. Watermelon arrived from Africa even earlier, in the seventeenth century. Given Catesby's interest in unusual plants, okra and watermelon would seem to be natural subjects for his description and depiction; their absence is notable.

Apart from respecting their knowledge of food and medicine, Catesby also cited the opinions of Africans in the course of a notable scientific enterprise which he described in the *Natural History*. "At a place in Carolina called Stono, was dug out of the Earth three or four Teeth of a large Animal, which, by the concurring Opinion of all the Negroes, native Africans, that saw them, were the grinders of an Elephant," Catesby wrote. He agreed with them: "in my opinion could be no other; I having seen some of the like that are brought from Africa." Not only is this another of Catesby's firsts—it is easily the earliest technical identification of a mammoth fossil, or of a vertebrate fossil of any kind, in America (in 1724 or early 1725 at the latest)—but it also shows Catesby treating enslaved Africans as credible sources for natural history information.

Thus, this naturalist, who was ostensibly in America only to study plants and wild animals, would leave to posterity a scant but valuable ethnographic study of the first African Americans. Like his friend Alexander Skene, he embodies his time's conflicted ideas about a society and economy that enslaved humans. His is the first, and one of the few, detailed looks into what knowledge of plants and animals these embattled, resourceful, resilient people had to help them survive in their early eighteenth-century enslavement. But his research, his time spent learning about these human beings, did not translate into resistance to the idea of purchasing one.

Catesby repeated his request for money for the "Negro boy" to Sherard in February, having received no response to his first in the glacially slow transatlantic mails. In March, as he left the Lowcountry for the interior, he notified Sherard that he had gone ahead and drawn the funds. In May, he thought to write Sherard, "I hope my Brother has paid you the 20li [guineas] you were so kind to disburse for me." The subject is never mentioned again in his letters, and is totally missing from his *Natural History*—notably unlike his published description of the assistance given him by the Native Americans he hired on the frontier.

What are we to make of this? What would the boy's story have been? Did Catesby, having seen firsthand the cruelties of William Byrd in Williamsburg, act kindly toward this young person whom he legally owned? What did he do with the boy when he left North America? There's no record of a sale, or a gift, or of releasing the boy into the small society of free Blacks in Charleston. A likely recipient of such a gift might have been Thomas Cooper, whose home Catesby used as his base when in Charleston.

We probably will never know the answers to any of these questions about this lost history. But we owe it to the anonymous enslaved boy—on behalf of the thousands of other enslaved people whose stories are unknown and untold—to ask them.

9

FORT MOORE AND THE FRONTIER 1723-1725

On March 19, 1723, Catesby wrote to William Sherard, "I am now on my journey to Fort Moor a frontier garrison 140 miles up the Country." After almost a year of collecting in the lush and fertile Lowcountry coastal area, Catesby was eager to explore the colony's other geographic zones. In the *Natural History* Catesby would be one of the first to describe the five geographical regions which lay in bands roughly parallel to the Atlantic coastline. Beyond the narrow coastal zone lay the dark rivers of the coastal plain—the Combahee, the Edisto, the Santee, as well as the Ashley and Cooper—sometimes called "black rivers" from the high concentrations of tannic acid from the "decaying leaves, branches, and roots of hardwoods." Further inland rose the sandy hills, a narrow strip of wind-blown sand sheets and dunes, disturbed and overlaid repeatedly from 75,000 to 6,000 years ago, after the end of the last major glaciation. Finally came the Piedmont, from the Latin phrase meaning "foot of the mountains," rolling and scenic remnants from the erosion of the once-massive Appalachian chain, formerly as tall as the Alps, now known as the Blue Ridge.

South Carolina's biodiversity across these regions offered the naturalist spectacular landscapes filled with plant and animal species, from the palmetto and cypress trees, herons, and waterfowl of the wetlands to the rhododendron, panthers, and bison of the Piedmont. The Atlantic coast's marshes, barrier islands, and beaches also teemed with life, from pelicans and terns to osprey, from oysters to sharks.

Other than colonial militia who manned three forts along Carolina's frontier and those who traded with Natives, few Europeans had ever been where Catesby planned to go. It was said that so few Lowcountry residents ever ventured past the place known as Parish End, about fifty miles from Charleston in St. George, Dorchester Parish, that it could as well have been named World's End. Just as he had in Virginia a decade before, Catesby would encounter Native Americans who were largely unregulated by European law or might, far from the relative security of the area around Charleston.

The Spanish and French had preceded the British into the Carolina backcountry. The conquistador Hernando de Soto had passed very close to the future site of Fort Moore in 1540 on his way to the Mississippi River, and since the mid-1600s English-Spanish conflict in what is now Georgia had been constant. In the 1560s the French had explored the interior from their base on present-day Parris Island, which they called Charlesfort; the Spanish would found Santa Elena, the first capital of Spanish Florida, atop the abandoned French fort there. British trade with South Carolina's Natives had begun in 1674, after the colony formed an alliance with the Westo, a tribe which had only recently moved south from Virginia. The Westo, who were known for their ferocity in battle, provided the colony with slaves captured from their enemies the Cherokee, the Chickasaw, and the Creek. After the Westo were wiped out in battle with the Savannah Indians, the Yamasee moved north from Florida into the Savannah River area. Another important group of Natives in South Carolina were the Cherokee, who controlled the upper Piedmont and were powerful allies and trading partners of the colony.

Europeans and Native Americans on the frontier along the Savannah continued this complex dance of cooperation and tension. Natives provided hundreds of thousands of deerskins for shipment to England between 1674 and 1715; market demand in Europe for furs and hides would increase throughout the eighteenth century. In return, Native Americans received a wide array of goods including cloth and clothing, mirrors, blankets, scissors, metal tools, brass kettles, guns and ammunition, pipes and tobacco, salt, and rum.

They also delivered tens of thousands of enslaved Natives, typically women and children captured from enemy tribes in battle. By 1712 about twenty-five percent of South Carolina's slave population were Native Americans; before 1715 the colony exported more slaves than it imported, mainly to the West Indies. If Charleston is sometimes considered the Ellis Island of enslaved Africans arriving in the New World, it also marked the departure point for thousands of Native Americans headed for the Caribbean. The trade in enslaved Natives and pelts was crucial to the economy of early Carolina before the development of forest products, livestock, and rice; it gave those settlers the capital which later allowed them to invest in large-scale rice farming, enabled by enslaved African labor.

In reality, the colonial settlers depended on alliances with Native American tribes to protect their farms and plantations from attacks by other tribes outside the alliance. The colony had neither the population nor the resources to protect itself against the combined might of the area's Indigenous groups, and as the plantations spread and the colony became more prosperous, its defense became even more problematic.

The colony may have been dependent on the good will of the surrounding Native tribes, but individual traders felt free to behave differently. Authorities in Charleston were barraged with complaints of abuse on the part of the traders, who continually cheated, physically abused, and enslaved the Natives. This would cause the colonial government to blame the traders' abuses for starting the Yamasee War. Of course Charleston was glad to have this pretext for putting the private traders out of business altogether.

Though the worst hostilities of the Yamasee War ended in 1718, only four years before Mark Catesby's arrival in South Carolina, continuing skirmishes made travel into the Carolina backcountry hazardous for Europeans. In the wake of the war, the Native trade was made a public corporation administered by the colony and the private trade with Native Americans was prohibited. Before the war, about fifty thousand deerskins a year were exported out of Charleston; in the first year after it, only five thousand skins left Charleston harbor for Europe.

The conflict also effectively ended the Native slave trade, as Charleston merchants shifted even more to deerskins and, too often, to the importation of enslaved Africans.

It had been a close thing for the young colony. Plantations near Charleston had been raided and burned. Ninety percent of the English traders who had lived among the Natives were killed. Only within a thirty-mile radius from Charleston could colonists feel safe. The very future of South Carolina had been in doubt. The Yamasee War, a modern account suggests, "probably came closer than any other conflict on the Atlantic seaboard to throwing an established colonial power back into the ocean."

Into war's aftermath, and the far-from-settled dynamic between Europeans and the various Native tribal communities, Catesby made his way in the spring of 1723. His explorations near Fort Moore and higher into the Carolina Piedmont would give him ample opportunity to observe people as well as flora and fauna.

◆

Ancient Native trails etched the South Carolina landscape in the early eighteenth century, as they did the rest of the North American continent. These well-maintained, well-marked paths connected tribes and regions for the purposes of both trade and war. Natives often traveled great distances for game, shellfish, fish, and pearls, as well as for minerals such as salt for food, flint for weapons, and ochre for paint. (When siting the trails, Natives preferred ridges and drainages; the twentieth-century engineers who would lay out the first roads for automobiles shared that preference, which is why many modern roads and interstate highways closely follow Native routes.) As Europeans entered the area in the sixteenth and seventeenth centuries, they began using these trails, sometimes widening them to accommodate wagons and horses.

In South Carolina, major Native paths linked Charleston and the interior, including to Savanna Town, a Native settlement near the Savannah River. The colony would establish Fort Moore on the eastern bank of the river near Savanna Town to protect this major trade center. Other trails led from Charleston to trade centers such as Fort Congaree at the beginning of the Piedmont and the Cherokee town of Old Keowee at the foot of the Blue Ridge. As Catesby was intent on collecting plant specimens and exploring throughout the interior, it is likely that he traveled inland to Fort Moore, probably with a packhorse train organized by white traders.

A Native path ran near the front door of Boochawee Plantation, home of Catesby's friend Colonel James Moore. Moore, who had extensive experience both fighting and negotiating with Natives, shared anecdotes about them with Catesby: "Col. Moore, a Gentleman of good Reputation in Carolina, told me, that he has seen an Indian daub himself with the Juice of [the Purple Bind-weed]; immediately after which, he handled a Rattlesnake with his naked Hands without receiving any harm from it, though thought to be the most venomous of the Snake-kind." It may have been Moore's connections to the Native trade that put Catesby on horseback with Native traders headed to the frontier.

The typical Native trader used one packhorseman, usually an indentured servant though sometimes a Native or Black slave, to assist in handling six or seven horses and their packs. Cherokee horses, handsome and strong, were the preferred packhorses. Often traders would assemble in large numbers, for safety; these could include a hundred horses and fifteen or sixteen men. Catesby could feel relatively safe in such a group.

If the naturalist found himself on a Native trail that hadn't been altered by Europeans, he might have been surprised by its narrowness. The trail builders and users reasoned that having the resources of the land—plants and animals, food and medicine—easily available from the trails outweighed any reason to widen them. To keep the path's minimal width, the Cherokee would even walk heel-to-toe, like tightrope walkers.

The trails wound through forests that, like those of Virginia, stunned Europeans who rode or walked through them—not just because of the age and grandeur of the trees, but also because of the lack of undergrowth. Early observers frequently noted that the forest floors of the Eastern seaboard resembled those of an English park. The Cherokee regularly burned the woods, which would have cleared out many of the thickets of rhododendron and multiflora rose; to them, a modern forest might well look sloppy and unkempt.

William Bartram later described the woodlands of South Carolina:

> Continuing some time through these shady groves, the scene opens, and discloses to view the most magnificent forest I had ever seen . . . The ground is perfectly a level green plain, thinly planted by nature

with the most stately forest trees . . . whose mighty trunks, seemingly of an equal height, appeared like superb columns . . . I think I can assert, that many of the black oaks measured eight, nine, ten, and eleven feet diameter five feet above the ground.

Unlike Catesby, who had seen the Native practice in action, Bartram did not seem to realize that this scene was created by burning the undergrowth on a regular basis.

Not all the land was transformed so extensively by Native actions. Catesby noted that "on the Banks of these Rivers extend vast Thickets of Cane . . . between twenty and thirty Feet high, growing so close that they are hardly penetrable but by Bears, Panthers, Wild Cats, and the like." The abundance of wildlife and game was also described by the rector of St. George's Dorchester, Francis Varnod, who traveled to Fort Moore in 1724, perhaps along the same route as Catesby. "The woods under the noble canopy of Heaven was the place where I lay most nights, being supplied sufficiently with Deers & Tigers [perhaps panthers?] flesh & now & then with wild Turkeys," Varnod wrote. The clergyman's party were "disturbed in the nights only with the woolfs when we were apprehensive of the Yamasees Indians."

South Carolina's government sited Fort Moore where the Savannah River became navigable after tumbling over the rocky fall line of the Piedmont. William Bartram, exploring the area fifty years later, described the fort's placement atop "a stupendous bluff . . . rising out of the river on the Carolina shore, perhaps ninety or one hundred feet above the common surface of the water," which "exhibit[ed] a singular and pleasing spectacle to a stranger," offering "a view of prodigious walls of party-colored earths, chiefly clays and marls of . . . brown, red, yellow, blue, purple, white, &c. in horizontal strata, one over the other." Catesby was similarly impressed. "It is one of the sweetest Countrys I ever saw," Catesby wrote Sherard, describing the two-hundred-foot-high riverbank on the Carolina side and the prospect below. "I am so enamoured with the place that I can't forbear tireing you with a tedious relation of what I saw."

The fort itself was modest, a square built out of wooden planks, with no more than fifty soldiers at any one time. Inside its walls were barracks, outbuildings, and a storehouse for trade goods. The regulations were firm: "by direction of the governor, council and assembly, that on no account whatsoever you will admit any indian, of any nation or quality soever, into the fort." However, archaeologists have found a Native American grave inside the fort, as well as a finely crafted stone used for the popular Native game of chunkey.

Unlike later forts in "Indian Country," Fort Moore was always more important as a central location for Native trade than for any defensive purpose. Its isolation and supplies of goods made it a stopping-point for Native Americans on their seasonal travels as they alternated between periods in their villages and the deer hunts of fall and winter, which produced the hides they would bring to the fort to exchange.

By the time William Bartram came through in the 1770s, Fort Moore was no more. "In early times, the Carolinians had a fort, and kept a good garrison here as a frontier and Indian trading post," Bartram wrote; "but Augusta superseding it, this place was dismantled; and since that time, which probably cannot exceed thirty years, the river hath so much encroached upon the Carolina shore, that its bed now lies where the site of the fort then was."

◆

Just as his curiosity had drawn him to the enslaved Africans he found on the Charleston-area plantations, on the western frontier Catesby encountered and took notes on the Natives in the area. Even after the end of the Yamasee War, the frontier was far from secure from the settlers' perspective. Many Native Americans coexisted with the settlers, however, and participated in trade, especially the thriving business in deer hides. In his *Natural History* Catesby included extensive descriptions of the manners and customs of the indigenous peoples he encountered during his travels.

Missing, of course, are records of Native Americans' responses to Catesby as they encountered him in the upland frontier of South Carolina. How would they have reacted to this white man, less interested in hunting or trading than in collecting and drawing the plants and animals around him? Other indigenous Americans borrowed a term from their creation myths to describe such white people: *earth divers.*

◆

Meanwhile, Catesby bent to his work as the first naturalist ever to visit this part of North America. His accounts and illustrations were often the very first depictions of what he encountered. Sometime during this period, Catesby sketched the American buffalo, later pairing it in the *Natural History* with the rose locust tree. "I never saw any of these trees but at one place near the Apalatchian mountains, where Buffelos had left their dung; and some of the trees had their branches pulled down, from which I conjecture they had been browsing on the leaves." Once again Catesby focused on relationships between plants and animals. His studies and illustrations were precursors of the science of ecology.

From the immense buffalo to the smallest insect, Catesby's curiosity and attention drove him. He was the first to document indigenous North American dung beetles, or "tumble turds." Catesby painted two of them at the base of a Canada Lily (*Lilium canadense*). A common tumblebug (*Canthon pilularius*) is shown busily pushing a ball of dung with its rear legs, while a rainbow scarab beetle (*Phanaeus vindex*) meanders toward the edge of the page.

Catesby thrilled to the variety of plants, animals, and topography he encountered on his journeys. "I was much delighted to see Nature differ in these Upper Parts, and to find here abundance of Things not to be seen in the Lower Parts of the Country; this encouraged me to take several Journeys with the Indians higher up the Rivers, toward the Mountains, which afforded not only a Succession of new vegetable Appearances, but most delightful Prospects imaginable, besides the Diversion of Hunting Buffello's, Bears, Panthers, and other wild Beasts."

And he valued the knowledge of the Native Americans he traveled, hunted, and collected with. "Indians are wholly ignorant in Anatomy and their Knowledge in Surgery very superficial," he wrote, "yet they know many good vulnerary and other Plants of Virture, which they apply with good Success: The Cure of Ulcers and dangerous Wounds is facilitated by severe Abstinence, which they endure with a Resolution and Patience peculiar to themselves." It is noteworthy that Catesby never disputed Native reports or information in the *Natural History*. Nowhere did he cite a non-Native source who contradicted Native claims. To naturalists like Catesby, Natives' connection with nature and their observable prowess in the natural world made them ideal companions in the field. Like the enslaved Africans on Lowcountry plantations, Natives were worth listening to when it came to herbal medicines.

"To the Hospitality and Assistance of these Friendly Indians, I am much indebted," Catesby wrote, "for I not only subsisted on what they shot, but their First Care was to erect a Bark Hut, at the Approach of Rain to keep me and my Cargo from Wet." That cargo would include the "Box, in which, besides Paper and Materials for Painting, I put dry'd Speciments of Plants, Seeds, &c.—as I gathered them." Catesby made pen-and-ink or graphite sketches in the field, sometimes augmented by brief watercolors to indicate the colors of plants and animals; he would sometimes write color notes on these sketches, to remind himself when he returned to Charleston or one of the planters' homes.

What would Mark Catesby have worn on his collecting journeys? His gentleman's attire of breeches and stockings might not have worked in the rough conditions and weather extremes of the South Carolina backwoods. As he was traveling with Indian traders from Charleston to Fort Moore, and beyond, he may have adopted their dress. He could have found what he needed in Charleston, as shown in a notice in the *South Carolina Gazette*: "Mary Robinson Widow of Mr. Robinson deceased, still carries on his Trade in . . . Mr. Laurens's House Number (9) near the New-Markett, she has ready made Buck and Doe skin Breeches, either natural or black, purple and Cloth Colours . . . She also dresses Deer Skins with or without the Hairs, dyes, washes and mends Buck-skin Breeches."

A decade after Catesby landed in Carolina, a young Carl Linnaeus set out on a tour of Lapland, then the northernmost region of Sweden, now divided between that country and Finland. Linnaeus's description of the clothes and scientific equipment he took with him on his naturalist's journey could have been comparable to Catesby's:

> My clothes consisted of a light coat of . . . linsey-woolsey cloth . . . leather breeches; a round wig; a green leather cap, and a pair of half boots. I carried a small leather bag, half an ell in length, but somewhat less in breadth, furnished on one side with hooks and eyes, so that it could be opened and shut at pleasure. This bag contained one shirt; two pair of false sleeves; two half shirts; an inkstand, pencase, microscope, and spying-glass; a gauze cap to protect me occasionally from the gnats; a comb; my journal, and a parcel of paper stitched together for drying

plants, both in folio . . . I wore a hanger at my side, and carried a small fowling-piece, as well as an octangular stick, graduated for the purpose of measuring.

◆

For his ethnographic study of Native Americans Catesby followed what was an established and accepted practice in his time, borrowing from John Lawson's *A New Voyage to Carolina*. "Mr. Lawson . . . has given a curious Sketch of the natural Dispositions, Customs, &c. of these Savages," Catesby wrote. "As I had the same Opportunities of attesting that Author's Account as he had in writing it, I shall take the Liberty to select from him what is most material." He added, "I cannot but here lament the hard Fate of this inquisitive Traveller, who, though partial in his favourable Opinion of these Barbarians, died by their bloody Hands, for they roasted him alive in revenge for Injuries they pretended to have received from him."

For his part, Catesby had a dualistic view of Native Americans. Perhaps he was trapped by his intellectual framework; as a subscriber to the idea of the Great Chain of Being, Catesby may have assumed that America's indigenous people lacked the possibility of becoming "civilized" as he would think of that word. Yet he readily provided individual examples of their moral worth, their creative abilities, and their physical and mental prowess. It would be another century before the idea of evolution—of societies and individuals as well as of plants and animals—would be introduced by Alfred Russel Wallace and Charles Darwin.

A fascinating example of Catesby's mindset came during his discursion on Indigenous arts and culture. First, he claimed that all Indigenous tribes "inhabiting the whole Extent of North America," from the equator to Canada, "differ no otherwise from the Charibbeans than in being not altogether so swarthy, and generally somewhat of a larger stature." Then Catesby turned to the accounts of Spanish conquistadores and missionaries in Central and South America.

If the accounts of early Spanish explorers in America could be relied on, Catesby wrote, they would be "enough to excite in us a high Opinion of the Knowledge and Politeness of the Mexicans even in the more abstruse Arts of Sculpture and Architecture." But he looked askance at the fact that "all those stupendious Buildings which the Spanish Authors describe . . . should be so totally destroyed that an Hundred Years after its Conquest there should remain not the least Fragment of Art or Magnificence in any of their Buildings; Hard Fate!" He admitted to "Incredulity, suspecting much the Truth of the above-mentioned [Accounts]," which Catesby thought was designed "to aggrandize their Achievements in conquering a formidable People, who in reality were only a numerous Herd of defenceless Indians, and still continue as perfect Barbarians as any of their neighbors."

In other words, according to Catesby, if the Maya and Aztec peoples could build such wonderful edifices, why weren't they still standing? (Answer one: some were; answer two: the conquistadors had cannon.) To Catesby's thinking, the Spaniards (who couldn't really be trusted to give an honest account) were probably just trying to make themselves look good by inflating the abilities of the conquered people on Mexico, who actually (according to Catesby) were just as lacking in "civilization" as the rest of the Indigenous people in America.

It is interesting to speculate how Catesby would have responded had he been provided with incontrovertible evidence of the greatness of those Mesoamerican cultures, such as has been uncovered by archaeologists in the intervening centuries. Could he have changed his mind, admitted his mistake? Did his eighteenth-century "curiosity" extend so far?

◆

The Natives Catesby encountered on the frontier were "generally tall, and well shap'd, with well-proportioned limbs, though their Wrists are small, their Fingers long and slender; their Faces are rather broad, yet have good Features and manly Aspects." Native women were "generally finely shaped, and many of them have pretty Features. No people have stronger Eyes, or see better in the Night or the Day than Indians . . . they have generally good Teeth and a sweet Breath." Although they were not "so robust, and of so athletick a Form as is amongst Europeans . . . in Hunting they are indefatigable, and will travel further, and endure more Fatigue than a European is capable of." Native women served as "Pack-Horses, carrying the Skins of the Deer they kill, which by much Practice they perform with incredible Labour and Patience. I have often travelled with them 15 and 20 miles a Day for many Days successively, each Woma carrying at least 60, and some above 80 Weight at their Back."

One of the striking things about Catesby's descriptions is the close-in familiarity he had with Native Americans. In addition to traveling and hunting with them, he also spent nights in their company: "They are naturally a very sweet People . . . and as in travelling I have been sometimes necessitated to sleep with them, I never perceived any ill Smell; and though their Cabbins are never paved nor swept, and kept with the utmost Neglect and Slovenliness, yet are devoid of those Stinks or unsavory Smells that we meet with in the Dwellings of our Poor and Indolent." He even ate alligator with them: "The Hind-part of their Belly and Tail are eat by the Indians. The Flesh is delicately white, but has so perfumed a Taste and Smell, that I could never relish it with Pleasure."

Which is not to say that Catesby felt totally comfortable in this frontier zone. "There are two obstructions in travelling in these remote parts," he wrote Sherard in May 1723. "One is the fear of being lost the other is meeting with Indians." The latter had actually taken place "as five of us . . . were out a Buffelo hunting tho' they hapned to be those we were at peace with they were about 60." He was in a party made up of Chickasaw Natives and white men when they spotted a group of Cherokees; "tho' the Cherikees were also our friends, we were not altogether unapprehensive of Danger." The white men separated from the Chickasaw, the Natives "shortening their Way by crossing Swamps and Rivers," while the whites took a different route, "with much Difficulty and a long March," back to Fort Moore.

Overall, Catesby wrote, "The Indians (as to this Life) seems to be a very happy People, tho' that Happiness is much eclipsed by the intestine Feuds and continual Wars one Nation maintains against another." Catesby dwelt at length on Natives' customs of warfare, including leaders' tattooing images of serpents on their bodies to make themselves "more known and dreaded by their Enemies," and carving into trees a "dreadful Hieroglyphick" combining their likeness with an open-mouthed rattlesnake. The carving signified that "he whose Pourtrait is there displayed, hunts in these Grounds, where if any of his Enemies dare intrude, they shall feel the Force of his *Tommahawk*."

It was this continual warfare, Catesby wrote, which "probably has occasioned the depopulated State of North America at the Arrival of the Europeans." Additionally, by "introducing the Vices and Distempers of the old World" into the New, Europeans "have greatly contributed even to extinguish the Race of these Savages, who it is generally believ'd were at first four, if not six times as numerous as they now are."

For Catesby, interrelationships were the thing: not only the dynamic between the plants that were native and those introduced from elsewhere, but also the interplay among the people and cultures who were undergoing the same transplanting and intermingling, voluntarily or not. Seeing the world through a naturalist's lens, Catesby saw that just as with plants, the cross-pollination of peoples and cultures could produce both benefits and problems. The unintended consequences of this dynamic, he felt, were well worth pondering.

◆

Catesby returned to Charleston in May, then went back to Fort Moore for July and August. In November he wrote Hans Sloane,

"I now send you Sr what Plants I collected 300 miles from the mouth of the Savanno River a very pleasant Hilly country infinitely excelling the inhabited parts both for goodness of land and air." Catesby was already planning a return to the frontier: "Next Summer if God permits I design to visit the Cherikees a Numerous Nation of Indians inhabiting part of the Apalathean Mountains about 400 miles from hence." He would return to the western frontier, to Fort Moore and the Piedmont, in the spring of 1724.

These expeditions yielded specimens by the dozens, if not hundreds. In fact, Catesby had collected enough to send Sherard three or four of each variety of plant, for Sherard to share with Dale and Dubois. There were also plants, seeds, birds, and skins for Sloane, for Thomas Fairchild at the Hoxton nursery, and for Peter Collinson. In a typical letter, Catesby listed "these few Seeds and Acorns" he was sending to Collinson from "Mr Skeyns" (Alexander Skene's) in January 1723:

Black
Walnut
Hickory Nut
Pignut
[classified as "Okes":]
Live
Chesnut
Willow
Water
with 2 or 3 other sorts mixt
Dogwood

Cassena

Haws

Bay a new kind

Tuberose

Catesby added, "The time was so far spent before I was able to goe out that it was with difficulty we got these it being Mid: December."

As in the Lowcountry, water was a primary means of travel to and from the frontier. The Savannah was wide enough to be easily navigable, especially when heading downstream, and was described by a prominent soldier and planter of the time as "the ordinary thorowfare to the Westward Indians." Rowing against the current from the Atlantic at Port Royal up to Fort Moore took about twenty days, but the reverse downstream journey needed only four or five days' travel. Floating downriver by periagua would have been the logical way for Catesby to cart all his specimens, his collecting gear, and his art equipment back to Charleston.

Catesby also found room in his baggage for Native American artifacts which he collected to send to Hans Sloane and others, impressed by the Natives' skills. He described a Cherokee split cane basket destined for Sloane, held today in the British Museum, as one of "their masterpieces in mechanicks . . . made of cane in different forms and sizes, and beautifully dy'd black and red with various figures; many of them are so close wraught that they will hold water." He also acquired clay pipes, an "Indian apron" of mulberry bark cloth which he sent to Sloane, and a "waistcoat" or vest, designed to be worn with the furred side either in or out, depending on the season, which Catesby sent to his brother.

◆

Before taking his long-planned trip to the Bahamas, Catesby had another plan, one which might have drastically changed what is known about the history of the American West. As he wrote Sherard, "Here is a gentleman with whom I have contracted a friendship, who has a strong inclination to see the remoter parts of this Continent perticularly Mexico in order to improve Natural Knowledge." The gentleman was Catesby's friend and host Thomas Cooper; "his practice is Phisick, and he is from Wadham College in Oxford. He is the only one so qualified in this Country." Catesby added, "I intreat you'l pleas to send me your sentiments concerning it." Neither Sherard nor Sloane, who received a similar letter, ever answered Catesby's request, and the journey to Mexico never happened.

Meanwhile the friction between Catesby and his subscribers over what, and how much, he was expected to send to them came to a head. In the summer of 1724 he wrote Sloane:

> My sending Collections of plants and especially Drawings to every of my Subscribers is what I did not think would be expected of me. My designe was Sir (til you'l please to give me your advice) to keep my Drawings intire that I may get them graved, in order to give a general History of the Birds and

other Animals, which to distribute separately would wholly Frustrate that designe . . . Besides, as I must be obbliged to draw duplicates of whatever I send, that time will be lost which otherwise I might proceed in the designe.

Catesby continued, referring to one of his patrons, "I beg Sir, if you (as I flatter myself you will) think this reasonable, that you will pleas, to satisfy Lord Percival, who no doubt will be influenced by what you say." Five months later, he would write of the most incessant of his patrons, "The discontent of Mr. DuBois and the trouble he gives my friends in receiving his Subscription is such that I would rather be without it."

This letter to Sherard of January 1725 is the last we have written by Mark Catesby from America, and his last from anywhere for the next five years. He would live for another quarter century, producing his great work and leaving a legacy of acclaim and accomplishment. But his voice from the New World was now muted, when not altogether silent, except in the pages of his *Natural History*.

◆

That same month, Catesby had written Sir Hans Sloane of his plans. "I am Sr preparing to goe to the Bahama Ilands to make a further progress in what I am about. This will add another year to my continuance in America." Aware that in a sense, he was going outside of his brief by leaving South Carolina, and unsure just how far his sponsors would enable him, he added,

"And tho' I doe not expect a continuance of my full subscriptions yet I hope partly by your interest and continuance of your Favours, I may expect the greater part of it." Without waiting for a response, Catesby turned his attention once more to the subtropical islands of the West Indies.

10

BAHAMAS 1725–1726

The sailboats taking people and cargo between South Carolina and the Bahamas in the 1720s were typically square-topsail sloops, their decks about sixty feet long and eighteen feet wide. Shipwrights crafted these boats in Jamaica, Bermuda, and everywhere along the American coast from Charleston to Canada for shorter voyages closer to shore. Because the Spanish in Florida were notorious for harassing British ships that strayed too close to their coast, the sloops would sail east away from Charleston, cross the powerful ocean river known as the Gulf Stream, and then head south to the Bahamas.

Their likely first landfall, Grand Bahama Island, lay just fifty miles east of the coast of Florida. From there the Bahama archipelago arced across six hundred miles of ocean. Catesby described them as "a Tract of small Islands extending from the Gulph of Florida in a South East Direction almost the whole length of Cuba." The islands, he wrote, numbered "some Hundreds, most of them very small."

Unlike Jamaica, with its volcano-remnant mountains rising steeply above seven thousand feet, the low-lying Bahamas consisted of fossil coral beds topped with limestone and thin topsoil. The highest point in the Bahamaian atoll stood on present-day Cat Island, 207 feet above sea level. Like most of the other islands in the Caribbean, the Bahamas featured karst formations that form sinkholes in the eroded limestone, including the deep "blue holes" that today attract divers.

The two thousand cays and seven hundred islands of the Bahamas were surrounded by about 85,541 square miles of shallow-water marine habitats; the Spanish called them the Gran Bajamar, "Great Shallows." The Bahamas contained more of such habitats than all the other Caribbean islands combined, measuring ten times the size of the islands' above-ground area.

Green and loggerhead turtles thrived in the marine banks, while parrotfish, grunts, and jacks swam in the coral reefs. Further offshore fishermen caught snapper and grouper, while tuna and swordfish could be found in the true deepwater. Whales also sounded where the ocean floor plunged to depths of thirteen thousand feet, what Catesby described as "the unfathomable Abyss of the Ocean." William Dampier's *A New Voyage Round the World* (1697) mentioned the Bahamas as a place where sailors and beachcombers had found ambergris, the aromatic substance expelled by sperm whales and highly sought for perfumes; Catesby echoed that claim in the *Natural History*, adding that "Amber-Griss" was "formerly found more plentiful" on the islands.

The original Caribbean people, the Taino, lived amid more than twelve thousand marine species, the greatest concentration in the Atlantic Ocean. Living off the largesse of the coral reefs, the most complex and diverse marine ecosystems on earth, the Taino grew tall and healthy. The Lucayans, the branch of Taino who populated the small, low-lying, arid Bahamas, could preserve what they caught in their nets, thanks to readily available salt. They also had grown maize, or corn, in the Bahamas since at least AD 800. The Lucayans knew their surroundings well enough to draw the positions of adjacent islands in the sand for Christopher Columbus, whose first landfall in America was on one of several disputed islands in the Bahama archipelago.

Catesby arrived in the Bahamas sometime in 1725; a passage in the *Natural History* places him on a sloop in the waters off Andros Island that September. No letters survive from his time there; his narrative and description in the *Natural History* are our only sources for his visit, besides the seeds and dried plants he sent or brought to England, and the watercolor sketches of fish, bird, and plants that he painted while in the islands. He had visited Bermuda, Hispaniola, and Puerto Rico during his previous visit to the New World, and had explored Jamaica. Now, in his more focused role as a professional naturalist, Catesby cast a keen eye on the Bahamas' plants and animals. He would be the first European naturalist to visit and work in the islands.

As had happened in Charleston, Catesby had connections in the Bahamas to high-ranking residents. He had been invited there by Woodes Rogers, one of Catesby's future "Encouragers" who would underwrite the publication of the *Natural History*. Rogers had twice served as governor of the island where he achieved a significant feat: it was he who had ended the pirates' reign of terror and intimidation based in the Bahamas, which had spread from there across the Caribbean and Atlantic.

◆

In December 1718, a gallows was erected in Nassau, the capital of the Bahama Islands, in anticipation of the mass hanging of nine pirates. The skull and crossbones flag, that infamous symbol of buccaneers in the Caribbean and worldwide, hung mockingly overhead. Woodes Rogers had just arrived on the island that year, having been named governor, captain general, and vice-admiralty judge of the Bahamas. He had been specifically tasked with ending piracy on the islands.

Nassau had long been a literal safe harbor for pirates, as well as what a modern writer terms "a tropical pleasure dome of unchecked debauchery." In 1670 the English monarchy had granted the Bahamas to the Lords Proprietary government of the Carolinas. This absentee authority and lack of government in the Bahamas, as well as its position near the shipping lanes of the Gulf Stream and the Old Bahama Channel, attracted pirates by the hundreds.

Anglo-American pirates were so successful in their attacks on merchant ships between 1716 and 1726 that the might of the nascent British Empire was sent against them. From 1680 to 1760, while the slavers and merchants were building a maritime system to maximize trade and profits, the pirates had created that system's total opposite: a society that was democratic, egalitarian, and multiracial. But because it threatened the slave trade and the larger Atlantic economy, the Golden Age of Piracy had to be brutally exterminated.

By 1718 King George II had received sufficient complaints about the Bahamas that he commissioned Rogers to bring the islands under control. By now, it had become clear that the mythology of the swashbuckling buccaneers obscured some cynical truths. The pirates seldom seized anything of value, much less treasure such as gold and silver. On the other hand, they were a huge drain on the overseas trade between America and Europe, causing massive losses to shipping. In the end, when pirates disrupted the triangular trade of sugar, tobacco, and cotton from America, textiles and guns from Europe, and enslaved people from Africa, the British Navy ended their presence on the high seas.

Rogers's efforts in the Bahamas were part of this larger British campaign against piracy, one that was gruesomely effective. Pirates at first left the Bahamas for the Carolinas and Africa, but they eventually ran out of places to hide from British fleets. Corpses dangled in chains in British ports around the world "as a Spectacle for the Warning of others." As many as 500 to 600 Anglo-American pirates, including those nine in Nassau, were executed between 1716 and 1726. The Golden Age of Piracy was over. Not coincidentally, Britain was now "the supreme nation in the Atlantic region."

By the time Catesby arrived in the Bahamas, however, Rogers was in an English debtors' prison. The governor had invested heavily in his vision of the Bahamas, and the British government in London had refused to bail him out. Rogers would spend several years in jail before the timely (for him) publication of

Captain Charles Johnson's *General History of the Robberies and Murders of the Most Notorious Pyrates* made him a national hero. His debts forgiven and in possession of a pension from the king, Woodes Rogers would return in 1728 to the Bahamas and a second term in the governor's office.

◆

Now, in 1725, George Phenney served as governor. He welcomed Catesby to stay at the governor's mansion in Nassau on the island of New Providence, where the naturalist was "entertain'd by him with much Hospitality and Kindness." Catesby found the Bahamas to be "blessed with a most serene Air," which "induces many of the sickly inhabitants of *Carolina* to retire to them for the Recovery of their Health."

In the *Natural History* Catesby describes watching Governor Phenney search his feet for "Chegoes," or chegoe fleas, and the two men then viewing the fleas through a microscope. In doing so Catesby made what is apparently the earliest recorded description of the use of a microscope in the Americas. While the governor's guest, Catesby also noted that in December 1725, "it was two days so cold, that we were necessitated to make a fire in the Governors Kitchen to warm us." (The eighteenth was a cooler century: the Little Ice Age, between the fifteenth and nineteenth centuries, caused periods of drought and freezing temperatures for the Jamestown colonists and other early American explorers.)

From Nassau Catesby sailed to the adjacent islands, "particularly Ilathera [Eleuthera], Andros, Abbaco and other neighboring Islands." He had come, mainly, for the marine life: he wrote of the Bahamas that "as they afford but few Quadrupeds and Birds, I had more time to describe the Fishes." He had seen sturgeon "leaping some Yards out of the Water" on the Savannah River and depicted a few shells and fish while in South Carolina, but purposely deferred most of that aspect of his project until reaching the more abundant prospects offered in the islands of the tropics. Not only would Catesby find a greater number of marine species in the Bahamas; he was also canny enough to realize his opportunity for distinction as the first to publish them: "there being not any, or a very few of them described by any Author."

Under the immense Caribbean sky, where massive banks of cumulus clouds gave way to multicolored sunsets, Catesby "collected many Submarine productions, such as Shells, Corallines, Fruitices Marini, Sponges, Astroites, &c." In the shallow waters just offshore, "so exceedingly clear, that at the Depth of twenty Fathom [about one hundred feet], the rocky Bottom is plainly seen," Catesby "distinctly and with much Pleasure beheld [a] Variety of Fish sporting amidst Groves of Corallines and numerous other submarine Shrubs."

He had been told more than once about the spectacular coloration of Caribbean fishes. "Yet," he wrote, "I was surprised to find how lavishly Nature had adorn'd them with Marks and Colours most admirable." These stunning colors of the Bahamian fish were ephemeral, though, quickly fading the moment specimens were removed from the water. Catesby addressed the problem with varying degrees of success. "Fish which do not retain their Colours when out of their Element, I painted at different times, having a succession of them procur'd while the former lost their Colours," he wrote. Not that this strategy was always available to him: "Some kinds I saw not plenty of, and of others I never saw above one or two." Catesby used this technique to capture the deep oranges and blues and iridescent green of the spotlight parrotfish (*Sparisoma viride*), the intricately mottled reds of the red rock crab (*Grapsus grapsus*), and the purple body and gold stripes of the lane snapper (*Lutjanus synagris*).

Catesby had more options when it came to other marine life, whose markings and other characteristics didn't deteriorate once they were out of the water. He gathered close to eighty-six shells, corals, crustaceans, starfishes, and sea urchins to send to Sloane, most of them clearly linked to the Bahamas. He also sent Sloane specimens of marine algae for his herbarium.

Specimens on land also attracted Catesby's time and attention. Of the over four hundred species in the *Natural History*, Catesby illustrated 124 from the Bahamas. Half of those were flowering plants, thirty were fishes, and fifteen were birds; the rest were insects, crustaceans, turtles, one lizard, and one mammal. He observed that "the Barrenness of these rocky Islands, and the little Soyl they contain, imploys not many hands in its Culture: therefore the greater part of the Inhabitants get their Living other ways." In addition to living from the sea by fishing and shipping, Bahamians hunted "Guanas" and cut "Brasiletto Wood" (Mexican logwood, *Haematoxylum brasiletto*), "Ilathera-Bark" (cascarilla, *Croton eluteria*), and "that of wild Cinamon."

In the *Natural History* Catesby described the three major soils of the Bahamas: "White Ground," coral sand; "Black Land,"

Bahama black loam; and "Red Land," Bahama red loam. He displayed his range as a naturalist, pointing out each soil type's suitability for agriculture accurately; "made successive Collections of dry'd Plants and Seeds"; and offered his considered sense of ecology, of the interrelationship between soils and plants. The black soil, he noted, was very productive at first, but soon exhausted; the red soil, though having "no good aspect," was more durable than the black; while the white was "a light-coloured Sand," best for growing cotton.

Catesby was on hand to observe a quirky annual phenomenon: the annual breeding migration of purple land crabs (*Gecarcinus ruricola*). He watched the crabs "descend the Hills in vast Numbers to lay their Eggs near the Sea." While en route, "whatever they meet with in their Passage they go over, never going aside let Houses, Churches or what will stand in their Way: They have been known to enter in at a Window, and on a Bed, where People who had never before had seen any, were not a little surprised."

One of Catesby's most notable illustrations combined land and sea creatures in an innovative fashion. For his watercolor sketch, which he eventually turned into a colored etching in the *Natural History*, Catesby yanked from the ocean a tall, treelike gorgonian called the double-forked plexaurella (*Plexaurella dichotoma*) and placed it on dry land behind his American flamingo (*Phoenicopterus ruber*). Gorgonians are not plants, as Catesby thought (he named it *Keratophyton Dichotomum fuscum* and wrote, "This plant ariseth from a short stem" on the sea bottom). Instead, they are actually marine animals called cnidarians, related to jellyfish, sea anemones, and corals. Catesby's willingness to go beyond simple relationships, to place unrelated plants and animals together on occasion for the sake of art, was never more obvious than here. The resulting composition looks strikingly modern.

As in South Carolina and Jamaica, Catesby often examined the commercial uses and possibilities for the specimens he collected. Mahogany was well known in England for its "Excellency . . . for all Domestick Uses," but it was also known in the Caribbean for its ability to grow in the rocky soils of the islands. It was also "in no less Esteem for Ship-building, having properties for that Use excelling Oak, and all other Wood," such as "Durableness, resisting Gunshots, and burying the Shot without splintering." Catesby found logwood growing on the Providence plantation of Mr. Spatches, "a Person of more than common Curiosity." This valuable source of dye had been the cause of "bloody Disputes . . . between the Spaniards and English," he wrote; "I could wish that the Inhabitants of our Southern Plantations could be induced to propagate it," both for their own use and to supply English markets when the Spanish cut off the supply.

Catesby continued another practice while in the Caribbean. As with the enslaved Africans and Native Americans he interacted with and learned from in South Carolina, Catesby gave respect and attention to the knowledge possessed by Bahamians. While governors and English merchants, intent on being as English as possible, dismissed the "lazy" Bahamians, whose dialect battered the King's English almost beyond recognition and (as Catesby described) ate poisonous fish, Catesby recognized that they were the true experts on the flora and fauna of the subtropical Caribbean.

He perhaps should have heeded native wisdom when encountering one particularly notorious native tree. Catesby had been told that the manchineel tree "causes a general Fear, or at least Caution, in felling them," but he proclaimed himself "not sufficiently satisfied" about this caution. But while "cutting down a Tree of this Kind on Andros Island, I paid for my Incredulity, some of the milky poisonous Juice spurting in my Eyes, I was two Days totally deprived of Sight, and my Eyes, and Face, much swelled, and felt a violent pricking Pain, the first twenty-four Hours," which "abated gradually . . . without Remedy."

Catesby's stoic recounting of this accident, along with the near-miss with the rattlesnake in his bed and the illness of his first autumn in Carolina, are the closest we come to any detailing of personal suffering while in the field. The humidity of the Carolina Lowcountry, the blinding sun of the Caribbean, the bug bites and poison ivy that were and are the everyday costs of being a naturalist, were not to Catesby worth mentioning. While at least one author of the time spent pages detailing the discomforts of heat, cold, damp, and sun, Catesby seems either unaffected by external conditions or determined to overlook them. He might merely have been too focused, or too busy, to notice.

Catesby made plain his disappointment at the brevity of his time in the Bahamas. Though he had managed to describe and illustrate "the Figures of the most remarkable Trees, Shrubs, &c. of the Bahama Islands," he admitted that "many Things remain undescrib'd for want of a longer Continuance there." As examples, he noted "four kind of Palms," which he considered "a Tribe of Trees inferior to none, both as to their Usefulness and majestick Appearance." Always hoping to be first to describe a specimen, Catesby regretted omitting "especially . . . the Silver-Leaf and Hog-Palms, of which, I think, no Notice has been taken."

Mark Catesby's writings are almost all the information we now have on conditions in the Bahamas early in the eighteenth century; they remained the standard reference work on Bahamian flora for two hundred years. In his observations Catesby showed the inclinations of a proto-ecologist, noting for example how the harvesting of brasiletto trees to make dye had caused a "Scarcity of it on the Bahama Islands," sending Bahamians across to Florida in search of more. Based on the detailed notes and sketches he made, he gave the Old World its first glimpse of many of the birds, fish, and plants of the New; his descriptions and illustrations of the Greater Antillean bullfinch (*Loxigilla violacea*), the loggerhead turtle (*Caretta caretta*), and the striking lily thorn (which would be named for him, *Catesbea spinosa*) would fascinate all who first found them in the pages of the *Natural History*.

Catesby's description of his encounter with the loggerhead turtle poses a mystery. In the *Natural History* he relates how "our boat was hoisted out, and a Loggerhead Turtle struck as it was sleeping on the Surface of the Water." This took place, he wrote, in April 1725, halfway between the Azores and the Bahamas, at 30° latitude. But that position is thousands of miles east of the Bahamas. If the encounter actually happened in April 1725, then Catesby at some point would have had to sail a huge distance—halfway to Europe—then back to the Bahamas by September 1725, before then returning to England a year later.

It also seems unlikely that Catesby meant to write 1722, on his way to America. He notes that on that voyage he spotted the owl, as mentioned in chapter 2, at 26° north latitude. That's almost three hundred miles south of the turtle's location at 30° north, though if the winds were from the southwest, his ship may have had to zigzag that far to make way toward Charleston.

What also seems plausible is that Catesby actually encountered the turtle on his way home from the Americas, in April 1726. The fact that ships tended to arc south toward the Caribbean when coming from Europe, and then bend north on the way back due to currents and trade winds, supports this possibility.

Catesby left the Bahamas for England in 1726, never to return to the Caribbean or North America. He had spent more than a quarter of his forty-three years exploring the woods, marshes, and shores of the New World; he had sent hundreds of plants, seeds, and animals back to his patrons in England, and to his friends in the business of commercial gardening and horticulture. Now he had to create a new life for himself, perhaps in London, where his knowledge and experience, as well as his connections, would best serve him. With little of his family and less of his estate remaining after his extensive journey of exploration in America, Catesby would be starting over in his native country.

He had another equally pressing and no less important task: how to finance, and then create, a book sufficient to display all that he had seen, learned, and captured on paper during his travels. On that work would rest his status in England and abroad for his remaining years of life, and his future standing among naturalists.

II

FORERUNNERS
1585–1709

A barefoot French monk dissecting fish in the Antilles. An eminent London physician's visit to Jamaica. An ahead-of-her-time Dutch artist investigating butterfly metamorphosis in Surinam. A pirate-turned-celebrity-author inspiring two of the greatest novels of the age.

Mark Catesby returned across the Atlantic to England having achieved various firsts. He had been the first naturalist to explore what was then the southwest frontier of the British colonies along the Savannah River and to the foothills of the Blue Ridge Mountains, and to visit the Bahama Islands. The result of his explorations would be the first full-color illustrated book depicting North American plants and animals. The *Natural History* also would stand as the first published work to combine color illustrations with detailed descriptions of the flora and fauna of the Caribbean, including marine life. But there were artists, explorers, and writers who at least in some respects had been there before him—sometimes figuratively, at other times literally.

Linnaeus himself, that giant of eighteenth-century science, referred to Catesby's era as a Golden Age of Botany. Increasing freedom of travel and communication allowed naturalists to experience a whole new range of habitats and climates, and to correspond with an ever-wider circle of scientists and collectors about those experiences. The burgeoning international trade, the dawning development of the scientific method, and the relative ease of portability of plants combined in a staggering expansion of knowledge and classification of flowers, herbs, shrubs, and trees. A similar explosion of encounter and acknowledgment occurred for insects, aquatic animals, reptiles, and mammals throughout the world. These phenomena produced an outpouring of both words and images, some of which predated and influenced Catesby.

In 1585, the newly knighted Sir Walter Raleigh was planning and organizing England's first mission of colonization to Virginia. In addition to a title, Queen Elizabeth I had granted this favorite of her courtiers a license to explore and settle in North America, the loan of a ship, and the right to give the name Virginia to whatever land he found, in honor of the Virgin Queen. As Catesby would do over a century later, Raleigh put together a syndicate of nobles to finance his venture. Unlike Catesby, however, Raleigh anticipated an additional source of revenue: loot captured from the Spanish.

Raleigh was careful to include an artist and what we would now call an ethnographer in this expedition to America, to depict and describe what the explorers would find. The ethnographer, Thomas Harriot, was a polymath who later made the first drawing of the moon as seen through a telescope, was the first to observe sunspots via a telescope, and first formulated the theory of refraction of light. The artist, whose artistic impressions of the New World would win him lasting renown, was John White.

White emerges from relative obscurity into the light of history between 1585 and 1592, then disappears again from all known records again, except for one brief mention in 1593. He is assumed to have been born sometime in the 1540s, and is listed as a member of the Painter-Stainers' Company in 1580. There is evidence that White traveled to North America in 1577 and 1584 before being named official artist of the 1585 expedition.

White would be granted a coat of arms in 1587, the mark of a gentleman and courtier; its heraldry was also proof of an ancient pedigree with Cornish connections. In this time of social mobility in England, Raleigh may have persuaded the Queen to find John White worthy by virtue of his service in America. However, he was already gentleman enough to have armor, books, and maps with him on his first voyage, and was used to having servants.

In May 1585 the *Tiger*, the expedition's flagship, landed in Puerto Rico. There White drew a pineapple and a banana, as well as many other plants, reptiles, fish, and insects. From there the *Tiger* sailed to Hispaniola, then through the Bahamas (where

White probably saw the pelican he later painted) en route to the Carolinas.

The expedition explored the Pimlico Sound and the Chesapeake Bay, with White steadily sketching the wildlife and the Native American culture he observed. He also made thorough maps of Raleigh's Virginia featuring not only geographic features, but also zoological and botanical information. The explorers were to be picked up by Sir Francis Drake's ships for the return to England. However, when Drake sent his pinnaces, the small boats used for ferrying between ship and shore, "the weather was so boysterous, and the pinnaces so often on the ground, that the most of all wee had, with all our Cardes, Bookes and writings, were by the Saylors cast over boord." Some, perhaps most, of White's work was lost, including whatever descriptions he might have made of his plants and animals.

But White did rescue and bring back to England a series of watercolors from his journeys in the New World. He painted the Natives and their customs and homes, as well as the birds, plants, and fishes that he saw. He labeled the animals with their Algonquin names: the striped bass is "Mesickek," the skink is "Memeskson," and the sturgeon is "Coppáuseo." White added no descriptions to his images other than brief notes on the drawings themselves. Across the top edge of his Portuguese man-o-war image, for example, White wrote, "This is a lyuing fish, and flote upon the Sea, Some call them Carvels," noting their resemblance to caravels, the nimble sailing ships used by the Dutch and Portuguese. Though White's paintings were not done with a scientists' eye, they were nevertheless the "first reports" back to the Old World, and their impact was sizable and immediate.

In 1587 Raleigh named White governor of a follow-up expedition to plant the "Cittie of Raleigh" in Virginia (this was when he gained his coat of arms). Among the colonists were White's daughter and her husband; while there, she gave birth to White's granddaughter, Virginia Dare, the first English child born in North America. White noted in his journal, "The first night we were on the island we caught five giant tortoises, some of them so large that sixteen of our strongest men were exhausted by carrying one the short distance to our cabins."

After establishing the settlement, White returned to England for more supplies, but events including the 1588 attack of England by the Spanish Armada prevented any ships from sailing back to Virginia until 1590. When White's expedition finally returned that year, they found only an uninhabited palisade with a post at the entrance; on it was the word CRO-ATOAN. The approaching hurricane season prevented White from staying to look for the colonists on Croatoan, probably modern-day Hatteras Island in the Outer Banks of North Carolina. None of the colonists were ever found, nor any evidence of their lives after leaving their homes. Thus began the legend of the Lost Colony of Virginia.

In 1590, the same year White returned to a vanished Roanoke colony, Theodor de Bry published Thomas Harriot's *A Briefe and True Report of the New Found Land of Virginia*. It contained etched versions of White's paintings of Southeastern Algonquian Native Americans and their culture, as well as a detailed map entitled "The Arrival of the Englishmen in

Virginia." De Bry printed about five hundred copies of the *Briefe and True Report*, perhaps as a prospectus for the Queen and the patrons of Raleigh's expedition. Herriot's account and White's illustrations portrayed North America as fertile and verdant, and its indigenous people as friendly and welcoming. White's images would become iconic, their portrayal of exotic Native Americans copied again and again in the eighteenth century.

But the *Briefe and True Report* did not include White's natural history illustrations. In fact, although these watercolor drawings of American flora and fauna were the first of their kind, they remained unpublished for three centuries. The images were known among English collectors and writers in the early 1600s, however; woodcuts of two of them, White's milkweed and a butterfly, appeared in 1597 and 1658. The last evidence of John White is his 1593 letter to the explorer Richard Hakluyt, recollecting the events surrounding the Lost Colony of Roanoke: "my fift & last voiage to Virgina . . . was no lesse unfortunately ended then frowardly begun," he wrote, "and as luckless to many, as sinister to my selfe."

In the early 1700s Hans Sloane learned of a sheaf of drawings purported to be White's, owned by his descendants. Unable at first to purchase the artworks, Sloane had them copied; later the tireless collector acquired the original drawings. These included forty-four images of birds, fish, and reptiles thought to have been executed by White in the area around Roanoke. Sloane copied one of them, the man-o-war jellyfish, for his *Natural History of Jamaica*. White's original watercolors were purchased by the Earl of Charlemont in 1788 and not seen again until the 1870s, nor were they published until the twentieth century.

Catesby would come across John White's images in Sloane's immense collection at Chelsea Manor in west London. He used seven of them in the *Natural History*, typically when he had observed an animal or plant but not made sketches of his own. Catesby copied White's catfish, *Ameiurus catus* ("Keetrauk" in Algonquin), though it was one of the least accurate of the images, as well as White's gar pike, *Lepisosteus osseus* ("Kowabetto").

Catesby's version of White's checkered pufferfish (*Sphoeroides testudineus*), which he called "The Globe Fish," figured in another of his unusual compositions. As with his flamingo, Catesby chose to combine creatures of sea and land. His pufferfish, a faithful copy of White's, floats on the page in front of two terrestrial plants (Lancewood, *Nectandra coriacea*, and red milk-pea, *Galactia rudolphioides*). Catesby never explained his choices: he might have wanted his viewers to be jolted into a new way of seeing—or he could have simply combined leftover specimens to fill one of his large sheets of "finest Imperial" paper. Whatever the reason, once again Catesby combined the artist with the scientist in his portrayal of America's natural wonders.

Almost a century elapsed after the Elizabethan voyages to America before another Englishman would publish detailed descriptions of the New World's natural wonders. That Englishman's life and career could scarcely have been more different than that of the gentleman-courtier John White.

◆

Early naturalists would eventually summon to the popular imagination familiar stereotypes: picture the aged Darwin puttering in his garden, or the shy nineteenth-century Anglican parson with his butterfly net. But in the late 1600s, the path of British natural history was blazed by a self-taught observer of natural phenomena who also happened to have been, at several points in his life, a pirate.

William Dampier's early life, like most in the seventeenth century, left little historical record. He was baptized on September 5, 1651, at East Coker in Somersetshire. Although he lost both parents early on, he managed to receive some education. At seventeen, the year after the death of his mother, he became an apprentice on board a ship which sailed to France and to Newfoundland, where the English fished the immense schools of cod. Dampier's adventurous and curious spirit, and his distaste for what he called "the rigours of that cold climate," led him to quit the apprenticeship in 1671 at about age twenty.

From there Dampier's service with the East India Company, the Royal Navy, and private concerns took him to Java, Jamaica, and the Gulf of Mexico. In 1679 he joined up with the buccaneers John Coxon, Richard Sawkins, and Bartholomew Sharp. Over the next twelve years his travels and adventures took him on the first of his three circumnavigations of the globe. Among his exploits was one of the early traverses by a European of the brutally wild stretch of the isthmus of Panama known today as the Darien Gap, due to a break there in the Pan-American Highway. Voyages to Mexico, Virginia, and West Africa followed. His was the first European party to reach the Galapagos Islands, in 1684; four years later Dampier reached northern Australia, the first

European to make contact with the Aboriginal people there. By September 1691 he was back in England.

All the while Dampier had been studying and recording what he saw. According to his biographers Diana and Michael Preston, "Like Catesby, Dampier was an instinctive, intuitive naturalist. He pioneered what today is known as descriptive botany and zoology, in other words, the careful, detailed, and objective recording of the world's living things." The publication in 1697 of *A New Voyage Round the World* caused a literary sensation, and made Dampier a celebrity, worthy of mention by the diarist John Evelyn: "I dined with Mr. Pepys, where was Captain Dampier, who had been a famous buccaneer . . . and printed a relation of his very strange adventure, and his observations."

Dampier himself had little doubt of his book's worthiness:

> After all, considering that the main of this Voyage hath its Scene laid in long Tracts of the Remoter Parts, both of the East and West Indies, some of which very seldom visited by English-men, and others as rarely by any Europeans, I may without vanity encourage the Reader to expect many things wholly new to him, and many others more fully described than he may have seen elsewhere; for which not only . . . this Voyage, tho' it self of many years continuance, but also several former long and distant Voyages, have qualified me.

Dampier also, it turns out, was a friend of John Woodward, the naturalist who had written the directions for dealing with specimens collected overseas (see chapter 1). Dampier sold or gave specimens to Woodward, including the very first artifacts collected by any European from Pacific peoples. These artifacts still exist as part of Woodward's collection in the Sedgwick Museum of Earth Sciences in Cambridge.

The literary and cultural effects of *A New Voyage* can hardly be exaggerated. It inspired Jonathan Swift's *Gulliver's Travels* and Defoe's *Robinson Crusoe* and caught the attention of members of the Royal Society, who invited him to address them. Dampier's rational, logical approach to explaining natural phenomena exactly fitted the Society's philosophy. The literary world also embraced him. In six succeeding books Dampier compiled information on currents, winds, and tides across all the world's oceans, and influenced Alexander von Humboldt, Charles Darwin, and Alfred Russel Wallace. His influence on the English language is nothing less than astonishing. As Preston and Preston point out,

> About one thousand entries in the *Oxford English Dictionary* come from Dampier's publications. To take only the first three letters of the alphabet, he gave to the English language such words as avocado, barbecue, breadfruit, cashew, and chopsticks. He was the first to write in English about southeastern Asia, describing the taste and manufacture of soy sauce and of what we now know as Thai fish sauce. Anyone researching the places Dampier visited . . . often finds him cited as the earliest and frequently the only authority for this period.

Like the apothecary and botanist James Petiver, Dampier was able to operate outside the constrictions of a caste-bound British social structure because of his achievements in the realm of natural history. The tenant farmers' orphan was accepted, at least intellectually, by the London scientific and literary elite.

It would be remarkable if the ubiquitous Sir Hans Sloane had not acquired copies of Dampier's work. As it happens, among Sloane's collections is a draft of the *New Voyage* with revisions in Dampier's handwriting. Catesby would have had little trouble accessing Dampier's bestselling works, from Sloane or elsewhere, and he cites them several times in the *Natural History.*

Writing about "The Booby" (brown booby, *Sula luecogaster*), Catesby noted, "They frequent the Bahama Islands, where they breed all months in the year . . . Dampier says, they breed on trees in an Island called Bon-Airy, in the West-Indies, which he believes not to have seen elsewhere." Catesby also quoted an extended passage from Dampier about the gathering of pods from the cacao tree (*Theobroma cacao*), and spreading them in the sun for harvest. Again, in Catesby's description of "The Mangrove Grape Tree" (seagrape, *Coccoloba uvifera*): "Dampier says the Wood of this Tree makes a strong Fire, therefore used by the Privateers to harden the Steels of their Guns, when faulty."

William Dampier was an important precursor to Mark Catesby. He both created and fed the British fervor for far-flung travel narratives involving exploration, danger, and exotic locales. As Britain's global reach grew along with the eighteenth century, the desire for descriptions of the places being colonized would furnish a market for Catesby's planned comprehensive treatment of North American flora and fauna. To Dampier's vivid descriptions Catesby would add powerful and ground-breaking illustrations. And in time to come, Catesby and Dampier would be recognized as being similar personalities, possessing a singular form of curiosity, as well as being, in the poet Samuel Taylor Coleridge's words about Dampier, "of exquisite mind."

◆

Of all the early naturalist-explorers to visit the New World, Charles Plumier might be the most unusual. Plumier entered the world of natural history not through social status, nor by piracy. For him, the route to advancement as a naturalist lay through an austere monastic order of the French Roman Catholic Church.

Plumier was born in Marseilles on April 20, 1646. The son of a wood turner, he received his early education from a parish priest, and at age sixteen he entered the Order of Minims. In addition to poverty, chastity, and obedience, the friars of the Minims (whose order still exists) abstained from meat and dairy products, and either went barefoot or wore sandals.

While staying in a convent in Rome, Plumier met two great Italian botanists, Francesco Onophrüs and Silvio Boccone. He soon proved to have an interest in and talent for botany, and was invited to the Alps to study plants with Joseph Pitton de Tournefort, inventor of the term "herbarium" who became Plumier's mentor.

In 1689 Plumier became a member of an expedition sent by King Louis XIV to the West Indies with the particular task of studying and illustrating the flora there. Plumier returned to

France to write his account of this trip, *Description des Plantes de l'Amerique* (1693), the success of which earned him an appointment as royal botanist and a pension. That same year, he returned to America by order of the king, and he would make a third voyage in 1695.

Plumier described his ambitions in fierce terms in the preface to another never-published book, addressing his benefactors: "For I, by His benign favor, as long as I am mindful of myself, as long as breath directs my limbs, shall sail through waves and through pathless rocks, and I shall lay nature bare by laboriously eviscerating her wonders for the satisfaction of your eyes."

Exploring and collecting in Martinique and Haiti along with shorter forays to Guadalupe and other islands of the Lesser Antilles, Plumier made about 6,000 drawings of specimens. Most of them were plants, but 1,550 of his illustrations were of animals, including 345 plates of fish. He identified and named the *Fuschia* genus of flowering plants, which he discovered on Hispaniola. Plumier also named the magnolia which he found in Martinique for Pierre Magnol, eminent French botanist and professor at the botanical garden at Montpelier. In 1703–1704 he published his landmark book *Plantarum Americanarum Genera* (*New Species of American Plants*), a massive work of botanical research based on his in situ observations of New World plants. He had finalized plans for printing another book when he died suddenly in 1704.

Plumier's notes and meticulous renderings included color indications when not done in watercolor. His images of fishes often added anatomical details such as pieces of skeleton or the swim bladder, indicating that he had dissected the specimens he illustrated. His groundbreaking work identifying and naming the one hundred genera with seven hundred species in the *Plantarum Americanum* was later adopted almost unchanged by Linnaeus.

For the scientific names of plants which he included in the *Natural History*, Catesby most frequently cited the works of Leonard Plukenet, an English botanist and collaborator with John Ray, with those of Plumier second, followed by those of Sloane. Plumier's astonishing and thorough depictions of the plants and animals of the Antilles were fit models for Catesby as he sought to complete a similarly ambitious work three decades later.

◆

Mark Catesby was not the first European naturalist-artist to explore the mainland of the New World. Nor was he the first to arrange Western Hemisphere plants and animals on paper in symbiotic relationship. Those honors instead go to a brilliant and trailblazing Dutch woman who in 1699 sailed to Surinam with her young daughter, Dorothea, unaccompanied by any man. The book that resulted from this highly unusual voyage of discovery, *Metamorphosis Insectorum Surinamensium* (*The Transformation of the Insects of Surinam*, 1705), offered new possibilities in illustrating the interdependence of flora and fauna.

Maria Sibylla Merian was already a prominent artist in Amsterdam when she left Europe for the small Dutch colony on the northwest coast of South America. She had lived a rather unconventional life; born in Frankfurt-am-Main in

1647, Merian grew up in an artistic household—her father was a famed botanical artist, her stepfather the owner of a book-printing business. She left her husband to join a strict Pietist sect, the Labadites, who believed in communal living, strict discipline, and minimal personal possessions. They also considered the natural world to be a divine source of wonder. Merian left the sect after six years and returned to Amsterdam.

There Merian visited the virtuosi's cabinets of curiosities, but the specimens on exhibit, even the bizarre and colorful, left her unsatisfied. They were out of context, pinned in a tray without the details of where and when and how. "The insects' origin and propagation were absent, that is, how they transformed from caterpillars into pupae and so forth," she would write. Like Catesby a little later, she wanted to learn about what we now call the ecology of species, the environment in which they are born, live, and die. So, in the words of her biographer, she "launched herself to a place no one, much the less a woman, had been before: setting out on a purely scientific journey to do field research in a foreign country."

Surinam in 1699 was run by the Dutch East India Company. There Merian spent three years making collections and completing many of her paintings of plants and animals.

It was a time when scholars still didn't quite comprehend the cycle of insect life history, from egg to adult and back to egg. The theory of spontaneous generation prevailed in many quarters. Daniel Sennet's *Thirteen Books of Natural Philosophy* (1660) stated that although butterflies develop from caterpillars, "experience shows that such Worms and Caterpillars are bred out of Dew and Rains falling down upon Plants."

Maria Merian had studied the life cycles of insects since the age of thirteen, raising generations of butterflies and learning their lifecycles: from egg to larva, then chrysalis and butterfly. Her time in Surinam would produce colorful and beautiful artistic affirmation of her knowledge, as she created plates for the *Metamorphosis* containing all these life stages—sometimes in a single composition.

But the larger world did not escape her notice. In Plate 45 of her *Metamorphosis*, Merian described the peacock flower, *Caesalpina pulcherrima*, the beauty of which hid a dark story: its poisonous seeds were used by enslaved women "as an abortifacient so that their children would not become slaves as they are." In one of the book's few non-scientific comments, Merian wrote that the slaves "must be treated benignly," to prevent such acts. The peacock flower is the national flower of Barbados, where the British would perfect the sugar plantation economy at the expense of enslaved Black bodies.

Like Mark Catesby, Merian was described as "Curious," in several senses of the word. And also like Catesby, she would be honored by scientists by having species named after her, including *Catasticta sibyllae*, a black butterfly so rare it has no common name, discovered only in the 1980s, and the Argentine black and white tegu, *Salvator merianae*, a dramatically colored lizard up to three feet in length which Merian featured in one of her plates.

Just as Mark Catesby paid attention to non-European voices in America and the Caribbean, Merian utilized African and Amerindian collectors and informants for their knowledge of plants and animals. From them she learned which seeds could be soaked and dried to produce red body paint, and which fruit made black dye which lasted on skin for nine days; "before then," she wrote, "they cannot be washed off with any soap." Like the enslaved people Catesby spoke with in South Carolina, Merian's sources revealed to her the medicinal plants they knew: the leaves which were used for wrapping wounds, the seed oil utilized for healing, and the sap which would stop itching.

To create the *Metamorphosis* Merian had learned the art of engraving, as Catesby would learn etching for the *Natural History*. Merian and Catesby both chose to include where possible the common names given to their specimens by the indigenous, enslaved, and European residents. And, as Catesby probably did, she owned slaves. Her house in Paramaribo was tended by both enslaved Africans and an Indigenous servant.

But most of all, Merian's influence on Catesby lay in the way her illustrations portray interactions between insects and plants, as well as the various phases of insects' lives—a holistic view that would characterize Catesby's work as well. The *Metamorphosis* is riotous with color, Merian's compositions teeming with energy and movement. In one, a large black and yellow striped caterpillar of the Tetrio Sphinx moth, with bright red ends and legs, grabs the viewer's attention as it perches on a leaf of a cassava plant; a Rustic Sphinx moth hovers in air, its black-and-white wings outstretched to display their swirls of pattern; and an Amazon Tree Boa, with tiger-like markings, its stomach distended with a meal, curls menacingly around the plant's main stalk.

In another plate Merian perches a Teucer Giant Owl Butterfly, with its shimmering aqua and bronze above and large "owl eyes" below on its wings, on the bright yellow of a banana, while another Giant floats above in space; another reptile, this one a blue-green Rainbow Whiptail Lizard, lurks below. A third displays the vivid long crimson petals and graceful curling leaves of the Heliconia flower, inhabited by the Potter Wasp in its life stages, as well as several Owlet Moths and small butterflies—in all, nine insects in the frame. As in all sixty of the book's oversized plates, though, the composition of the Heliconias is uncrowded, on a white background, in an almost-modern way that prefigures some of Catesby's work.

It was that botanical gadfly James Petiver who connected Merian with England, writing her in 1703 and eventually promoting her Surinam book to the Royal Society. Hans Sloane took notice. After Merian had returned to Amsterdam, he acquired sixty of her Surinam paintings. This notable addition to Sloane's holdings also substantially boosted Merian's reputation—and her finances.

As we've seen, while in England from 1719 to 1722 between his trips to America, Mark Catesby visited Sloane's London collections, which eventually included two albums of Merian's original watercolors. Catesby's stylistic choice of combining plants and animals in the same frame may have been influenced by his noting Merian's similar practice in her paintings owned by Sloane. Catesby also cited Merian's works in the *Natural History*: plotting the range of "The Opossum," Catesby mentioned that "Merian has described them at Surinam," and rather gently critiquing Merian's cashew tree, he pointed out how the fruit appears "between the foot-stalk and the nut," and "not as Madam Merian has unluckily placed hers, placing the fruit at the end, and the nut joining to the stalk instead of the fruit."

He had one substantive quibble with her work, however. When reviewing another work on insects for the Royal Society, Catesby quoted the author's opinion of Merian: "Madam Merian's pictures are fine, but want descriptions."

◆

A decade before Merian went to Surinam, Hans Sloane himself had traveled to the New World. Between 1687 and 1689, before attaining his status in London as eminent physician, collector, and president of the Royal Society, he spent fifteen months as physician to the governor of Jamaica. The resulting book, *A Voyage to the Islands Madera, Barbados, Nieves, S. Christophers and Jamaica with the Natural History of the Herbs, and Trees, Four-footed Beasts, Fishes, Birds, Insects, Reptiles &c. of the Last of Those Islands* (commonly called *The Natural History of Jamaica*) was published in two volumes in 1707 and 1725. Catesby of course had access to Sloane's book; in fact, it was the most commonly cited source in Catesby's *Natural History* and was an impetus for Catesby to visit the island in 1714, during his first trip to America.

The first volume of *The Natural History of Jamaica* was concerned mainly with plants such as grasses and bushes, with some corals and other sea creatures such as the copy of John White's Portuguese man-o-war. Volume two contains more plants as well as trees, seashells, caterpillars, spiders, and butterflies. Fish, birds, and lizards round out the Sloane illustrations. Together the two volumes contain 285 engraved plates, all of them uncolored engravings and all single specimens (or groups of the same type of specimen) composed against a blank background.

Sloane's *Natural History* was an expensive, luxury publication fit for its author's position in British society, "the Royal Society secretary's indispensable guide to what was fast becoming the British Empire's indispensable colony." It is easy to see how Sloane's work would have influenced the style and packaging of Mark Catesby's own lavishly illustrated natural history guide.

◆

Another forerunner of Mark Catesby covered some of the same actual ground, not long before Catesby himself. In fact, had tragedy not intervened, it might have been John Lawson, not Mark Catesby, whose book on the natural history of the Carolinas became famous.

Lawson, a surveyor by training, decided to travel to America in 1700 after meeting "a Gentleman, who had been abroad" and who "assur'd me, that Carolina was the best Country I could go to." He arrived in Charleston (his impressions of which were noted in chapter 7), then departed on December 28, 1700, by boat up the Santee River to begin a two-month, 550-mile clockwise arc of a journey into Carolina as far inland as the Piedmont, then back to what is now the North Carolina coast.

Lawson had been chosen by the Lords Proprietors of the Carolina Colony to make a reconnaissance survey of the interior of their holdings. He took extensive notes on the natural history of the region, and was especially attentive to the customs of the Native Americans he encountered, much of which would be "borrowed" by Mark Catesby for his *Natural History*. Settling in the town which would become New Bern, North Carolina,

Lawson worked as a surveyor while also immediately beginning a correspondence with James Petiver. Nearly three hundred of the plant samples he sent back to Petiver in England survive today in the Sloane Herbarium of the Natural History Museum in London, many with tags in Lawson's handwriting giving the date, location, and notes on habitat.

In 1709 Lawson returned to London to finalize the publication of his book. *A New Voyage to Carolina* was published in 1711, the year before Mark Catesby first sailed for North America; the book's success launched a wave of new immigration to the Carolinas.

Lawson returned in 1710 to North Carolina, where he became involved in efforts to settle hundreds of German refugees in New Bern. He also worked to resolve the longstanding boundary dispute between North Carolina and Virginia in his role as Surveyor-General, which brought him into contact with Richard Byrd II. Yet another role of Lawson's saw him help in suppressing the Cary Rebellion, an uprising aimed at overthrowing the government of Edward Hyde, first governor of the separate colony of North Carolina.

In September 1711, Lawson and his traveling companion Christoph von Graffenried, 1st Baron of Bernberg, were captured by the Tuscarora while on an expedition up the Neuse River. Von Graffenried claimed protection from the Great White Queen and was spared, but Lawson was tortured and killed. Had Lawson lived, he may have scooped Catesby, as Lawson fully intended to write a fuller version of his *New Voyage*. He had written Petiver that he hoped the specimens he sent to him "& such Ingenious Gentlemen of the Royal Society" would be "a foundation toward a Compleat History of these parts, wch. I heartily wish I may live to tell you." As it was, his book greatly influenced and was quoted at length in Catesby's *Natural History*, especially its accounts of indigenous culture in Carolina.

In London, the bookseller James Knapton, who had published Dampier's *New Voyage*, printed Lawson's *New Voyage* in serial form, which Catesby would also choose to do with his *Natural History*. A modern scholar has written that Lawson's "accounts of customs, society, and vocabularies are among the best records of Native American culture from the early eighteenth century."

Catesby owned a 1714 edition of Lawson's *New Voyage*, which had been renamed *The History of Carolina*; it contained marginalia in Catesby's hand when it was bequeathed to Peter Collinson after Catesby's death. In his book, Catesby gave Lawson what was probably high praise: Lawson was, wrote Catesby, an "inquisitive *Traveler*."

❖

John White's depictions of Native Americans, the first ever seen in England, became the standard images of the seventeenth century, but his watercolors of flora and fauna remained unpublished for centuries. However, White's natural-history work served as models for two of Catesby's plates in the *Natural History*.

The life and works of William Dampier inspired not only Catesby, but also Daniel Defoe, Jonathan Swift, and the members of the Royal Society. His remarkably detailed accounts of the plants, animals, and indigenous inhabitants of the places he visited during his three circumnavigations of the globe served as examples for Catesby to follow, and Dampier's technical writings on such topics as turtle migration are echoed in Catesby's own musings on the lives of the creatures he portrayed.

The friar Charles Plumier set a standard for artwork, scientific analysis, and classification of genus and species during his forays to the Antilles in the Caribbean. Catesby's writings and illustrations of North American plants benefited from Plumier's example, as the monk's genus and species names bolstered the scientific worth of Catesby's work.

Maria Sibylla Merian's astounding images, brilliant as they were, focused almost exclusively on insects in an isolated part of South America. Catesby, by contrast, collected on a much larger scale, both in terms of kinds of specimens—bird, insect, plant, mammal, and fish—and over a broader range of territory. And because his book dealt with North America, where the British in the early 1700s had a clear and compelling interest, Catesby was bound to receive more attention. Nevertheless, Merian inspired Catesby to combine plants and animals on the page in striking and sometimes unorthodox ways.

Lawson's and Sloane's books, on the other hand, though wide-ranging in their way, lacked something that Catesby's *Natural History* offered: a raft of beautiful, colored etchings. Though Sloane's had a number of engraved illustrations, they lacked context and evidence of ecological awareness. The first edition of Lawson's book had few illustrations, but it would provide much of the information on Native Americans that found its way into Catesby's own work. And, in Sloane, Catesby had not only a benefactor, but a naturalist and writer who had shown how books on natural history could be expensive, sought-after items in the London of the day.

Catesby, back in London from America, would consult all these sources while writing his *Natural History*. Now the forty-three-year-old Catesby could bring the information and inspiration of these forerunners together with the fruits of his own exploration, research, and collection. He was ready to create his own masterwork.

Mark Catesby was born in this house in Castle Hedingham, Essex, on March 24, 1683. His mother Elizabeth chose to have him in her family home, where her uncle Nicholas Jekyll would have a botanical garden and extensive natural-history library.

One of England's most renowned clergyman-naturalists, John Ray, lived near and was close friends with Catesby's uncle, Nicholas Jekyll, who kept a botanical garden at his estate in Castle Hedingham, Essex. Ray has been called "the father of natural history in Britain."

ABOVE: An outdoorsy young member of the landed gentry, such as Mark Catesby of Sudbury and Castle Hedingham circa 1710, may well have dressed in the manner of Robert Andrews, subject of this 1750 portrait by Thomas Gainsborough. Painter and subject, as it turns out, were also from Sudbury. BELOW: Coffee houses were the social, commercial, and intellectual centers of London in the late 17th and early 18th centuries. Each profession or interest had its own chosen establishment; botanists gathered at the Temple Coffee House near Fleet Street "to pore over plant specimens and discuss the latest botanical discoveries."

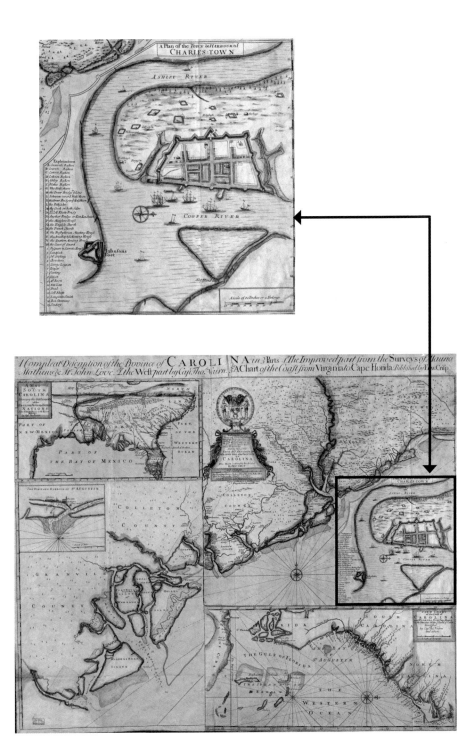

Detail from Crisp Map of 1711 showing Charleston Harbor. In May 1722, Catesby landed here; for the next three years this fledgling city in the colony of South Carolina would be his base of operations for exploring the Lowcountry and the western frontier.

Catesby's time in America coincided with the Golden Age of Piracy. Edward Teach, aka Blackbeard, blockaded Charleston Harbor four years before Catesby's arrival. Upon learning that a ship carrying his specimens to England had been attacked, Catesby wrote, "I dread the mischief the Pirates have done to the things I sent."

Un Anglais de la Barbade, vend sa Maitresse

British planters imported the slave system of production to South Carolina from the West Indies. By the time of Catesby's arrival, enslaved Africans outnumbered whites two to one in the colony. Catesby himself likely purchased a "Negro Boy" to help him with collecting his plant and animal specimens. He also visited enslaved people's personal gardens, and respected their knowledge of medicinal plants, citing their observations in *Natural History*.

"To the Hospitality and Assistance of these Friendly Indians, I am much indebted," Catesby wrote. He valued the knowledge of the Native Americans he hunted, camped, and collected with. In his *Natural History* Catesby included extensive descriptions of the manners and customs of the indigenous peoples he encountered during his travels.

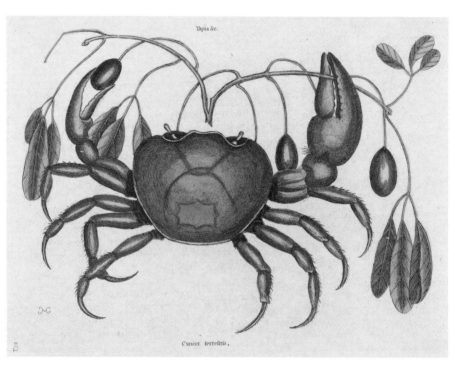

Tapia &c.

Cancer terreftris.

In 1725, Catesby sailed to the Bahamas, the first naturalist to visit the islands. He focused mainly on marine life, but also observed the annual migration of purple land crabs (*Gecarcinus ruricola*) in "vast Numbers" to lay their eggs near the sea: "They have been known to enter in at a Window, and on a Bed, where People who had never before had seen any, were not a little surprised."

Sir Hans Sloane, Catesby's sponsor and one of the towering collectors and patrons of the age. His holdings would become the foundation of the British Museum. Catesby visited his Chelsea mansion to examine works by Maria Sibylla Merian, John Smith, and Georg Dionysius Ehret, among other prominent artists.

Peter Collinson, a Quaker merchant and botanist in London, was important to the world of natural history and to Mark Catesby's career. Collinson had more than a hundred correspondents in America and Europe, and used his trade connections to accumulate exotic specimens for his gardens, especially American varieties.

THE ROYAL SOCIETY'S HOUSE IN CRANE COURT (*see page* 104).

The Royal Society of London for Improving Natural Knowledge was founded in 1663. Sir Isaac Newton became president of the Society in 1703; in 1710 it moved into its first permanent headquarters on Crane Court, Fleet Street, where a lamp would be hung over the entrance to the court on meeting nights. The Royal Society would be Mark Catesby's intellectual home base after his return to London from the New World.

Catesby dedicated the completed Volume I of *Natural History* to Queen Caroline of Ansbach, wife of King George II. Caroline surrounded herself with artists, architects, and intellectuals; as a modern historian put it, "The women of the Hanoverian court were as intellectual as the men were crude. While the dukes collected mistresses and plotted murder, their duchesses occupied themselves with philosophy."

William Dampier's writings inspired not only Catesby, but also Daniel Defoe, Jonathan Swift, and the members of the Royal Society. The former pirate's three circumnavigations of the globe produced remarkably detailed accounts of the plants, animals, and indigenous inhabitants of the places he visited. The publication in 1697 of his *A New Voyage Round the World* caused a literary sensation.

The brilliant and trailblazing Maria Sibylla Merian sailed to Surinam in 1699 with her young daughter, Dorothea, unaccompanied by any man. Her illustrations, riotous with color and teeming with energy and movement, gave Catesby an example of natural-history art which portrayed the interactions between insects and plants.

ABOVE: Catesby's *Natural History*, described in the Royal Society's *Journal Book* as a "Curious and Magnificent Work," was a sensation among scientists, botanists, and nurserymen in London. Issued in eleven sections between 1731 and 1746, the *Natural History* cost twenty guineas—a little more than a year's wages for a "general labourer" in England or Wales at that time. *Natural History* was a stunning and lavish luxury item of a book, which set out to be innovative as well as informative. BELOW: On the evening of March 5, 1746, Catesby presented a paper to the Royal Society in which he described the night migrations of "the rice-bird" (bobolink, *Dolichonyx oryzivorus*). His remarks made him one of the earliest proponents for the idea that birds migrated rather than hibernating.

Phoenicopterus.   *Keratophiton &c.*

One of Catesby's most notable illustrations combined land and sea creatures in an innovative fashion. Catesby yanked from the ocean a tall, treelike gorgonian called the double-forked plexaurella (*Plexaurella dichotoma*) and placed it on dry land behind his American flamingo (*Phoenicopterus ruber*). The resulting composition looks strikingly modern.

Catesby introduced the southern magnolia (*Magnolia Grandiflora*) to Britain upon his return from the New World in 1726. "This stately tree," he wrote, "perfumes the Woods, and displays its Beauties from May till November."

ABOVE: The iconic American bullfrog, later named for Catesby: *Lithobates catesbeianus*. "The Noise they make has caused their Name," he wrote, "for at a few Yards Distance their Bellowing sounds very much like that of a Bull a quarter of a Mile off."

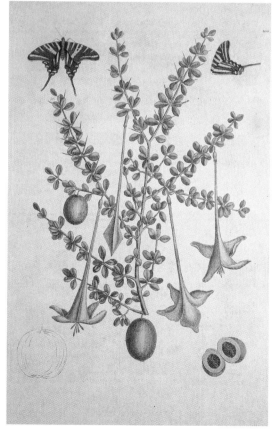

RIGHT: Catesby brought back seeds of the lily thorn from the Bahamas in 1726; the plant was later named *Catesbaea spinosa* in his honor by the Dutch botanist J. F. Gronovius. He had found the tree "near the Town of Nassaw," its flowers "in Form of a Roman Trumpet."

Two of the birds first painted by Catesby are now extinct, with another on the edge of oblivion. The last Carolina parakeet (*Conuropsis carolinensis*), "a creature of brilliant green, yellow, and orange coloration," died in captivity in 1918. Four years before, the sole living passenger pigeon (*Ectopistes migratorius*), flocks of which once darkened North American skies, had met the same fate. The fate of the ivory-billed woodpecker (*Campephilus principalis*) continues to cause controversy to the present day. No one has made a verified sighting of an ivory-billed woodpecker in North America since the 1940s, and the U.S. Fish & Wildlife Service in September 2021 declared the bird extinct. However, in April 2022, scientists proclaimed that the ivory-billed woodpecker was in fact alive in the remote swamps of Louisiana.

12

LONDON AND THE *NATURAL HISTORY* 1726–1731

Mark Catesby faced several challenges when he returned to England in 1726. Now nearing his mid-forties, Catesby had spent the previous four years and twelve of the last fourteen exploring and documenting what he found in North America and the Caribbean, from the Blue Ridge of western Virginia to Barbados in the Caribbean. Working in the field as a naturalist, he had undertaken the arduous task of collecting, observing, and sketching the plants and animals he found. Those years had been somewhat uncomplicated ones, if extremely demanding of his time and energy. Now, however, Catesby needed to plot his future course in light of his changed circumstances.

Foremost for him would be the technical difficulties involved in transforming his extensive fieldwork on flora and fauna into a book of the sort he envisioned. He had sketched and painted hundreds of birds, plants, fish, and insects while in the New

World and had made extensive notes on their distinctive features, behavior, and habitat; now he had to turn his notes and sketches into a book, transforming his watercolors into reproducible images. But who would do the necessary engravings of his illustrations, and turn his notes into columns of printed copy on numbered pages?

Then, Catesby would need to secure funding for the printing of the groundbreaking book which he envisioned. Before the advent of the modern publishing house, upfront costs for putting a book into the world were often sizable. Those costs were certain to be so for Catesby, who was determined to bring to fruition a large-scale, fully illustrated work. But that meant expensive paper and ink and copper plates for the illustrations, not to mention paying the craftsmen who would do what Catesby could not: the typesetters, printers, engravers, and colorists.

Beyond all that lay a much more basic question: where and how would he live? He seems never to have contemplated residing anywhere other than London, "the centre of all science," as he called it. But his financial and social circumstances could hardly have been more different than those of the young naturalist who had left for Virginia in 1712. The comfortable living that had been bequeathed him by his father was apparently gone, spent in Virginia, Carolina, and the Caribbean. There were no Catesby family properties in central London, no Suffolk estates. His only surviving brother, John, fourteen years Mark's junior, was an army officer with the 10th Regiment of Foot. A gentleman Mark Catesby might still tenuously be considered; landed, however, he almost certainly was not.

Catesby at first hoped to have the illustrations for his book engraved on the Continent, after the fashion of other prominent botanical and zoological works of the day. He would have known plenty of examples of European artistry, including the French engravings of the monk-naturalist Charles Plumier's illustrations and the Dutch work produced for Maria Sibylla Merian's *Metamorphosis*. As he described in the *Natural History*, however, the advice of his patrons made him change his plans: those "Gentlemen, most skill'd in the Learning of Nature . . . were pleased to think [my work] worth Publishing, but [thought] that the Expence of Graving would make it too burthensome an Undertaking." So, Catesby wrote, "I alter'd my Design of going to Paris or Amsterdam."

Apparently undaunted, Catesby decided to learn the art of etching and to produce the necessary illustrations himself. For his tutor he seems to have reached out to his patrons in the scientific and artistic worlds, for his teacher, Joseph Goupy, was well-connected indeed.

Goupy was born in London of French parents. After traveling and studying in Italy he settled in London around 1711; for a time he lived on Bond Street, around the corner from his friend the composer George Frederick Handel, with whom he would later have a very public falling-out. At a time when creating and owning well-rendered duplicates of famous artworks was accepted in fashionable circles, Goupy was popular among what was called "the Quality" for the copies he painted of works by Raphael and other masters and was patronized at the highest level of art and society. Goupy's patrons included the Duke of Chandos and Lord Oxford, both of whom were "Encouragers" of Catesby's trip to South Carolina, as well as the Dukes of Devonshire and Rutland. He painted sets for Handel's operas for the Royal Academy of Music, and "small pictures on Snuff Boxes" for George I. But Goupy was not only a prominent copyist and theater painter. He was also a famous printmaker; a modern art historian described Goupy's etchings as "beautiful in their own right" with "a remarkably sophisticated touch, the best of any etcher in London at a time when etching was uncommon."

Etching, in the intaglio method used by Catesby (from the Italian *intagliere*, "to cut or engrave," from which we get the English word "tailor"), involves incising lines on copper sheets with an etching needle. Ink is worked into the etched lines, and then paper is pressed against the copper plate. "At length," Catesby wrote, "by the kind Advice and Instructions of that inimitable Painter Mr. Joseph Goupy, I undertook and was initiated in the way of Etching them myself."

Catesby's decision to learn the art of etching gave him more than an affordable way to bring his book to life. He also achieved artistic independence and flexibility, allowing him to experiment and add to his illustrations until late in the process. He borrowed small elements from books he owned, such as an edition of *Aesop's Fables*, adding small animals to the plates. Other artists' depictions of plants and animals also found their way into the *Natural History*: a Dutch artist's drawing of a flying squirrel is copied exactly in Catesby's illustration, nibbling on a persimmon.

Catesby may have learned etching to illustrate the *Natural History* himself, but funding the book would not admit of a similar solution. Instead, he tackled his funding problem in two ways, reaching out to his extensive connections among the influential merchants, scientists, and aristocrats who had sent him to the frontier and the West Indies. As the volumes of the *Natural History* gradually saw the light of day, Catesby would be forthright in using these connections—including those among the British royal family.

A Londoner attending a meeting of the Royal Society or of the recently formed Society of Gardeners in 1728 or 1729 might have been handed a printed broadsheet with the title *Proposals, for printing an essay towards a natural history of Florida, Carolina and the Bahama Islands.* The prospectus described a planned book which would include "the FIGURES of Birds, Beasts, Fishes, Serpents, Insects, and Plants; particularly, the Forest-Trees, Shrubs, and other Plants, not hitherto described, remarkable for their Rarity, Virtues, &c . . . By MARK CATESBY." The author, the document stated, "went to Carolina in the year 1722, where, after having described the Productions of the low and flat Parts of the Country, he went from thence several hundred Miles within Land, performing the same amongst the Mountainous Parts." Then, after three years in Carolina "and various Parts of Florida," the author "went to the Bahama Islands; amongst which he made as much Search into the like natural Productions, as nine months would admit of."

Below this were listed Catesby's patrons for the Carolina voyage of exploration, with the Duke of "Chandois" first and including Hans Sloane, Governor Nicholson of South Carolina, and William Sherard. The prospectus promised that "as Figures convey the strongest ideas . . . we shall take care to exhbit every thing drawn by the Life, as well as described in the most particular manner." Catesby's plan was straightforward if ambitious: "to publish every Four Months Twenty Plates, with their Descriptions," on the same paper as the *Proposals* but not colored, for one guinea; and, "for the satisfaction of the Curious," copies printed "on the finest Imperial Paper, and the Figures put in their Natural Colours from the Original Paintings," for two guineas.

Notably, the proposal assured "Encouragers of this Work" that "no Money [is] desired to be paid 'till each Sett is deliver'd," so that there would be "no Ground to suspect any Fraud, as happens too often in the common way of Subscription." The prospectus would go through at least three printings as Catesby continually hustled for subscribers even as he set to work on the book itself.

The shrewd decision to solicit subscriptions not only gave Catesby cash flow for printing the volumes of the book; it also allowed interest to grow as subsequent sections were published. By the time the final section was released, the list of subscribers to the *Natural History* had grown from the twelve original patrons to 155 men and women who would underwrite the entire project. Seven of the patrons of his American explorations became subscribers, including Hans Sloane, Francis Nicholson, and the Earl of Oxford ("2 books"). So did William

Byrd, Samuel Dale, the "Envoy extraordinary from her Imperial Majesty of Russia," the queen of Sweden, and Woods Rogers of the Bahamas.

Counting the purchasers of multiple copies, he seems to have sold as many as 180 copies, all told. But the subscription model certainly had its drawbacks: a third of those 155 subscribers would be dead before the work was completed. This was, in a modern historian's words, "an example of subscription publishing in which the author took a major risk." Fortunately, the book's format and what quickly became obvious as its growing cachet helped Catesby's cause. His subscribers not only acquired a rare, expensive, and beautiful book for their libraries; they also acquired some of the book's luster by association. They positioned themselves as men and women of taste, learning, and "curiosity" by becoming patrons of the *Natural History*.

Subscriptions would not fully cover the startup costs of producing the *Natural History*, however. For that, Catesby would rely on the generosity of two of his most ardent supporters.

In his copy of the *Natural History*, Peter Collinson wrote notes which comprise some of the most in-depth background information we have about Catesby. According to Collinson, Catesby was "at great loss how to introduce this valuable work to the world," until Collinson lent him "a considerable amount of money without interest." Catesby was thus able to publish his book "for the benefit of himself and family"; otherwise, it would have "fallen prey to the book sellers" who were likely to have different ideas about what Catesby's book should be.

Collinson was not the only benefactor who came to Catesby's aid as he struggled to launch the production of his great work.

Dr. Richard Mead was a Fellow of the Royal Society who in 1727 became physician to George II. Mead's collection of books and manuscripts was second only to Hans Sloane's; he was a highly respected medical professional of whom Samuel Johnson said, "he lived more in the broad sunshine of life than most any man." In the *Natural History* Catesby would give the name *Primula meadia* to the shooting star, a flowering member of the primrose family: "To this new Genus of Plants I have given the name of the learned Dr. Richard Mead . . . in gratitude for his zealous patronage of Arts and Sciences in general, and in particular for his generous assistance towards carrying the original design of this work into execution."

Between the subscriptions raised and the support of Collinson and Mead, Catesby was able to release the first volume of the *Natural History* in late May 1729, but the thrice-yearly schedule promised in his proposal would prove wildly optimistic. Succeeding volumes would be presented to the Royal Society in January and November 1730, November 1731, and November 1732 to complete the first volume. Catesby's reputation, and the *Natural History*'s place in scientific history, would rest upon the Society's reception.

◆

For some time now, while in England and on his overseas explorations, Catesby had cultivated another kind of connection. Even before he left for Williamsburg, he had fostered relationships in the horticultural world of England among the nurserymen and gardeners who would help him in his plan to promote the planting and growing of American plants in British gardens. From them he would find his physical place in the London he had returned to after so long away.

Thomas Fairchild, author of *The City Gardener* and receiver of seeds and plants from Catesby since at least 1715, had a famously productive half-acre nursery in the village of Hoxton. This rural enclave, eventually to be subsumed into greater London, lay just north of the City, near enough for Fairchild to supply his customers. Catesby apparently lived and worked in Hoxton, perhaps even on Fairchild's property, where he seems to have had his own garden plot; Catesby's *Proposals* for the *Natural History* stated that his original watercolors could be viewed "at Mr. Fairchild's, in Hoxton." One indication of Catesby's closeness to the nurseryman is his serving as a witness to Fairchild's will, in which Fairchild left him a bequest of "one guinea for a Ring." At Fairchild's Catesby might supplement his income by working in horticulture while working on his book, and gather additional information on the plants he meant to include in the *Natural History.*

Fairchild, who was around sixty when Catesby returned to London, died in 1729. Catesby apparently was able to continue the same arrangement at the nursery with Stephen Bacon, Fairchild's nephew and heir; the 1731 title page to Volume I of the *Natural History* informed readers that the books were available for sale "by the Author, at Mr. Bacon's in Hoxton."

When he first returned to London Catesby seemingly ignored everything but his work on the *Natural History*, including his family. His sister Anne's husband, George Rutherford, informed Catesby's niece Elizabeth Jones in 1728 that "your uncle Mr.

Mark Catesby is now in London but I can't tell you where he lodges." But it was ostensibly from Fairchild's that in a letter headed "Hoxton 1st March 1729/30" Catesby wrote his niece Elizabeth Jones in Virginia, asking for "Cones, Acorns & Seeds of all kinds." He was sending her an uncolored copy of the *Natural History*; "I can at present but ill spare those painted," Catesby told her, "the demand for them being quicker than I can supply."

It is not known exactly how long Catesby lived in Hoxton; sometime in the mid-1730s circumstances would force him to move to another nursery, in another part of London. The man who had traveled thousands of miles to explore the plants and animals of a new and strange continent would remain mostly within a ten-mile radius of the City of London for the remainder of his life.

◆

Settled in Hoxton, funded by Collinson and Mead, trained by Goupy, Catesby could now get to work. He began adapting the hundreds of watercolor sketches he had made in America with a keen eye to composition. Inspired by Maria Sibylla Merian, he arranged bold combinations of plants and animals which often told a story of interdependence: birds with the grains they fed on, or a tree which Catesby had found standing near where bison left their droppings. Sometimes, however, the naturalist gave way to the artist; there are plates in which there is no connection between the elements except aesthetic or design considerations, such as the flamingo posed before the outstretched fan of the gorgonian.

He had clear intentions behind his methods of etching and coloring. "As I was not bred a Painter I hope some faults in Perspective, and other Niceties, may be more readily excused," he wrote. But then he defended his style: "for I humbly conceive Plants, and other Things done in a Flat, tho' exact manner, may serve the Purpose of Natural History, better in some Measure than in a more bold and Painter like way." As for his etching style, once again he combined apology with defense: though he didn't etch his plates "in a Graver-like manner, choosing rather to omit their method of cross-Hatching," he had decided on a harder and better path: "to follow the humour of the Feathers, which is more laborious, and I hope has proved more to the purpose." That laborious work served his belief in the primacy of visual over verbal representation: "I have been less prolix in the Description, judging it unnecessary to tire the Reader with describing every Feather, yet I hope sufficient to distinguish them without Confusion." He knew what he was doing, and why.

Clearly the most important aspect of the book would be its validity as a work of natural history. Catesby noted about "the Paints, particularly Greens, used in the Illumination of Figures, I had principally a regard to the most resembling Nature, that were durable and would retain their Lustre, rejecting others very specious and shining, but of an unnatural Colour and fading Quality." He anticipated possible criticisms of the colors he choose: "Yet give me leave to observe that there is no Degree of Green but what some Plants are possess'd of at different Times of the Year, and the same Plant changes it's Colour gradually with it's Age." For example, "in the Spring the Woods and all Plants in General are more Yellow and bright, and as the Summer advances the Greens grow deeper, and the nearer their Fall are yet of a more dark and dirty Colour." If a reader found a discrepancy when comparing Catesby's illustrations with living plants, "the difference of Colour . . . may proceed from the above-mentioned Cause."

Catesby's passion for accuracy drove another choice regarding the production of the *Natural History*. "The whole was done within my house, and by my own hands," he wrote; "for as my honour and credit were alone concerned, I was resolved not to hazard them by committing any part of the Work to another person." Besides, Catesby wrote, "should any of my original Paintings have been lost, they would have been irretrievable to me, without making another voyage to America."

This is an interesting claim for Catesby to make. As Henrietta McBurney has pointed out, it would have been physically impossible for Catesby to have colored even the 1,200 plates for the first batch of copies of Part 1 before May 1729 while working on the plates for Part 2. In addition, there are also enough variations in the illustrations, both in appearance and method, to make it certain that Catesby had help with the *Natural History*. It is possible that the colorists worked for Catesby in his house, each painted page overseen and touched up by him, thereby satisfying at least in part the claim of "within my house, and by my own hands."

The *Natural History* was printed with two columns per page, with the French translation on the right. "As to the French Translation," Catesby wrote, "I am oblig'd to a very ingenious Gentleman, a Doctor of Physick, and a French-man born, whose

Modesty will not permit me to mention his Name." Some have speculated that the French-born gentleman was in fact Catesby himself.

◆

Part 1 of the *Natural History* began with a plate for the "Bald Eagle," described as "so formidable to all birds, yet suffers them to breed near his royal nest without molestation." The bird was shown snatching from the air a grey mullet (*Mugil cephalus*) as an osprey in the background looked on, probably having been spooked by the eagle into dropping the fish. (Notably, Catesby was one of the first to show birds in flight, depicting details of the birds' physiognomy not typically shown with more static poses and imparting energy to the composition.) Nineteen plates and descriptions followed, containing twenty-one birds and fourteen plants. The seven plates following the eagle featured static birds on white backgrounds, sometimes perched on a generic plant stem. Then, with Plate 9, things changed. The "Cuckow of Carolina" (yellow-billed cuckoo, *Coccyzus americanus*) is shown on a branch of the Allegheny chinquapin (*Castanea pumila*) in a much more lively composition. In all but one of the remaining plates in Part 1, Catesby combined birds and plants in his illustrations.

By coincidence Catesby described in Book 1 and the third plate of Book 2 three birds which have become historic for the most somber of reasons. As the first to describe and illustrate much of North America's wildlife, Mark Catesby unknowingly contributed tragic bookends to the stories of a handful of his subjects. Some of his firsts have in the intervening centuries been paired with lasts. The stories of two birds which Catesby unveiled to the readers of the *Natural History* have been concluded; neither will be seen in the wild again. And one has become so incredibly rare that even now, scientists debate its continuing existence.

There was once a native parrot in North America, though only centenarians living today could possibly have seen it. The Carolina Parakeet (*Conuropsis carolinensis*) "was once among the most familiar and lively birds of North America. It was a creature of brilliant green, yellow, and orange coloration, and it moved about in large, noisy flocks, giving the natural landscape a flamboyant touch." In Plate 11 of Book 1 Catesby described how "The Parrot of Carolina" would "feed on seeds and kernels of fruit; particularly those of cypress and apples," and "numerous flights of them" visited orchards in autumn, "where they make great destruction." Oddly, Catesby claimed that "their guts are certain and speedy poison to cats." This may have been because the parrots feasted on cockleburs, a highly toxic plant which can kill animals who ingest it—though not, for some reason of evolution or adaptation, the Carolina parakeet.

One reason for their disappearance can be guessed at by reading John James Audubon's description a century later of how Carolina Parakeets "are destroyed in great numbers, for whilst busily engaged in plucking off the fruits or tearing the grain from the stacks, the husbandman approaches them with perfect ease, and commits great slaughter among them. All the survivors rise, shriek, fly round about for a few minutes, and again alight on the very place of most imminent danger . . . I have seen several hundreds destroyed in this manner in a couple of hours." Today, scientists are also considering causes such as habitat loss and disease as causes for the bird's decline.

Whatever the reasons, what is certain is that on February 21, 1918, the last Carolina Parakeet, Incas, died in captivity in Cincinnati, in the same cage where the first bird to be the last of her kind, Martha the passenger pigeon, had breathed her last not four years before.

◆

Catesby was also the first European to describe and portray "the most abundant bird on the continent, if not the planet," in the words of a modern writer, which "may well have comprised 25 to 40 percent of American bird life." Catesby's "Pigeon of Passage" (passenger pigeon, *Ectopistes migratorius*) was "about the size of our English wood-pigeon," with a patch of feathers on the wing "that shines like gold." Like many who wrote about the passenger pigeon, Catesby described their "incredible numbers," recalling that "in Virginia I have seen them fly in such continued trains three days successively, that there was not the least interval in losing sight of them." A century later, they were numerous enough for James Fenimore Cooper's Natty Bumppo to deride the people killing them indiscriminately in *The Pioneers:* "'This comes of settling a country!' he said—'here have I known the pigeon to fly for forty long years, and, till you made your clearings, there was nobody to skear or to hurt them . . . Well! the Lord won't see the waste of his creaters for nothing, and right will be done to the pigeons, as well as others, by-and-by.'"

Less than a century after the publication of *The Pioneers*, the last passenger pigeon shot in the wild is believed to have been brought down by a hunter in Laurel, Indiana, on April 3, 1902. The unrelenting slaughter had continued past the point of the bird's recovery as a species. Martha, the last passenger pigeon in captivity, died on September 1, 1914, her "drooping wings atremble with the palsy of extreme old age." Martha's body was sent to the Smithsonian Institution to be stuffed and mounted.

◆

"The Largest White-bill Wood-pecker" was Catesby's name for the ivory-billed woodpecker (*Campephilus principalis*), the immense ghostly avatar of North American birds, which he chose for Plate 16 of Book 1. Those familiar with the pileated woodpecker and its vivid black, white, and scarlet plumage have some idea of the presence of the ivory-billed, though in the words of ornithologist Jerome Jackson, it made—makes?—the pileated look "puny." But, Jackson adds, "Seeing an ivory-bill is about more than size. The ivory-billed woodpecker is also a spectacularly patterned bird. It is the equivalent of a tuxedoed aristocrat."

Ivory-bills preferred heavily wooded lowlands and marshland such as the Santee River Swamp, and once were common in South Carolina and elsewhere across the Southeast. In his *American Ornithology* (1811), Alexander Wilson described how the ivory-billed woodpecker "seeks the most towering trees of the forest; seeming particularly attached to those prodigious cypress swamps, whose crowded giant sons stretch their bare and blasted, or moss-hung, arms midway to the skies. In these almost inaccessible recesses, amid ruinous piles of impending timber, his trumpet-like note, and loud strokes, resound through the solitary, savage wilds, of which he seems the sole lord and inhabitant."

"The bills of these birds are much valued by the Canada Indians," Catesby wrote in the *Natural History*, "who make coronets of them for their princes and great warriors." Because the ivory-billed's range did not extend to "their cold country," the natives "purchase them of the southern people at the price of two, and sometimes three buck-skins a bill." In Illinois, Nebraska, and Texas, archaeologists have found ivory-billed woodpecker remains in Native American sites dating back to the fifteenth or sixteenth century. To at least some of the Indigenous people of North America the bird was a powerful symbol, with spiritual dimensions to its display.

No one has made a verified sighting of an ivory-billed woodpecker in North America since the 1940s, and the last official sighting anywhere happened in Cuba in 1987. The U.S. Fish & Wildlife Service in September 2021 declared the bird extinct.

However, in April 2022, scientists proclaimed that the ivory-billed woodpecker was in fact alive in the remote swamps of Louisiana, furnishing grainy photographs and other evidence in a scientific article. "They don't want people close to them because they've been shot at for 150 years," said one biologist. "They have better eyes than we do, they are high in the trees and actively flee people. They aren't great thinkers but they have developed a pretty simple strategy to avoid people." Regardless of this hopeful news, the ivory-billed woodpecker lives today mostly in videos and books, following in the tradition of its first description and illustration in English, in Catesby's *Natural History*.

◆

In the preface to the *Natural History* Catesby would explain his system of naming the plants and animals he studied in America. "Very few of the Birds having Names assign'd them in the Country, except some which had Indian Names; I have call'd them after European Birds of the same Genus, with an additional Epithet to distinguish them," he wrote. Since "the Males of the Feather'd Kind (except a very few) are more elegantly colour'd than the Females, I have throughout exhibited the Cocks only, except two or three," with "a short Description of the Hens, wherein they differ in color from the Cocks." The lack of such descriptions, Catesby added pointedly, "has caused great Confusion in works of this Nature."

"As to the Plants," Catesby wrote, "I have given them the English and Indian Names they are known by in these Countries." For the Latin names Catesby relied on "the above-mention'd Learned and accurate Botanist Dr. Sherard." Like his predecessors in America John White and John Lawson, Catesby made use of his sources among the Native American and colonial communities he had visited while exploring the country. Shrewdly, Catesby also described certain American plants as thriving, or at least living, in English gardens and commercial nurseries. In this way he could name-check his patrons, subscribers, and colleagues such as William Sherard,

Peter Collinson, Christopher Gray, and Thomas Fairchild's Hoxton nursery.

In Parts 2 through 5 Catesby balanced the number of birds and plants fairly evenly, posing his "blew Gross-beak" (blue grosbeak, *Passerina caerulea*) stretching up for a seed of a sweetbay magnolia (*Magnolia virginiana*) or what he called the "blew Linnet" (indigo bunting, *Passerina cyanea*) on a leaf of the wildflower which would be named for him: *Trillium catesbaei*, the bashful wakerobin. Part 5 concluded Volume I, which was finished by November 1732 and sent to subscribers with a title page and dedication page. Catesby wrote his niece Elizabeth Jones in December 1731, "I have sent you a continuation of my Nt. Hit . . . the second, third, and fourth parts are all I have published."

Beginning Volume II with Part 6 he turned to the marine life of the Bahamas, from Plate 1's barracuda and bonefish to Plate 20's green moray eel (*Gymnothorax funebris*). He continued in this vein in Part 7, adding a few plants to the twenty plates of fish and crustaceans. Parts 8 through 10 returned him to terrestrial plants, lizards, frogs, snakes, and butterflies. These were some of his most famous illustrations: snakes sinuously curled around branches of shrubs; the dramatic trumpets of the lily thorn (*Catesbaea spinosa*, its genus named for Catesby) circled by zebra swallowtail butterflies (*Eurytides marcellus*); and the iconic American bullfrog, also named for Catesby, *Lithobates catesbeianus*.

His ten original sections and two hundred plates finished, Catesby turned to the additional material he had planned, including a preface, a map, and what he called "An Account of

Carolina and the Bahama Islands." Catesby had included a note to his subscribers at the end of Volume 1 alerting them that this material was coming: "There being a Frontice-Piece, Preface, and Maps of the Country's, to be added at the conclusion of the Work. It is desired, not to bind up any of the Sets, 'till the whole are finished." At least some of Catesby's subscribers ignored his wishes; many copies of the *Natural History* extant today have the additional material bound in the second volume.

After the preface, in which Catesby described his travels in the New World and the methods by which he collected and illustrated his subjects, he began "An Account" with a short history of Carolina ("Carolina was first discovered by Sir Sebastian Cabot, a Native of Bristol . . . about the year 1500"), then described its weather in "Of the Air of Carolina" ("thus happily situated in a Climate parallel to the best Parts of the Old World, [it] enjoys in some Measure the like Blessings. It is very little incommoded by Excess of either Heat or Cold").

Sections headed "Of the Soyl," "Of the Water," and "Of the Aborigines of America" followed. Of the Indigenous people of North America, Catesby wrote, "there has been various Conjectures how that Part of the Globe became inhabited." He mentioned the likelihood of the peopling of the continent "from the northern Parts of Asia," then, citing his "many Opportunities of seeing and observing the various Nations of Indians inhabiting the whole Extent of North America," Catesby rather breezily lumped all Native tribes together, only noting "some little Differences . . . in the Industry of one Nation" or "a small mechanick Knowledge" between them.

Next followed the section "Of the Indians of Carolina and Florida," in which Catesby quoted John Lawson at length, as discussed in chapter 8. He then turned to the agriculture of Carolina, with sections on corn, rice, wheat, barley, oats, "Bunched Guinea Corn," "Spiked Indian Corn," and kidney beans, before turning to "The common European Culinary Plants." Brief accounts of America's trees and berry bushes came next, after which Catesby described "The Manner of Making Tar and Pitch." The beasts and fish of the New World got their turn, followed by "Some Remarks on American Birds" ("The Birds of America generally excell those of Europe in the Beauty of their Plumage, but are much inferior to them in melodious Notes"). Insects rated a half-page before Catesby proceeded to his lengthy passage on the Bahamas, along with "the Sea, and its Productions." Finally, like an afterthought, Catesby added two "Addenda" including "the American Partridge" and three catchall paragraphs naming wild turkeys, pheasants, the "Whipper-will," and American domestic fowl such as "Pea-Fowls, Turkeys, Geese, and Ducks."

The text and plates for Part 10, the preface, and "An Account" were all finished by December 1743, when they were presented to the Royal Society. But Catesby wasn't done.

In what he called an "Advertisement" which he sent to his subscribers, Catesby noted that the 200 plates in Volumes I and II "are all that were at first designed." But as it turned out, he had "ample Materials for another Set of Twenty Plates," which he proposed to add as an appendix. The "Animals," "Insects," and "Vegetables" which he listed to be included were "such curious Subjects, that for the Reputation of the Work, I am loath to omit, and for no other Reason."

It took four years. Finally, in 1747, the Appendix was complete. "I confess it is now time to conclude this extensive and laborious Work," Catesby wrote. "The greatest deliberation and caution were necessary in the whole progress, since errors must have been apparent to the judicious Reader." The entire work contained 220 plates, illustrating 109 birds, thirty-three amphibians and reptiles, forty-six fishes, thirty-one insects, nine quadrupeds, and 171 plants. The engraved and colored plates and facing text were elephant folios, twenty-one by fourteen inches in size.

"Catesby's noble work," Peter Collinson wrote Linnaeus, "is finished."

◆

With the *Natural History of Carolina* Mark Catesby had created a landmark work, presaging by a century the ecological thinking of Alexander von Humboldt. His dynamic and lively compositions of the plants, mammals, fish, and insects of the New World were stunning works of art, and his studious and exacting notes on appearance, behavior, diet, and habitat furnished firsthand information which would be valued by his immediate successors in natural history and by naturalists and artists for centuries to come.

He had ventured to the edge of the nascent Empire, serving as nature's messenger to a British public which yearned to know more about the territories it was rapidly adding to its possessions. That public had thrilled to the stories of Dampier's voyages and the pirate tales of "Captain Charles Johnson," and tasted the exotic appeal of America's natural wonders in Hans Sloane's *Voyage to Jamaica* and Maria Sibylla Merian's *Metamorphosis*. Catesby would give them something different and more complete; his deliberate conjunctions of animals and plants marked a sharp departure from his predecessors. He examined the interplay of recently introduced species as well as native specimens; he established connections between species through diet and other factors in a large portion of his illustrations. And he gave the general public in Britain and America (if a relatively small and fairly wealthy slice of it) their first illustrations of many of the plants and animals in the British colonies. The wealthy merchant in the City of London, the landed aristocrat, and the Hoxton nurseryman now knew what a southern magnolia looked like, and a great blue heron, and a timber rattlesnake.

Many of Catesby's readers were well-read observers of events in North America and the Caribbean, involved in business ventures and commodities trading—and all too often, profiting from the trafficking of human beings from Africa. They knew that the landscapes of Barbados and Jamaica had seen wholesale destruction and reconstruction on an industrial line, as the production of sugar overwhelmed all other priorities on the islands. They were also aware that the rice economy was steadily transforming the topography and ecology of the Carolina Lowcountry. This knowledge among the well-informed back in England only increased their hunger for information about the native plants and animals living in the Caribbean and in the southeast of America. Catesby's *Natural History* supplied this information, in glorious and brilliant detail.

Catesby fully understood the value of providing the first color illustrations of American flora and fauna. "The Illuminating [of] Natural History," he wrote, "is so particularly essential to the perfect understanding of it, that I may aver a clearer Idea may be conceiv'd from the Figures of Animals and Plants in their proper Colours, than from the most exact Description without them."

13

THE "CURIOUS AND MAGNIFICENT WORK" 1731–1746

In late May 1729 an announcement appeared in British newspapers:

> LONDON—The last week Mr Catesby (introduced by the Right Honourable the Lord Carteret) presented to Her Majesty the first Volume of his Natural History of Florida, Carolina, and the Bahama Ilands; containing a great Variety of the Animal and Vegetable Productions of those Countries, which the Author hath been several Years collecting and delineating from the Life.

Lord Carteret was one of Catesby's subscribers; he also owned land on the border between North and South Carolina. The book Catesby presented to Queen Caroline was already starting to provoke reactions: the *Newcastle Courant*'s version of the royal announcement added, "This is said to be a Work superior to any Thing of its Kind."

Catesby's *Natural History*, which would be described in the Royal Society's *Journal Book* as a "Curious and Magnificent Work," was a sensation among scientists, botanists, and nurserymen in London. "The illustrations were so unique," modern historian Andrea Wulf noted, "that even gardeners with a small salary bought what was, at twenty guineas, the most expensive botanical book of the age":

> Plant-lovers were entranced by the pictures of magnolia buds which unfolded into enormous, flawless white petals against a background of shiny green leaves . . . They were gripped by Catesby's depiction of the lilac blossom of American wisteria . . . The aromatic bark of Carolina allspice, Catesby tantalizingly promised, was like cinnamon.

Twenty guineas was a little more than a year's wages for a "general labourer" in England or Wales at that time. A standard novel, by comparison, would cost at least seven shillings, six pence (twelve pence made a shilling, and twenty-one shillings equaled a guinea); a work of history or literature one guinea.

❖

Catesby apparently succeeded at St. James's Palace in earning "Your Royal Protection and Favour to my slender Performance" from Caroline of Ansbach, wife of George II. He dedicated the completed Volume I of the *Natural History* to Queen Caroline: "I esteem it a singular Happiness," he wrote, "that I am the first that has had an Opportunity of presenting to a Queen of Great Britain a Sample of the hitherto unregarded, though beneficial and beautiful Productions of Your Majesty's Dominions." Once again Catesby had taken pains to note that he was doing something for the first time.

The choice of queen rather than king as object of the dedication spoke volumes about the intellectual situation within the British royal family. As a modern historian put it, "The women of the Hanoverian court were as intellectual as the men were crude. While the dukes collected mistresses and plotted murder, their duchesses occupied themselves with philosophy."

Caroline was probably more savvy about the leading players of the period than her husband the king. Her youth had been spent in the intellectual atmosphere of Sophia Charlotte of Hanover, wife of Frederick III, Elector of Hanover, and sister of George I. The vivacious and quick-witted Caroline's portraits suggest a self-contented woman, with a somewhat playful gaze for the portraitist. She acted as regent when George II would return to Hanover, to the dismay of her son Frederick, Prince of Wales, with whom she and the king were constantly at odds. We have very few direct quotations from Caroline, although she was known to reply to the diplomat, courtier, and author Lord Chesterfield, "You may have more wit, my lord, than I, but I have a bitter tongue, and always repay my debts with exorbitant interest."

Queen Caroline was well received by her British subjects; she may in fact have done more than any of the Hanoverians to win over British hearts and minds at a time when there was public resistance to the idea of a royal court with a Germanic background. Caroline surrounded herself with artists, architects, and intellectuals, and in the words of modern royal historian Joanna Marschner, she "play[ed] an important part in Britain's agenda as it forged lucrative, but also highly problematic, relationships with the wider world."

An eighteenth-century memoirist wrote that Caroline's "charms of her person were far surpassed by the endowments of her mind. She possessed quickness of apprehension, a natural good understanding . . . and a considerable knowledge in many branches of useful and polite literature." Caroline's interest in politics led her to champion Robert Walpole, the Whig politician generally considered the first British prime minister.

In England Caroline had her own cabinets of curiosities; among her collected objects, later part of Queen Augusta's cabinet, were "a stuffed hummingbird, vases of rock crystal, and branches of red and white coral." Caroline also took her children to see Hans Sloane's collections.

Yet another of her interests made her a likely target of Catesby's attentions. Between the time of her husband George II's accession in 1727 and her death a decade later, Caroline's interest in gardens made her a natural patroness for Catesby, Sloane, and the rest of the botanical and horticultural set in England. At the royal residences in Kensington and Richmond, she led the fashion for the new "natural" style. This bucolic, less formal style was perfectly suited for the American trees, shrubs, and flowers being promulgated and promoted by Catesby and his coterie. A modern scholar has argued that "if pervasive influence is taken as the criterion, [Caroline's] part in encouraging . . . the development of the English garden may be her most significant contribution to the modern world: the idea of assisting, rather than replacing, Nature in creating a garden has shaped the styles of landscaping in most country estates, urban parks, suburban towns, and cemeteries down to the present day."

Princess Caroline having died in the interval, Catesby dedicated the second volume of the *Natural History* to Augusta, wife of Frederick, Prince of Wales and son and heir of George II. Unlike with Caroline, there's no record of Catesby's being received by Princess Augusta. Not quite Caroline's equal in intellect or personal charm, Augusta nevertheless followed in her predecessor's footsteps as a student and patroness of natural history. Together with Frederick, she developed the grounds of the White House, their country house located adjacent to Richmond Lodge, which had been acquired in 1730. Augusta also developed another interest in the natural world: her passion for native songbirds led to the creation of the royal Aviary Flower Garden, which would be the predecessor of the Royal Botanic Gardens at Kew.

◆

Meanwhile, reviews of the *Natural History* were being published by the Royal Society in the *Philosophical Transactions*. "Our Author proposes in this Work," the first review began, "to give the Figures of the Birds, Beasts, Serpents, Insects, and Plants, the greatest Part whereof have never been described by any Author, or no good Figures given of them." It promised to "just hint some few of the remarkable Things which occur in the Descriptions of them." Catesby began attending the society's meetings, and on February 1, 1733, while a guest of Peter Collinson, he was nominated to be a Fellow of the Royal Society:

> Mark Catesby a Gentleman well Skill'd in Botany and Natural History who travell'd for Several years in Various parts of America where he Collected Materials for a Natural History of Carolina and the Bahama Islands which Curious and Magnificent Work he has presented to the Royal Society Is desirous to become a member thereof.

After the required ten meetings' posting of the nomination, Catesby became an F. R. S. on April 26, 1733. As a fellow he not only promoted his own ideas and writings at Society meetings, but also provided illustrations for journal articles and reviews of others' writings for Society periodicals. Another Society practice in which he joined was the reading of letters to fellows from naturalists elsewhere—in Catesby's case, a missive from William Byrd in Virginia, read by Catesby to the Society on January 12, 1738, detailing Byrd's opinion that good wine could be made in Virginia, and that the senega snakeroot, contrary to Catesby's considered opinion, actually had curative properties including the cure of snakebite.

The Royal Society had at various times collected not only ideas and printed words, but also artifacts, from fossils to plant specimens to "curious" and bizarre items such as embalmed two-headed calves. Catesby added to the society's store in 1734 with the skin of a polecat from South Carolina, and in 1741 with a poison ivy plant from Virginia which he had raised in his nursery. (No mention is made of precautions to be taken, or whether the fellows present acquired itchy rashes from the experience.)

During this time Catesby deepened his involvement with the Royal Society. He produced "Draughts of Plants and Animals . . . to be inserted with the copies of the Papers they related to in the Register Books" of the Society, in return for which his membership dues were forgiven. And he was chosen to be on the committee dealing with the Society's repository, at a time when the organization was attempting to shed its past tendencies toward the bizarre and sensational among its collections for a more lofty and scientific tone. Catesby continued to mine his knowledge of the New World for presentation to the society; he read an account of "The Aborigines of America" over two meetings, and submitted papers on the making of tar and pitch in Carolina and "the striking of Sturgeon according to the practice of the Indians."

◆

The same year Catesby put FRS after his name, he traveled to Holland. Leiden, the country's second-largest city after Amsterdam, boasted a university city's energy and a history of accomplishments in medicine and science. In Leiden Catesby could have visited his friend Johan Gronovius, professor of botany at Leiden University and one of Catesby's subscribers. It's easy to imagine Catesby presenting Gronovius with a copy of Volume I of the *Natural History*, touring Leiden's renowned botanical garden, and perusing Gronovius's specimens and manuscripts.

Three years later, the Swedish naturalist Carl Linnaeus came to London. He made a poor impression: on his initial visit to London in 1736, Johann Dillenius, holder of the Sherardian Chair of Botany at Oxford (named after its benefactor), told William Sherard, "This is the man who has thrown all botany into confusion." His arrogance and willingness to take credit which was at least partly due to others, such as Willughby, was not designed to go over well in Georgian society. Willughby's modern biographer wrote, "when Carl Linnaeus, who is much better known than either [Ray or Willughby], came to write his *Systema Naturae*, he failed (or refused—arrogant man that he was) to recognise that the arrangement created by his two predecessors was superior to his own." But the power of Linnaeus's ideas, and the virtues of Linnaean classification, would eventually persuade most of his skeptics.

It was a time of peak confusion around how to name the creatures of the natural world. As more and more new discoveries were made in lands newly visited by Europeans, the deficiencies of the system then in place became ever more glaring. A 'new' American plant might be given different names in Paris, London, and Leiden. Nor, in the absence of clear and concise illustrations or specimens of the plants themselves, could botanists be sure which plants were distinct and which were in fact the same as others that had already been given names.

Not until 1753, four years after Catesby's death, would the problem begin to be resolved. That year saw the publication of the first edition of Linnaeus's *Species Plantarum*, with the binomial system of genus and species that is standard today. Together with the expanded tenth edition of Linnaeus's *Systema Naturae* in 1758, this saw the beginnings of the modern form of taxonomy for both botanical and zoological species.

But although Catesby didn't live to see Linnaeus's methods take over the field of taxonomy, he left his own imprint on the Swedish naturalist's work. Of the 187 plants figured by Catesby in the 220 published plates of his *Natural History*, Linnaeus would cite 131 of them in the *Species Plantarum*, giving them his new binomial names. Linnaeus bestowed the names of seventeen of these new species using nothing but Catesby's plates and descriptions, and he used another seventeen Catesby plates as specimens' nomenclatural types—chosen as representative of their genus or species. Catesby is commonly accepted as one of the largest single influences on Linnaeus's work—though Linnaeus would undoubtedly be too proud to admit as much.

Catesby and Linnaeus seem never to have met, nor does Linnaeus's library include a copy of the *Natural History*. Through his work cataloguing the royal libraries of Sweden, Linnaeus may have seen the copy bought by Queen Ulrika Eleonora; he also had access to the book through a wealthy friend of his, an industrialist and amateur naturalist. One letter from Catesby to Linnaeus survives. Sending "a Case of American Plants in Earth" to Linnaeus in 1745, Catesby wrote Linnaeus that "if but a few of them be acceptable, I shall be much pleased. And whatever other American Plants in this inclosed Catalogue will be acceptable, you may freely command any that I am possessed of."

◈

Catesby had traded the raw landscapes of Carolina and the Bahamas for the urban roar and frenzy of London. Even while tending his urban garden and working assiduously on the *Natural History*, however, he continued to think like a naturalist, still pondering the relationships and interconnections inherent in the natural world which to him seemed so obvious.

It was in the early 1740s that Catesby began corresponding with John Bartram, initially offering to send Bartram the books of his *Natural History*, in return for which Bartram would send him plants from Pennsylvania. Catesby never lost his enthusiasm for new information about plants and animals, pestering Bartram for details about his region: "I am told of an animal in Pensilvanea called . . . by some a Ground Hog. It lives and burrows under ground, and Sleeps much is about the Size of a Rabbit. I shall be glad of what you know concerning it." He also asked Bartram, "Have you observed any other of the Deer kind, besides the Moose, Elk, and Common Deer? Do you think that the black Fox, common in North America is a different Species, or only varying in Colour from the common gray Fox?"

For his part, Bartram seemed delighted to have the chance to communicate with the British naturalist. "The reading of thy acceptable letter incited in me the different passions of joy, in receiving a letter of friendship and request from one so much esteemed, and sorrow in considering what time we have lost, when we might have obliged each other," he wrote Catesby. "It's a pity thee had not wrote to me ten years earlier. I should by this time have furnished thee with many different species of plants, and, perhaps some animals; but the time past can't be recalled."

In a lengthy 1736 letter to Johann Dillenius, Catesby gave a thorough and exacting account of his observations of cedar trees from North America and the Caribbean, concluding, "I infer from this that many plants of the same species growing at great distancies in different Climes & Soil spourt into various little differences tho' much too small to deem them a different kind." A decade after his return to Britain Catesby was still making use of his explorations and research to further the cause of discovery. One of his keen observations from his time in the New World, though, would cement his place in the history of science.

◆

On the evening of March 5, 1746, Catesby appeared before the Fellows of the Royal Society in their meeting hall in Crane Court, London. He read to the eminent group a paper he had written entitled "Some Remarks on American Birds," which would be published in the *Philosophical Transactions* as "Of Birds of Passage." Catesby argued that age-old ideas about birds were mistaken. Aristotle, for instance, believed that swallows hid in holes during the winter; others thought birds could lie frozen under lake ice. Ray and Willughby, in their *Ornithology* of 1678, thought it "more probable that they fly away into hot countries."

Basing his arguments on his firsthand observations of bird behavior in the Carolinas and the Caribbean, Catesby went beyond academic speculation to scientific documentation. More than twenty years before, bound for Charleston, Catesby had wondered how an owl had reached his ship in the mid-Atlantic. Throughout the *Natural History*, he had noted the absence of presence of the birds he described and illustrated. Some, he wrote, were absent in fall, others in winter, while others remained year-round.

Catesby described to the Society the night migrations of the bobolink, or "rice-bird":

> Lying on the Deck of a Sloop on the North Side of Cuba, I, and the Company with me, heard three Nights successively Flights of Rice-Birds (their Notes being plainly distinguishable from others) passing over our Heads northerly, which is their direct Way from Cuba, and the Southern Continent of America, from whence they go to Carolina annually at the time Rice begins to ripen; and, after growing fat with it, return South back again.

In short, he told his audience in Crane Court, "when, by the Approach of our Winter, they find a Want of Food," many birds then "are directed, by Instinct, to report to some other Parts of the Globe, where they might find a fresh Supply." Catesby also pointed out that grains which had been newly introduced in North America were "found out, and coveted by some of these migratory Birds." His "ingenious Friend Dr. Mitchel" reported the resulting appearance in Virginia of "exotic Birds" that "had never been observed there before." Catesby thus not only gave a firsthand account of bird migration to the Royal Society; he also reported on such migration as an adaptation to a changed environment.

These observations placed him in the forefront of the debate on bird migration versus hibernation. The debate would continue, however, and would be settled only in the nineteenth century, and sooner in England than in America. Nor did Catesby's writings on bird migration spread widely after publication; William Bartram apparently was ignorant of them decades later. In his *Travels* Bartram wrote of the zoologists he had consulted, "These authors have done very little towards elucidating the subject of the migration of birds, or accounting for the annual appearance and disappearance, and vanishing of these beautiful and entertaining beings, who visit us at certain stated seasons. Catesby has said very little on this curious subject."

◆

Catesby's *Natural History,* the Appendix, and his continuing involvement in the Royal Society placed him firmly in the intellectual and social circles of mid-century London. The artist, the scientist, and the gentleman coexisted comfortably in Catesby. Even though he had "so impoverished himself through his devotion to natural history that he was essentially déclassé," in the words of his biographers Frick and Stearns, he still "mixed with the great in the Royal Society or in the informally organized, but nevertheless real, worldwide society of naturalists."

In the overlarge elephant-folio pages of his book Catesby had produced an innovative and groundbreaking work of natural history. He had taken the conventions of natural-history illustration found in Lawson's book about Carolina and Sloane's on Jamaica and blown them up, with colorful inspiration from Maria Sibylla Merian. The *Natural History* was a stunning and lavish luxury item of a book which set out to be innovative as well as informative, historic even as it followed in the tradition of Catesby's forerunners.

Modern scholar Shepard Krech III says of Catesby's artistry, "He had faults. He placed birds awkwardly in compositions. Several etchings are graceless, from feet atop leaves and legs split at extreme angles to clutching branches with feet that do not fully grasp and standing erect in poses rare in nature." Nevertheless,

> A number of Catesby's images stand out as portraits on aesthetic, postural, or behavioural grounds. A pied-billed grebe stretches one foot and leg above the water's surface. A green heron tenses in anticipation of its prey. A hooded merganser erects the feathers on its head as it calls with bill open and tongue distended. A red-eyed vireo cocks it head as if looking for an insect on the underside of leaves. A blue jay screams, tongue thrusting between open mandibles. A territorial red-winged blackbird flashes its epaulets.

Peter Kalm, a thirty-two-year-old Finnish naturalist, botanist, explorer, and agricultural economist, called on Catesby before leaving for America. On May 23, 1748, he spent "nearly the whole afternoon" with Catesby, by his account. Catesby, Kalm later wrote, "is very well known for his *Natural History* . . . in this work he has incomparably well represented with lifelike colours . . . the rarest [creatures] which are there found." Kalm felt that Catesby's illustrations were so lifelike that "no one can see that they are not living where they stand with their natural colors on the paper."

◆

When the last copy of the Appendix was delivered to a subscriber in 1747, more than two decades had passed since Mark Catesby had left behind the rigors of the naturalist's fieldwork for London and the tools of an author, etcher, and illustrator. In the last paragraph of the *Natural History*, having noted "the strong inclination I had to these kinds of subjects, join'd to the love of truth, that were my constant attendants and influencers," Catesby could look back proudly on "the circumspection and advantages I was blessed with in the compiling of my History, and which I flatter myself are in some measure conspicuous therein."

He would have only two years left to live.

14

NURSERYMAN AND EXPERIMENTAL HORTICULTURALIST 1731–1749

In the years Mark Catesby had been away from England, the country's passion for gardens and plants of all kinds, but especially for exotic botanical prizes from America, had only grown. Even as Catesby tended and released the *Natural History*, the plantings and seeds he had sent on perilous and uncertain voyages from America took hold in the gardens of high and low alike. The descriptions in Latin which were shared among the literate botanical elite were eventually translated into the catalogues of wholesale nurserymen on the outskirts of London; and the precious single specimens from Catesby's voyages were propagated wholesale, becoming fashionable additions to gardens across England, and beyond. He would once again become nature's messenger, in a different role: this time, supplying seeds to the nursery trade in order, in the words of a modern writer, to "turn the rare exotics of his *Natural History* into the affordable commodities of the nurseryman's catalogue."

The craze for North American plants in English gardens in Catesby's time would remind some of the mania for tulips in seventeenth-century Europe. Catesby's *Natural History* contributed to this continuing mania. His experience with cultivating American plants in their home locales in Virginia and Carolina would make him a respected voice about the planting and care of the English plants propagated from American seeds or seedlings. In this Golden Age of Botany, Catesby's work supplying plants and scientific knowledge to Britain and the Continent was fundamental. He helped create and sustain what has been described as "a vast network of intellectual and material exchange that served a burgeoning culture of gardeners, botanists, politicians, and artists."

In the mid-1730s Catesby shifted his base of horticultural operations. When Stephen Bacon died, his Hoxton nursery was sold to John Sampson, who has no known connection either to Catesby or to North American plants. Perhaps because Sampson didn't share his botanical interests, Catesby then moved to Christopher Gray's nursery on the opposite side of London. Gray had been born in the 1690s in Fulham to a nurseryman father and had his nursery in the King's Road (now New King's Road) there. Peter Kalm in 1748 described Fulham, only four miles southwest of London: "all round . . . the country consists wholly of gardens and market-gardens."

It was through Gray that Mark Catesby's next printed work was published. The single-sheet broadside, "A Catalogue of American Trees and Shrubs that will endure the Climate of England," contains Catesby's etching of the southern magnolia (*Magnolia grandiflora*) surrounded by an alphabetical listing of plants' Latin names, with English names also included. Although the broadside is undated, various clues place its date of origin as 1742. The catalogue advertised the plants that Gray offered in his Fulham nursery. But it also helped advertise the *Natural History*: thirty-five of the seventy-two plants had the letters "H. F." before their names, referring readers to their descriptions in the "Nat. Hist. of Florida."

Catesby's prominent center etching, based on an engraving by Georg Dionysius Ehret, was chosen to catch the eye of the reader. The magnolia's glossy green leaves and large cream-colored petals made it the most expensive and desirable of the exotic American plants available for growing in England. "This stately Tree perfumes the Woods, and displays its Beauties from May until November, producing first its fragrant and ample Blossoms, succeeded by its glittering Fruit," Catesby wrote. The magnolia was "so far naturalized and become a Denizon to our Country and Climate, as to adorn . . . the Garden of that worthy and curious Baronet, Sir John Collinson, where for these three years past, it has produced Plenty of Blossoms."

◆

Many details of Catesby's life during his time in London, as in the rest of his life, are vague. By 1730 he had left Fairchild's and was apparently living with Elizabeth Rowland in the parish of St. Giles-without-Cripplegate, on the eastern side of the City of London, just south of Hoxton. There the Catesbys' first son, Mark, was born in April 1731 and another, John, in March 1732, though he lived only four months; a daughter Caroline arrived in May 1733, but was buried that August. A second daughter, Anne, was baptized in December 1737 at St. Luke's Church, Old Street, indicating that the family had moved there from the parish of St. Giles. Sadly, the baptizing in 1740 of a second Catesby boy named Mark indicates that the first did not survive childhood.

In 1747, Catesby married Elizabeth in Keith's Chapel, Hyde Park Corner, though they had been together for at least seventeen years by then. The marriage may have been for legal purposes, as Catesby would not have much longer to live. So-called "irregular" marriages required a Church of England clergyman, but not the publishing of banns or other expenses; though not legal under Church law, they were valid under British common law for determining inheritance and proof of legitimacy. A nineteenth-century chronicler of such marriages noted that "May Fair stands . . . perhaps pre-eminently, so far as regards the number of fashionable clandestine marriages." There the Rev. Alexander Keith "fitted up a house as a chapel," and advertised that "the License on a Crown Stamp, Minister and Clerk's fees . . . amount to one guinea . . . at any hour until four in the afternoon." To ensure his chapel could be recognized, Keith pointed out the "porch at the door like a country church porch." There Catesby and Elizabeth were married by the Rev. John Grierson, one of Keith's curates. By the time of Ann's baptism they had taken up residence in the house behind St. Luke's, less than a mile north of St. Giles, where Mark Catesby would live out his days.

The character of the British landscape had been changing since Mark Catesby's youth. Aristocrats, country squires, and newly wealthy merchants with social aspirations all desired rural holdings as a mark of their status. They created or modified something like three hundred county seats between 1660 and 1735. The growth of the British economy, and rising values of land due to burgeoning population growth, underwrote massive improvement projects on Britain's estates—especially to their gardens.

Accidents of geography had left prehistoric Britain with surprisingly few plants native to the islands—well under two thousand, compared to eighteen thousand native plant species in North America. The Romans had imported grapevines, and rosemary had been brought over in the fourteenth century. Firs, pines, and plane trees could be found in Britain four centuries later. But it was the expansion of European exploration that caused a concurrent explosion of new species into Britain and the rest of Europe. This colonial expansion, combined with the strength of the economy, the efforts of botanical explorers such as Mark Catesby, and the ascension of garden design as intellectual exercise by men such as Alexander Pope and Capability Brown, led to a widespread fixation concerning all aspects of the British garden.

To give advice on all those gardens, there were critics such as Batty Langley, the Twickenham gardener's son who published a number of books on gardening and architecture. In his *New Principles of Gardening: or, The Laying Out and Planting Parterres, Groves, Wildernesses, Labyrinths, Avenues, Parks, &c.,* published in 1728, the eccentric garden designer laid into the prevailing formal style of the garden: "To consider how many authors . . . have wrote on Gardening, and the vast Numbers of fine Plants that are . . . raised in our Nurseries about London, would make a Foreigner . . . believe, that they excell'd all others in the World." However, Batty claimed, "to our great Misfortune, *our Gardens are much the worst of any in the World,* some few excepted, that have been laid out by *Gentlemen,* who have a grand and elegant Taste in Designing, known to very few Gardeners."

Batty left no doubt as to his definition of "grand and elegant Taste." Nothing, he wrote, is "more *shocking* than a *stiff regular Garden*; where after we have seen one quarter thereof, the very same is repeated in all the remaining parts, so that we are tired, instead of being entertained" (all emphases his). Instead, Langley wrote, "when we come to copy, or imitate Nature, we should trace her Steps with the greatest Accuracy that can be." To him, that meant planting trees in irregular clumps, "and that no three Trees together range in a strait Line, excepting now and then by Chance, to cause Variety." These practices would create "Designs that are *truly Grand and Noble,* after *Nature's own Manner.*"

Batty Langley was only one of the forces behind the rise of the naturalistic style that took over English landscape gardening in the early eighteenth century. According to landscape historian Todd Longstaffe-Gowan, the naturalistic style was "associated with patriotism and rustic virtue," and was "adopted on the estates of aristocratic patrons . . . as well as Alexander Pope's villa at Twickenham. It rejected formal geometry, instead using winding paths, long vistas, and artfully placed groves to achieve its effects." Imitating nature could be expensive. In 1734 Frederick, Prince of Wales, paid the equivalent of $48,800 for a twenty-five-foot tulip poplar tree (*Liriodendron tulipifera*) from North America.

Another authority on garden design and planting was Philip Miller, of the Chelsea Physic Garden, who in 1731 began publishing *The Gardeners Dictionary*. In it Miller praised the rebirth of interest in gardening during the reign of King William; "yet we find the Taste at that Time extended little farther than to small Pieces of Box-work, Finish'd Parterres, and Clipp'd Greens, all which are generally banish'd out of the Gardens of the most polite Persons of this Age, who justly prefer the more extended Rural Designs of Gardens, which approach the nearest to Nature." The *Dictionary* would go through eight editions during Miller's lifetime, the last appearing in 1768, thirty-seven years after the first and three years before Miller's death.

In many ways *The Gardeners Dictionary* was the opposite of Catesby's *Natural History*. Rather than being an outlandishly expensive wish book funded and purchased by the well-to-do, the *Dictionary* offered nurserymen and gardeners of all classes advice "on every aspect of horticulture from how to protect tender flowers against frost or pests, to which species suited particular areas of the garden, such as north-facing plots, avenues or groves," Andrea Wulf has written. "Its concept was so insightful that it became an instant success, influencing every gardening book that followed it." Mark Catesby, who had sent Miller seeds from America, and Peter Collinson bought copies of Miller's book.

The Chelsea Physic Garden embodies the transformation of botanical interest in Britain during the eighteenth century. The very name references its origins as a resource for the Society of Apothecaries and its apprentices, intended to teach them the uses of various herbs. By 1731, Miller had transformed the Chelsea Physic Garden into a more comprehensive botanical resource, from which he gleaned the detailed, practical information that he made available through *The Gardeners Dictionary*. Miller's description of the "Bastard Indigo" (*Amorpha fruticosa*) acknowledged Catesby's role: "the seeds of this Plant were sent from Carolina by Mr. Catesby, in the Year 1724, which were sown in many Gardens; and Numbers of the Plants were raised from them, some of which produced their Flowers in a few Years after." By 1755, Miller could state that the plant was "pretty common in most of the Nursery Gardens about London, being propagated and sold as a flowering Shrub, with many other sorts."

The Royal Society's inquiries into natural history, and its repository of specimens of plants, also contributed to the rise of a more naturalistic gardening style. Gardeners used the influx of "wild" trees, shrubs, and flowers from Britain's diverse colonial holdings to break up the traditional native English landscape to create "American" gardens. Peter Collinson wrote John Bartram in Pennsylvania, "The Trees & Shrubs raised from thy first seeds is grown to great maturity," creating such an impression that a visitor "cannot well help thinking He is in North American thickets."

One prominent example of Catesby's contributions to British "American gardens" was the catalpa tree (*Catalpa bignonioides*),

which Catesby first introduced to the colonists in South Carolina before shipping seeds to Britain. "Catalpah called so by the
Indians," Catesby wrote on a specimen label, describing
the white flowers "with a mixture of yellow and purple" which
"hang in bunches after the manner of the hors chestnut
which at a distance it resembles tho' much more beautiful." The
seeds "hang prodigiously full in clusters. They grow by the sides
of Rivers very remote from the Settlements in rich land."

The catalpa, Catesby noted, "was unknown to the inhabited
parts of Carolina, till I brought the seeds from the remoter parts
of the Country. And tho' the Inhabitants are little curious in
Gardining, yet the uncommon Beauty of the Tree has induc'd
them to propagate it." He predicted in the *Natural History* that
just as the catalpa had become "an Ornament to many of their
Gardens," it "probably will be the same to ours in England," and
he could later write in the *Hortus* that indeed "it is since become
naturalized in England; and did in August 1748 produce, at Mr.
Gray's, such numbers of blossoms, that the leaves were almost
hid thereby."

The magnolia tree was another successful Catesby introduction to Britain. He had sent seeds of *Magnolia grandiflora* to
Sherard from Charleston in 1724; when he returned to London,
magnolias growing there provided the models for illustrations
used in the *Natural History*.

Even the weather seemed to be on the gardeners' side. The
1720s and 1730s were exceptionally favorable in Britain for
cultivating the new American plants. The "Little Ice Age" of the
sixteenth and seventeenth centuries was ending, and gardeners
such as Fairchild, Miller, and Catesby found themselves in a

climate which overall was trending favorably for their efforts. In the decade and a half between the "dismal summer" of 1725 and the winter of 1739–40, the coldest in English temperature records (which were begun in 1659), these nurserymen and gardeners were given mild weather to support their ambitious botanical programs.

◆

Mark Catesby had one more substantial publication in him. In the late 1740s, toward the end of his life, Catesby completed his *Hortus Britanno-Americanus*, a selection of eighty-five hardy North American plants which Catesby believed were suitable for planting in English gardens. The volume included sixteen hand-colored etched plates, all of them details of plates in the *Natural History*, with parts of the plant squeezed into the smaller frame of the plate. Four new images of plants were included, including two not included in the *Natural History*: the palmetto tree (which would become a symbol of South Carolina) and "Jove's Beard," the false indigo that Philip Miller had grown in the Chelsea Physic Garden from Catesby's seeds. Seventeen more plants not in the *Natural History* were given descriptions, but not illustrations. The *Hortus* was both scientific reference and catalogue for English horticulturalists, furthering Catesby's interest in the commercial possibilities of American native plants. The eighty-five "Curious Trees and Shrubs" included perhaps Catesby's proudest horticultural achievement, which he called "Magnolia altissima . . . The Laurel-Tree of Carolina," and which we know as *Magnolia grandiflora*—the southern magnolia.

Why the *Hortus* was not published until 1763, fourteen years after Catesby's death, is a mystery. Four years after that, it was reissued as *Hortus Europae-Americanus*, in a nod to the growing demand for these plants in Europe outside of Great Britain. Catesby biographers Frick and Stearns described the *Hortus* as "this monument, this self-composed epitaph to Catesby the gardener and Catesby the experimental horticulturalist—for he was more than a mere gardener."

In this, the last of his published writings, Catesby continued the mission which had animated a lifetime of exploration, collection, and publishing on natural history: the widespread dissemination not only of plantings, but also of knowledge about the workings of nature. Though "many kinds of American plants" have been "hitherto in the possession of the opulent and curious," Catesby wrote, "they, it is to be hoped, will for the benefit of their country be excited to encourage [plants'] propagation and increase, that both Faunas and Flora may be consulted, as well for the benefit of our woods, as for ornaments to our gardens."

◆

By the mid-1740s Catesby had become a respected elder member of British natural-history circles. His opinions on North American flora and fauna were given great weight, and visiting naturalists such as Peter Kalm made a point of meeting him. On December 29, 1743, Catesby was elected an honorary member of the prestigious Spalding Gentlemen's Society in Yorkshire, joining Sir Isaac Newton, Sir Hans Sloane, and Alexander Pope.

Emanuel Mendes de Costa, botanist and clerk to the Royal Society, left us a sketch of Catesby in his later years, depicting him as "tall, meagre, hard favoured, and [with] a sullen look." Typically, Mendes de Costa wrote, Catesby "was extremely grave or sedate, and of a silent disposition; but when he contracted friendship was communicative and affable." As Mark Catesby was in his sixties when Mendes de Costa described him, with only a year or two to live, it might not do to extrapolate all these qualities backward, as it were, into being lifelong character traits.

One of Catesby's last letters, to John Bartram a year before Catesby's death, was very different in tone and subject matter. First, he responded to the idea that he has been a neglectful correspondent, saying "I will not vindicate my silence but pray attribute it to the indolence of 60" (he was in fact 65). He continued, "How much greater occurrencies must a few Villages afford among which you reside, than our grand Metropolis, which tho' the most opulent on the Globe is but a member of those mighty powers by which the late Catastrophe has been brought about, which I pray God may answer all ends." (Henrietta McBurney has suggested that Catesby here refers to the War of Austrian Succession, known in America as King George's War.) The letter is notable, perhaps even unique among Catesby's extant letters, for containing no references to the natural world.

By 1749 the robust health which had allowed Catesby to spend years collecting specimens in all weathers had left him. A letter from Thomas Knowlton to Dr. Richard Richardson in July of that year noted that "poor Mr. Catesby's Legs swell and he looks badly, Drrs. Mead & Stack said there were little hopes for him long on this side the Grave." That December, according to his friend George Edwards, Catesby while "Crossing the way in holbore . . . fell and was taken up Senceless and So continued 2 or 3 days, when he dyed. He receiv'd in his fall a bruse in his head"; and "he had his son with him, a Boy of 8 years old, who could give not Satisfactory account." Two years after formalizing his marriage to Elizabeth, and two years after presenting the Appendix of his *Natural History* to the Royal Society, on December 23, 1749, Mark Catesby died at the age of sixty-six in his home behind St. Luke's.

He was buried in the church's graveyard, to be joined there in 1753 by Elizabeth. Both of their gravesites have been lost. The *Gentleman's Magazine* published this tribute in its January 1750 issue:

On Saturday morning the 23rd of December died at his house, behind St Luke's Church in Old-Street, the truly honest, ingenious, and modest Mr. Mark Catesby, F. R. S. who, after travelling through many of the British dominions, on the continent, and in the islands of America, in order to make himself acquainted with the customs and manners of the natives, and to collect observations on the animals and vegetables of those countries, which he very exactly delineated, and painted on the spot, he returned with these curious materials to England, and compiled a most magnificent work, intitled, A natural History of Carolina, Florida, and the Bahama Islands, which does great honour to his native country, and perhaps is the most eloquent performance of its kind that has yet been published; since not only the rare beasts, birds, fishes, and plants etc. were drawn, engraven, and exquisitely coloured, from his original paintings, by his own hands, in 220 folio copper plates but he has also added a correct map and a general history of that world. He liv'd to the age of 70, well known to and much esteemed by, the curious of this and other nations, and died much lamented by his friends, leaving behind him two children and a widow, who has a few copies of his work, undisposed of.

In a more personal vein, George Edwards wrote of Catesby:

He was in his behaver much of Gentleman and gained the respect of all his acquaintance[. H]e was to[o] Modest to rise in the world by pushing his interest amongst the great, to many of whom he had Acces[. H]e was under the frowns of fortune yet through his Great prudence and oeconomy Steared his cours to the end without either running in debt or being troublesom to his friends[. H]e dyed regretted by all who knew his merits.

Where did Mark Catesby fit in the social order? He was educated, somehow, in Latin and French. His family owned enough land for him to be considered a 'gent.' He corresponded with Sloane and Collinson, and was welcomed into the grand homes of Byrd and Nicholson. Yet he scraped by in London, living in less-fashionable neighborhoods, dying with little estate. He also had a common-law wife for almost two decades before finally marrying her late in life. It seems that his intellect, personal qualities, and achievements lent him a social fluidity that allowed him into the Royal Society without his having to cultivate any of the other commonly accepted markers of gentility.

Perhaps the key to Catesby's relationships within the often-rigid British class system can be found in the description of him penned by Richard Pulteney, a physician and botanist, in 1790. Catesby, Pulteney wrote, "lived in acquaintance and friendship with many of the most respectable members of [the Royal Society,] being greatly esteemed for his modesty, ingenuity, and upright behavior." A man of such qualities and accomplishments as Catesby's might well have been looked at as existing outside of any consideration of personal wealth, social position, or caste. And his ability to accept the natural-history knowledge of those American outsiders, the Natives and enslaved Africans, may well have derived from his unusual status in English society. From the available evidence, it appears that in London as in the New World, Mark Catesby created his own course, and followed his own path.

EPILOGUE

Mark Catesby's will has not survived, but that of Elizabeth Catesby has. Dated January 4, 1753, her will left "to my loving cousin, Jekyll Catesby, a second volume of Mr Catesby's Natural History, to make his set complete" and "all the rest, residue and remainder of my estate . . . to my two loving children, Mark Catesby and Ann Catesby, to be equally divided between them." Jekyll Catesby was made executor, and Peter Collinson was one of the two witnesses. Collinson wrote that Elizabeth had been able to "[subsist] on the sale [of copies of the *Natural History*] for about 2 years."

It was one of Sloane's favorite natural-history artists, George Edwards, who had stepped forward at Mark Catesby's death. Edwards had remained one of Catesby's closest friends in his last years, and after the loss of her husband he assisted Elizabeth in the sale of Catesby's works to Thomas Cadell, a London bookseller. Edwards would write that Catesby's "whole fortune [—] household Stuff, Coppy of his histor, original drawings, and Copper plates [—] did not amount in the whole to 700£." Though sufficient to live on, even in London, it was surely a comedown for the son of landed gentry who had inherited London properties a few decades before.

It was also George Edwards who revised the *Natural History* for its second edition, published in 1754. The printing was largely unchanged from the original; Edwards removed the list of subscribers and made some correction and regularization of capitalization, punctuation, and spelling—as Frick and Stearns commented, "Catesby was always more erratic in these matters than was considered good form even in mid-eighteenth-century England." In 1771, four decades after the first printing, a publisher named Benjamin White brought out a third edition, with only one significant change: Linnaean names could now be given to all of Catesby's species. The *Natural History* remained in print throughout the eighteenth century; as late as 1818, a French reference work included an exact copy of Catesby's hermit crab.

The same month that Elizabeth Catesby's will was read, Sir Hans Sloane died in Chelsea. London's Sloane Square would be named after him (lending its name to the Sloane Rangers, a particular social set much critiqued in the 1970s and 1980s, London's counterpart to American preppies). Linnaeus gave the name *Sloanea* to a genus of flowering plants in his memory.

Nineteen years after Catesby's death, King George III bought all of Catesby's watercolors and sketches from Thomas Cadell for £120; today they reside in the Royal Library at Windsor Castle. That same year, Thomas Jefferson paid ten guineas, half the original price, for the *Natural History*, which he was "very anxious" to own. He later described it as the only "complete, reliable, illustrated natural history of America," and consulted it when compiling his list of common North American birds for his *Notes on the State of Virginia*. Meriwether Lewis and William Clark consulted the *Natural History* before launching their historic expedition to the American West.

In the 1770s, William Bartram of Pennsylvania, whose father John had forged extensive connections with Catesby, Collinson, and other botanists and nurserymen in England, explored the Carolinas, Georgia, and Florida. His *Travels through North and South Carolina, Georgia, East and West Florida, the Cherokee Country, etc.*, commonly known as *Bartram's Travels*, is today considered a classic of the field, and has largely surpassed Catesby's work in reputation.

It took another half-century for the most famous naturalist of his time, and probably of ours, to visit the Southeast. In October 1820, John James Audubon collected ornithological specimens in Mississippi, Alabama, and Florida; the next year, he settled in Louisiana. He began publishing his great work, *The Birds of America*, in 1827, and won fans and collectors in the US and Britain: King George IV admired and supported Audubon's work, just as his father George III had collected the watercolors of Mark Catesby.

Catesby undeniably sits in the shadow of Audubon, however unfairly. Perhaps Audubon was simply better at self-promotion; perhaps the enhanced communications media of his day gave (and give) him an unfair advantage. Partisans of Catesby can point out that unlike the Englishman, Audubon did not engrave and color the plates of his own masterpiece, *The Birds of America*; instead, he hired teams of commercial artists to produce the prints. For his part Catesby, unlike Audubon, is not known to have propped up freshly shot birds with wire in order to capture their likenesses with his brush.

◆

The question then arises, why isn't Mark Catesby better known? He was, after all, a kind of trailblazer, the first white man to roam the Carolina woods and hills with a naturalist's eye and an artist's skill. His masterwork, the *Natural History*, caught the attention of the British royal family as well as the Royal Society, selling well in spite of its immense size and astounding price tag.

Historians tend to agree that Mark Catesby's status for posterity suffered from his living and working too early in the timeline of natural history, of the study, illustration, and description of the flora and fauna of Earth. The rise and general acceptance of Linnaeus's system of botanical nomenclature beginning with his *Systema Naturae* in 1736 made Catesby's work, with its pre-Linnaean names for the birds, plants, and animals he portrayed, less accessible and less valuable as a reference.

Under the Linnaean system, non-Linnaean classifications were disqualified, and whoever coined the proper Linnaean two-part name, such as *Homo sapiens* for our species, could claim to be the namer of the species in question. Catesby had named the ivory-billed woodpecker "the Largest White-Bill Woodpecker, *Picus maximus rostro albo.*" Linnaeus later consulted the *Natural History*, shortened the name to *Picus principalis,* and with typical Linnaean self-regard took credit as the namer of the species.

Catesby was also the victim of a fundamental shift in how science was being done. A new way of seeing nature, arising alongside and to some degree aided by the ascendancy of the Linnaean system, was developing. It focused more on individual organisms, and less on the surrounding environments in which they lived or the interconnections between them. Illustrations of plants and animals began appearing without backgrounds; the illustrations of Maria Sibylla Merian, Catesby, and Bartram, placing species in their natural contexts, were not considered scientific. As Merian's biographer wrote, "In Linnaeus's wake, scientists wanted to know how creatures related to those similar to themselves . . . In the short term, natural scientists would be less interested in . . . what a given caterpillar might eat, the relationship of an organism to its environment . . . than they were with marking each species off from the others."

This shift was part of a larger project, the movement to professionalize the sciences. Amateur parson-naturalists and apothecary hobbyists would eventually have little place in the development of botany, ornithology, and entomology. The age of the virtuosi was coming to an end. Universities and laboratories, populated with specialists often brandishing credentials from those very same institutions, would increasingly be the ones to produce the discoverers and namers of species, and the authors of the papers about them.

Sloane's *Voyage to Jamaica* and Catesby's *Natural History of Carolina* thus faded from the literary history of the early Americas and the Atlantic world. Their ways of cataloguing and presenting information were soon out of date, too literary for scientific works and too detailed for pleasurable reading.

Merian's and Catesby's visions of a comprehensive natural history would have to be realized in the future, first by such farsighted explorers as Alexander von Humboldt, then with the environmental movement of twentieth century. Today, the holistic study of nature, of flora and fauna and their ecosystems, enjoys a popularity which Catesby would find gratifying—though the excesses of human alteration of the natural world and the onset of the Anthropocene would be less well received by the naturalist.

◆

Outside of the ebbs and flows of literary and intellectual fashions, Mark Catesby is and has been still remembered and lionized, not least in the scientific community. He has been called the "founder of American ornithology": no one before him had published illustrations together with detailed information about North American birds. The same can be said of his work with plants, mammals, insects, and aquatic species of the American Southeast and the Caribbean.

But Catesby's reputation as a naturalist rests not only on his being the first to identify and illustrate the plants and animals he found in the New World. Given the wholesale revamping of taxonomy under Linnaeus and the ongoing research into speciation using the latest scientific techniques, Catesby's ability to discriminate between species—and perhaps as important to science, his ability to avoid creating separate species where he shouldn't have—was noteworthy. Most of the animals he chose to name as distinctive have been acknowledged as valid species in the intervening years. A modern herpetologist has written, "Among amphibian and reptile species, for example, thirty-two of the thirty-five that [Catesby] illustrated are recognized scientifically today. Statistically, this is a far better record than almost every other naturalist who has worked in America up to the present day." In 1920, when Nathaniel Britton and Charles Millspaugh authored *The Bahama Flora*, they were able to identify all but one plant that Catesby cited in the *Natural History* as Bahamian specimens. Until their book, Catesby had remained the reference on Bahamian plants for almost three centuries.

Botanists and zoologists since Catesby's time have shown their regard for him in the time-honored way of scientists. Catesby's Dutch friend Johan Gronovius named the lily-thorn genus, *Catesbaea*, while Catesby was still alive. The American bullfrog (*Lithobates catesbeianus*) was originally named the *Rana catesbeiana* by George Shaw, an English zoological compiler, in the early nineteenth century. Stephen Elliot, a South Carolina planter and botanist, chose the name Catesby's Trillium (*Trillium catesbyi*) in 1817 for a rare wildflower of the Southeast whose purple or pink blossoms nod downward toward the woodland floor. And in 1968 J. E. Böhlke and D. G. Smith named *Catesbya pseudomuraena,* an eel inhabiting the reefs of the Bahamas, citing "Mark Catesby, whose [work] marks the beginning of our knowledge of Bahaman fishes."

The greater public has also rediscovered the naturalist and his art. In 2013, "Mark Catesby: Watercolours from the Royal Collection" debuted at Gainsborough's House in Sudbury, Catesby's hometown. Charleston's Gibbes Museum of Art in 2017 mounted "Artist, Scientist, Explorer: Mark Catesby in the

Carolinas," an exhibit featuring forty-four paintings from the British Royal holdings.

A tiny few of the actual specimens Mark Catesby sent back to England can be viewed today. The West Indian topsnail, which Catesby illustrated in Plate 33 of the *Natural History*, can be found in the Natural History Museum in London, along with a Jurassic shark vertebra and a viperfish preserved in spirits in an eighteenth-century glass jar. Over nine hundred of his dried plants now reside in the Sherard, Du Bois, and Dillenius Herbaria at Oxford University.

Nor is Catesby's botanical legacy limited to dead plants mounted on paper. The catalpa tree, which Catesby found in the wilder parts of Carolina, now grows as it has since at least the 1840s on the grounds of Westminster Palace. Cabinet ministers being driven into Parliament can see these "Indian Bean Trees" on Bridge Street in front of Big Ben, as well as in nearby Parliament Square. Britain's grand political stage is continuing witness to the "uncommon beauty" that Mark Catesby delivered from the New World.

◆

Another enduring inheritance from Mark Catesby's era is less green and leafy, less heartwarming, more sobering. Catesby was only able to be in America, only had ships carrying him and his specimens between Carolina and England, because of Britain's expansionist, colonial, imperial project. Sir Hans Sloane's biographer wrote an assessment which could also be said of Catesby: his work "embodied a fusion of empire and information in which the lofty dream of surveying the creation rested on the cunning mundanities of colonial and commercial ambition." Like Sloane's, Catesby's legacy is "an artefact of British imperial power."

The Royal Society morphed in the eighteenth century from a purely scientific body to an indirect (at least) supporter of voyages of conquest and commercial enterprise. The British Museum, as we've seen, began with the endowment of Sloane's collections, themselves tainted by the bleak shadow of his Jamaican sugar plantations worked by slaves. Nor should we ignore Catesby's own probable purchase of a young enslaved African boy, though we know so little about the event. Recently, researchers with Britain's National Trust, the body which maintains the UK's country homes and mansions, among other duties, aroused a firestorm of criticism after mounting a research project into the colonial and slaveholding connections of the nation's fabled country homes and mansions. "Scratch almost any institution with roots in Britain's era of global dominance," Maya Jasanoff has written, "and you'll draw imperial blood."

But Mark Catesby was ruled foremost by his curiosity, not his Englishness. He welcomed knowledge from everyone he met, not only white Englishmen. Although smart enough to include in his writings to his wealthy patrons information about the practical and commercial value of the plants he collected, Catesby wasn't the British Empire's commercial envoy. He was willing to let others fund his explorations as well as the printing of his book, but his agenda was overwhelmingly his own. To seek, to discover, to document: to satisfy his ravenous appetite for knowledge and experience: these were Mark Catesby's motives. And he wanted to be first—first to find, first to sketch, first to send back to the avid collectors in England. Finally, Catesby wanted to be the first to publish a book like *The Natural History of Carolina, Florida, and the Bahama Islands.* Though his ambitions tracked with the rise of British power and status, they were for himself, and not in the service of what would soon enough be called Empire.

In the spring of 2022, a second edition of the *Natural History* sold at auction with Arader Galleries in New York for $240,000. Today Mark Catesby is recognized more often as artist than naturalist. Three centuries of advances in science have rendered his descriptions of flora and fauna less important to our understanding of the natural world, but time has only enhanced Catesby's status as illustrator. His dynamic and engaging compositions still attract the eye and arrest our attention. He had written in his book proposal, "As figures convey the strongest Ideas . . . we shall take care to exhibit every thing drawn by the Life, as well as described in the most particular manner." This care has given us, even today, what all art can give: fresh ways of seeing the world—in this case, the world of eighteenth-century American wildlife.

But Mark Catesby left something else from his time exploring American fields, forests, and frontiers. By examining not only plants and animals, insects, and fishes, but also people, Catesby gave us an indelible glimpse into the clash of cultures spawned by British arrival in the New World. Native Americans and enslaved Africans appear in Catesby's accounts, their knowledge duly recorded, their roles implicitly acknowledged. Incomplete though it was, Catesby's inclusion of these other sources of information reminds us to look for all the voices present in a place and time. We can do no less, if we would aspire like Mark Catesby to comprehend "truthfully and accurately" the world around us.

ACKNOWLEDGMENTS

Sometime in the 1990s while reading William Bartram's *Travels*, I came across a small article about another naturalist who had roamed the Southeast: Mark Catesby. I remember looking for more about him in those pre-internet days, finding nothing, and moving on with a shrug.

Decades later, there is plenty to read, see, and learn concerning the man and his art. I'm fortunate to be riding a wave of critical, scholarly, and biographical creation about Catesby, especially in the last decade.

Henrietta McBurney's fabulous *Illuminating Natural History: The Art and Science of Mark Catesby* was foundational for my own telling of Catesby's story. Her research, and especially her transcription of all of Catesby's extant letters, made my work much easier, and she generously responded to my emailed questions. Another valuable reference was *The Curious Mister Catesby*, edited by E. Charles Nelson and David J. Elliott, particularly for the work in identifying Catesby's subjects by their modern common names and Linnaean taxonomy.

ACKNOWLEDGMENTS

Amy Meyers, formerly of the Yale School for British Art and editor with Margaret Beck Pritchard of the important *Empire's Nature: Mark Catesby's New World Vision*, encouraged me in the beginning of this project. One of the authors in *Empire's Nature*, Mark Laird, helped me figure out whether *Catalpa bignonioides* still grew in the shadow of Westminster Palace.

In the UK, Jeremy Archer shared his extensive genealogy of the Jekyll and Catesby families. Phillip Ludgrove, Beadle-Houseman of the Worshipful Order of the Skinners, gave me fascinating background about the Royal Livery Companies of London. Dr. Kim Sloan, Enlightenment scholar and former curator at the British Museum, sent me lengthy responses to my lengthy emails about John White, Sir Hans Sloane, and Mark Catesby. Paul Wood, researcher and blogger on Britain's trees, confirmed for me the existence in London of descendants of Catesby's catalpas.

In May 2022, I had the good fortune to attend the *Catesby at 300* symposium, hosted by The Catesby Centre at the University of South Carolina in Columbia in conjunction with the tricentennial of Catesby's landing in Charleston. David Elliott and the symposium speakers added greatly to my understanding of Catesby and his times. Suzanne Linder Hurley and Chris Judge were kind enough to answer follow-up emails about South history and Indigenous history and culture. Professor Hurley also was kind enough to read and comment on the South Carolina chapters. The Hollings library offered a stunning display of several different editions of the *Natural History*; Michael Weissenberg, guru of the special collections, was a patient and helpful resource.

Dr. Nic Butler, historian at the Charleston County Public Library, very generously shared his deep knowledge of early Charleston, shared unpublished chapters of his work, and answered my questions about early eighteenth-century life. His editorial comments on chapters 7–9 were invaluable. Nic's *Charleston Time Machine* podcast is a treasure. Toby Smith, cultural historian at McLeod Plantation in Charleston, met with me on-site and discussed the life of slaves in eighteenth-century South Carolina.

Here on the mountain in southeast Tennessee, Matthew Mitchell, professor of early modern British history at the University of the South in Sewanee, shared his comments and helped guide me. John McCardell, former vice chancellor at Sewanee and South Carolina historian, guided me toward those standard histories which were not to be missed, and read and critiqued chapters 7–9. Christopher McDonough, professor, classicist, local historian, and beer-drinking buddy, also cast his eye on various parts of the book in progress. Chris connected me with Jennifer Matthews, who gave me advice about Mark Catesby's possible sartorial choices, and Mishoe Brennecke, who set me straight about eighteenth-century portraits of Englishmen.

Thanks go once again to the awesome staff at Jessie Ball DuPont Library at the University of the South, especially Cari Reynolds, Penny Cowan, and Terri Limbaugh, who kept renewing overdue books for me.

Josephine McDonough of McDonough Fine Arts in Atlanta provided me with a modern collector and dealer's take on Catesby, as did Josephine Arader of Arader Galleries in California and New York, who shared the online link when a second edition of the *Natural History* sold at her auction for $240,000. Professor Marcus Rediker answered my query about pirates, even though I suspect he'd rather never talk about them ever again.

As I wrapped up the manuscript, I lost my best buddy of eleven years, Jackson aka J Dog, Bubba, and the Giant Mountain River Otter. While still grieving his departure, I am grateful to have had him in my life.

Once more, I am dedicating this to Susan, who's given me time and space and enabled me to do this work, particularly the last frenzied bit right up to the publisher's deadline. And speaking of publishers, Jessica Case and the people of Pegasus Books continue to treat this author (though here I'm tempted to add, like Catesby, that I'm "conscious of my own Inability") with respect and attention, as does my agent, Farley Chase of Chase Literary Agency.

I have also dedicated this book to my parents, Edwin and Maria Dean. Although I only knew them for the first thirteen years of my life, my mother's love of her big Italian family and my father's devotion to the life of the mind have become essential parts of their youngest son.

BIBLIOGRAPHY

Ackroyd, Peter. *Revolution: The History of England: From the Battle of the Boyne to the Battle of Waterloo.* New York: Thomas Dunne Books, 2016.

Anderson, John G. T. *Deep Things Out of Darkness: A History of Natural History.* Berkeley: University of California Press, 2013. https://www.jstor.org/stable/10.1525/j.ctt24hshw.

Anishanslin, Zara. *Portrait of a Woman in Silk: Hidden Histories of the British Atlantic World.* New Haven, CT: Yale University Press, 2016.

Armstrong, Patrick. *The English Parson-Naturalist: A Companionship between Science and Religion.* Leominster, UK: Gracewing, 2000.

Audubon, John James. *Ornithological biography: or An account of the habits of the birds of the United States of America; accompanied by descriptions of the objects represented in the work entitled The Birds of America, and interspersed with delineations of American scenery and manners.* Philadelphia: Judah Dobson, ca. 1831–1839.

Ball, Edward. *Slaves in the Family.* New York: Ballantine Books, 1999.

Bartram, William. *Travels and Other Writings.* New York: Library of America, 1996.

Bauer, Ralph. *The Alchemy of Conquest: Science, Religion, and the Secrets of the New World.* Charlottesville: University of Virginia Press, 2019. https://doi.org/10.2307/j.ctvsn3p7z.

Birkhead, Tim. *The Wonderful Mr Willughby.* London: Bloomsbury Publishing, 2018. Kindle edition.

Boswell, James. *The Life of Samuel Johnson, LL.D.* London: Printed by Henry Baldwin, 1791.

Bray, William, ed., *The Diary of John Evelyn*, vol. II. London: M. Walter Dunne, 1901. https://www.gutenberg.org/files/42081/42081-h /42081-h.htm.

Burn, John Southerden. *The Fleet Registers. Comprising the History of Fleet Marriages, and Some Account of the Parsons and Marriage-House Keepers . . .* London: Rivingtons et al., 1833.

Butler, Lindley S. *A History of North Carolina in the Proprietary Era, 1629–1729.* Chapel Hill: University of North Carolina Press, 2022.

Byrd, William. *The Secret Diary of William Byrd of Westover, 1709–1712.* Richmond, VA: The Dietz Press, 1941. Ebook, Internet Archive. https://openlibrary.org/books/OL6423476M.

Byrne, Marcus, and Helen Lunn. *Dance of the Dung Beetles: Their Role in our Changing World.* Johannesburg, South Africa: Wits University Press, 2019.

Carney, Judith A., and Richard Nicholas Rosomoff. *In the Shadow of Slavery: Africa's Botanical Legacy in the Atlantic World.* Berkeley: University of California Press, 2010.

Catesby, Mark. *The natural history of Carolina, Florida, and the Bahama Islands: Containing the figures of birds, beasts, fishes, serpents, insects, and plants: Particularly, the forest-trees, shrubs, and other plants, not hitherto described, or very incorrectly figured by the authors. Together with their descriptions in English and French. To which, are added observations on the air, soil, and waters: With remarks upon agriculture, grain, pulse, roots, & c. To the whole is prefixed a new and correct map of the countries treated.* 2 volumes. London: Published by the author, 1731–1743. https://www.biodiversitylibrary.org /item/126524.

———. *Hortus Britanno-Americanus: Or, A Curious Collection of Trees And Shrubs: the Produce of the British Colonies In North America; Adapted to the Soil And Climate of England . . .* London: Printed by W. Richardson and S. Clark for J. Ryall, 1763. https://catalog .hathitrust.org/Record/100971529/Home.

———. "Of Birds of Passage," March 5, 1746 *Philosophical Transactions.* Royal Society Vol. 44 (1746–1747), pp. 435–444.

Cobb, Charles R., and Stephanie Sapp. "Imperial Anxiety and the Dissolution of Colonial Space and Practice at Fort Moore, South Carolina." In Ferris, Neal, Rodney Harrison, and Michael Wilcox, eds., *Rethinking Colonial Pasts through Archaeology.* Oxford: Oxford University Press, 2015.

Coleridge, Samuel Taylor. *Table Talk of Samuel Taylor Coleridge and The Rime of the Ancient Mariner, Christabel, &c.* London: George Routledge and Sons, 1884. https://archive.org/details /tabletalksamuel01morlgoog/page/n150/mode/2up.

Cooper, James Fenimore. *Leatherstocking Tales, Volume I.* New York: Library of America, 1985.

Cowan, Brian. *The Social Life of Coffee: The Emergence of the British Coffeehouse.* New Haven, CT: Yale University Press, 2005.

Coxe, William. *Memoirs of the Life and Administration of Sir Robert Walpole, Earl of Orford.* London: Longman, Hurst, Rees, Orme, & Brown, 1816.

Crane, Verner W. *The Southern Frontier, 1670–1732.* Durham, NC: Duke University Press, 1928.

Dalrymple, William. *The Anarchy: The East India Company, Corporate Violence, and the Pillage of an Empire.* New York: Bloomsbury Publishing, 2019. Kindle edition.

Dampier, William. *A New Voyage Round the World.* London: Penguin Books, 2020. Kindle edition.

Delbourgo, James. *Collecting the World: Hans Sloane and the Origins of the British Museum.* Cambridge, MA: Belknap Press of Harvard University Press, 2017.

Defoe, Daniel. *The Compleat English Gentleman*, Karl D. Bulbring, ed. London: David Nutt, 1890.

———. *The Complete English Tradesman: In Familiar Letters; Directing Him in All the Several Parts and Progressions of Trade . . . Calculated for the Instruction of Our Inland Tradesmen; and Especially of Young Beginners.* London: Charles Rivington, 1726.

———. *Tour through the Eastern Counties of England, 1722.* Project Gutenberg eBook, https://www.gutenberg.org/files/983/983-h /983-h.htm. Accessed April 7, 2022.

Dennison, Matthew. *The First Iron Lady: A Life of Caroline of Ansback.* London: William Collins, 2017.

Dolnick, Edward. *The Clockwork Universe: Isaac Newton, the Royal Society, and the Birth of the Modern World.* New York: HarperCollins, 2011.

Drayton, Richard. *Nature's Government: Science, Imperial Britain, and the 'Improvement' of the World.* New Haven, CT: Yale University Press, 2000.

Dunn, Richard S. *Sugar and Slaves: The Rise of the Planter Class in the English West Indies, 1624–1713.* Williamsburg, VA: Omohundro

Institute of Early American History and Culture; Chapel Hill: University of North Carolina Press, 1972.

Edgar, Walter. *South Carolina: A History.* Columbia: University of South Carolina Press, 1998.

Eustace, Nicole. *Covered with Night: A Story of Murder and Indigenous Justice in Early America.* New York: Liveright Publishing Company, 2021.

Fairchild, Thomas. *The city gardener. Containing the most experienced method of cultivating and ordering such ever-greens, fruit-trees, flowering shrubs, flowers, exotick plants, &c. as will be ornamental, and thrive best in the London gardens.* Printed for T. Woodward, at the Half-Moon against St. Dunstan's Church in Fleet-Street, and J. Peele, at Locke's Head in Pater-Noster Row, 1722. Eighteenth Century Collections Online, link.gale.com/apps/doc /CW0109302458/ECCO?u=tel_a_uots&sid=bookmark-ECCO &xid= dd31f971&pg=1. Accessed September 8, 2021.

Feduccia, Alan, ed. *Catesby's Birds of Colonial America.* The Fred W. Morrison Series in Southern Studies. Chapel Hill: University of North Carolina Press, 1985.

Ferris, Neal, Rodney Harrison, and Michael V. Wilcox, eds. *Rethinking Colonial Pasts through Archaeology.* Oxford, UK: Oxford University Press, 2014.

Fishman, Gail. *Journeys through Paradise: Pioneering Naturalists in the Southeast.* Gainesville: University Press of Florida, 2001.

Floud, Roderick. *England's Magnificent Gardens: How a Billion-Dollar Industry Transformed a Nation, from Charles II to Today.* New York: Pantheon Books, 2021.

Fraser, Walter J., Jr. *Charleston! Charleston! The History of a Southern City.* Columbia: University of South Carolina Press, 1989.

French, H. R. "'Ingenious & Learned Gentlemen': Social Perceptions and Self-Fashioning among Parish Elites in Essex, 1680–1740." *Social History,* Vol. 25, No. 1 (Jan. 2000), pp. 44–66. https://www.jstor .org/stable/4286608. Accessed January 9, 2021.

Frick, George F., and Raymond P. Stearns. *Mark Catesby: The Colonial Audubon.* Urbana: University of Illinois Press, 1961.

Gallay, Alan. *The Formation of a Planter Elite: Jonathan Bryan and the Southern Colonial Frontier.* Athens: University of Georgia Press, 1989.

———. *The Indian Slave Trade: The Rise of the English Empire in the American South, 1670–1717.* New Haven, CT: Yale University Press, 2002.

Gill, Anton. *The Devil's Mariner: A Life of William Dampier, Pirate and Explorer, 1651–1715*. London: Sharpe Books, 2018. Kindle edition.

Gilleir, Anke, and Aude Defurne, eds. *Strategic Imaginations: Women and the Gender of Sovereignty in European Culture*. Leuven, Belgium: Leuven University Press, 2020.

Gleick, James. *Isaac Newton*. New York: Pantheon, 2003.

Greenberg, Joel. *A Feathered River Across the Sky: The Passenger Pigeon's Flight to Extinction*. New York: Bloomsbury USA, 2014.

Greene, Jack P., and Taylor Stoermer, eds. *The Natural, Moral, and Political History of Jamaica, and the Territories thereon Depending: From the First Discovery of the Island by Christopher Columbus to the Year 1746* by James Knight. Charlottesville: University of Virginia Press, 2021, p. 644, n. 4. https://www.jstor.org/stable/j.ctv1hhj104.19. Accessed June 12, 2022.

Harris, Jessica B. *High on the Hog: A Culinary Journey from Africa to America*. New York: Bloomsbury Publishing: Kindle edition, 2011.

Hart, Emma. *Building Charleston: Town and Society in the Eighteenth-century British Atlantic World*. Charlottesville: University of Virginia Press, 2010.

Heard, Stephen B. *Charles Darwin's Barnacle and David Bowie's Spider: How Scientific Names Celebrate Adventurers, Heroes, and Even a Few Scoundrels*. New Haven, CT: Yale University Press, 2020.

Holenstein, André, Hubert Steinke, and Martin Stuber, eds., *Scholars in Action: The Practice of Knowledge and the Figure of the Savant in the 18th Century*. Leiden: Brill, 2013.

Hoskins, W. G. *The Making of the English Landscape*. Dorset: Little Toller Books, 2013.

Hulton, Paul. *America 1585: The Complete Drawings of John White*. Chapel Hill: University of North Carolina Press, 1984.

Hunter, Lynette, and Sarah Hutton, eds., *Women, Science, and Medicine 1500–1700: Mothers and Sisters of the Royal Society*. Phoenix Mill, UK: Sutton Publishing, 1997.

Iannini, Christopher P. *Fatal Revolutions: Natural History, West Indian Slavery, and the Routes of American Literature*. Williamsburg, VA: Omohundro Institute of Early American History and Culture; Chapel Hill: University of North Carolina Press, 2012. Kindle edition.

Jackson, Jerome A. *In Search of the Ivory-Billed Woodpecker*. Washington, DC: Smithsonian Books, 2004.

Johnson, Captain Charles. *A General History of the Robberies and Murders of the Most Notorious Pyrates . . .* London: Printed for Ch. Rivington et al., 1724.

Johnson, Steven. *Enemy of All Mankind: A True Story of Piracy, Power, and History's First Global Manhunt.* New York: Riverhead Books, 2020. Kindle edition.

Kenny, Kevin. *Ireland and the British Empire.* Oxford: Oxford University Press, 2006.

Knight, James, and Trevor Burnard. *The Natural, Moral, and Political History of Jamaica, and the Territories Thereon Depending: From the First Discovery of the Island by Christopher Columbus to the Year 1746.* Jack P. Greene and Taylor Stoermer, eds., Charlottesville: University of Virginia Press, 2021. https://doi.org/10.2307/j .ctv1hhj104.

Laird, Mark, and Margaret Riley. "The Congenial Climate of Coffeehouse Horticulture: The Historia plantarum rariorum and the Catalogue plantarum." In *Studies in the History of Art, Vol. 69, Symposium Papers XLVI: The Art of Natural History: Illustrated Treatises and Botanical Paintings, 1400–1850,* pp. 226–259. Washington, DC: National Gallery of Art, 2010. Stable URL: https://www.jstor.org /stable/42622440.

Langley, Batty. *New principles of gardening: or, The laying out and planting parterres, groves, wildernesses, labyrinths, avenues, parks, &c. after a more grand and rural manner, than has been done before; With Experimental Directions For raising the several Kinds of Fruit-Trees, Forest-Trees, Ever-Greens and Flowering-Shrubs with which Gardens are adorn'd. To which is added, The various Names, Descriptions, Temperatures, Medicinal Virtues, Uses and Cultivations of several Roots, Pulse, Herbs, &c. of the Kitchen and Physick Gardens, that are absolutely necessary for the Service of Families in general.* Printed for A. Bettesworth and J. Batley in Pater-Noster Row; J. Pemberton in Fleet Street; T. Bowles in St. Paul's Church-Yard; J. Clarke, under the Royal Exchange; and J. Bowles at Mercer's Hall in Cheapside, MDCCXXVIII. [1728] [1727]. Eighteenth Century Collections Online, link.gale.com/apps/doc/CW0108660926/ECCO?u=tel_a _uots&sid=bookmark-ECCO&xid= b3d47876&pg=18. Accessed March 26, 2022.

Lawson, John. *A New Voyage to Carolina; Containing the Exact Description and Natural History of That Country: Together with the Present State Thereof. And A Journal of a Thousand Miles, Travel'd Thro' Several*

Nations of Indians. Giving a Particular Account of Their Customs, Manners, &c. London: 1709. Electronic edition. https://docsouth .unc.edu/nc/lawson/lawson.html. Accessed December 13, 2020.

Linder, Suzanne Cameron. *Anglican Churches in Colonial South Carolina: Their History and Architecture.* Charleston, SC: Wyrick & Company, 2000.

Linebaugh, Peter, and Marcus Rediker. *The Many-Headed Hydra: Sailors, Slaves, Commoners, and the Hidden History of the Revolutionary Atlantic.* Boston: Beacon Press, 2000.

Linnaeus, Carl. *Lachesis Lapponica, or A Tour in Lapland.* James Edward Smith, trans. London: White & Cochrane, 1811. https://archive .org/details/lachesislapponic01linn/page/n3/mode/2up?ref=ol.

Littlefield, Daniel C. *Rice and Slaves: Ethnicity and the Slave Trade in Colonial South Carolina.* Baton Rouge: Louisiana State University Press, 1981.

Lorant, Stefan, ed. *The New World: The First Pictures of America.* New York: Duell, Sloan & Pearce, 1946.

MacGregor, Arthur, ed. *Naturalists in the Field: Collecting, Recording, and Preserving the Natural World from the Fifteenth to the Twenty-First Century.* Leiden: Brill, 2018.

"The Maria Sibylla Merian Society." https://www.themariasibyllamerian society.humanities.uva.nl.

Marschner, Joanna, David Bindman, and Lisa L. Ford, eds. *Enlightened Princesses: Caroline, Augusta, Charlotte, and the Shaping of the Modern World.* New Haven, CT: Yale University Press, 2017.

Marshall, P. J., ed. *The Oxford History of the British Empire: Volume II: The Eighteenth Century.* Oxford, UK: Oxford University Press, 1998.

McBurney, Henrietta. *Illuminating Natural History: The Art and Science of Mark Catesby.* New Haven, CT: Paul Mellon Centre for Studies in British Art, 2021.

McKeon, Michael. *The Origins of the English Novel, 1600–1740.* Baltimore: Johns Hopkins University Press, 1987.

Merian, Maria Sibylla. *Insects of Surinam.* Los Angeles: Taschen America, 2009.

"Merianin." Website devoted to Maria Sibylla Merian. https://merianin .de/en/.

Meyers, Amy R. W., and Margaret Beck Pritchard, eds., *Empire's Nature: Mark Catesby's New World Vision.* Williamsburg, VA: Omohundro Institute of Early American History and Culture; Chapel Hill: University of North Carolina Press, 1998.

Miller, Lulu. *Why Fish Don't Exist: A Story of Loss, Love, and the Hidden Order of Life*. New York: Simon & Schuster, 2020.

Miller, Philip. *The Gardeners Dictionary: Containing the Methods of Cultivating and Improving the Kitchen, Fruit and flower garden*. London: n.p., 1733.

Mitchell, B. R. *British Historical Statistics*. New York: Cambridge University Press, 1988.

Moor, Robert. *On Trails: An Exploration*. New York: Simon & Schuster, 2016. Kindle edition.

Morgan, Philip D. *Slave Counterpoint: Black Culture in the Eighteenth-Century Chesapeake and Lowcountry*. Williamsburg, VA: Omohundro Institute of Early American History and Culture; Chapel Hill: University of North Carolina Press, 1998.

Morgan, Philip D., J. R. McNeill, Matthew Mulcahy, and Stuart B. Schwartz. *Sea and Land: An Environmental History of the Caribbean*. New York: Oxford University Press, 2022.

Nelson, E. Charles, and David J. Elliott, eds., *The Curious Mister Catesby: A "Truly Ingenious" Naturalist Explores New Worlds*. The Catesby Commemorative Trust. Athens: University of Georgia Press, 2015.

Nicholls, Steve. *Paradise Found: Nature in America at the Time of Discovery*. Chicago: University of Chicago Press, 2009.

Nobles, Gregory. *John James Audubon: The Nature of the American Woodsman*. Philadelphia: University of Pennsylvania Press, 2017.

Ogilvie, Brian W. *The Science of Describing: Natural History in Renaissance Europe*. Chicago: University of Chicago Press, 2006.

Parker, Matthew. *The Sugar Barons: Family, Corruption, Empire, and War in the West Indies*. New York: Walker & Company, 2011.

Parrish, Susan Scott. *American Curiosity: Cultures of Natural History in the Colonial British Atlantic World*. Williamsburg, VA: Omohundro Institute of Early American History and Culture; Chapel Hill: University of North Carolina Press, 2006.

Pepys, Samuel. *The Diary of Samuel Pepys*. https://www.pepysdiary.com/diary/1666/09/.

Picard, Liza. *Dr. Johnson's London: Everyday Life in London 1740–1770*. London: Phoenix, 2000. Kindle edition.

———. *Restoration London: Everyday Life in London 1660–1670*. London: Phoenix, 2013. Kindle edition.

Pietsch, Theodore Wells. *Charles Plumier (1646–1704) and His Drawings of French and Caribbean Fishes*. Paris: Publications Scientifiques du Muséum, 2017.

Porter, Roy. *English Society in the Eighteenth Century*. The Penguin Social History of Britain. London: Penguin Books, 1990.

Preston, Diana, and Michael Preston. *A Pirate of Exquisite Mind: The Life of William Dampier*. London: Transworld, 2010.

Rediker, Marcus. *Between the Devil and the Deep Blue Sea: Merchant Seamen, Pirates, and the Anglo-American Maritime World, 1700–1750*. Cambridge, UK: Cambridge University Press, 1989.

———. *Villains of All Nations: Atlantic Pirates in the Golden Age*. Boston: Beacon Press, 2004.

Robertson, Ritchie. *The Enlightenment: The Pursuit of Happiness, 1680–1790*. New York: Harper, 2021.

Rogers, George C., Jr. *Charleston in the Age of the Pinckneys*. Norman: University of Oklahoma Press, 1969.

Sansavior, Eva, and Richard Scholar, eds., *Caribbean Globalizations, 1492 to the Present Day*. Liverpool: Liverpool University Press, 2015.

Simon, Robin. *Hogarth, France, and British Art: The Rise of the Arts in 18th-Century Britain*. London: Hogarth Arts, 2007.

Slaughter, Thomas P., and William Bartram. *William Bartram: Travels and Other Writings*. New York: Library of America, 1996.

Sloan, Kim. *A New World: England's First View of America*. Chapel Hill: University of North Carolina Press, 2007.

Sloane, Sir Hans. *A voyage to the islands Madera, Barbados, Nieves, S. Christophers and Jamaica, with the natural history of the herbs and trees, four-footed beasts, fishes, birds, insects, reptiles, &c. of the last of those islands; to which is prefix'd an introduction, wherein is an account of the inhabitants, air, waters, diseases, trade, &c. of that place, with some relations concerning the neighbouring continent, and islands of America. Illustrated with figures of the things described, which have not been heretofore engraved; in large copper-plates as big as the life*. London: Printed by B.M. for the Author, 1707. Ebook, Internet Archive. https://archive.org/details/mobot31753000 820123.

Snyder, Noel F. R. *The Carolina Parakeet: Glimpses of a Vanished Bird*. Princeton, NJ: Princeton University Press, 2004.

Stuart, Andrea. *Sugar in the Blood: A Family's Story of Slavery and Empire*. New York: Alfred A. Knopf, 2013.

Tarter, Brent. *Virginians and Their Histories*. Charlottesville: University of Virginia Press, 2020.

Tinniswood, Adrian. *The Royal Society and the Invention of Modern Science*. New York: Basic Books, 2019. Kindle edition.

Todd, Kim. *Chrysalis: Maria Sibylla Merian and the Secrets of Metamorphosis*. Orlando: Harcourt, 2007.

Twitty, Michael W. *The Cooking Gene: A Journey through African American Culinary History in the Old South*. New York: Amistad, 2018.

Vickery, Amanda. *Behind Closed Doors: At Home in Georgian England*. New Haven, CT: Yale University Press, 2009.

Wadmore, James Foster. *Some Account of the Worshipful Company of Skinners of London: Being the Guild Or Fraternity of Corpus Christi*. London: Blades, East & Blades, 1902.

Weatherford, Jack. *Indian Givers: How Native Americans Transformed the World*. New York: Broadway Books, 2010.

Wood, Peter H. *Black Majority: Negroes in South Carolina from 1670 through the Stono Rebellion*. New York: W. W. Norton, 1996.

Wulf, Andrea. *The Brother Gardeners: Botany, Empire, and the Birth of an Obsession*. New York: Vintage Books, 2010.

——— . *Founding Gardeners: The Revolutionary Generation, Nature, and the Shaping of the American Nation*. New York: Alfred A. Knopf, 2011.

———. *The Invention of Nature: Alexander von Humboldt's New World*. New York: Alfred A. Knopf, 2015.

NOTES

Abbreviations:

MC   Mark Catesby

INH   *Illuminating Natural History*

Note: All letters from Mark Catesby are cited from Henrietta McBurney, *Illuminating Natural History: The Art and Science of Mark Catesby* (New Haven, CT: Paul Mellon Centre for Studies in British Art, 2021).

Prologue

p. xii   "to discribe the Natural productions of the Country": MC to the Earl of Oxford, August 20, 1724.

p. xii   "Observe the Rarities of the Country for the Uses and Purposes of the [Royal] Society": *Council Minutes of the Royal Society,* October 20, 1720; quoted in George F. Frick and Raymond P. Stearns, *Mark Catesby: The Colonial Audubon* (Urbana: University of Illinois Press, 1961), 18.

p. xv   "the ways in which English colonists, enslaved peoples of African descent, and native Americans were coming together": Amy R. W. Meyers, "Picturing a World in Flux: Mark Catesby's Response to Environmental Interchange and Colonial Expansion," in Amy R. W. Meyers and Margaret Beck Pritchard, eds. *Empire's Nature: Mark Catesby's New World Vision* (Williamsburg, VA: Omohundro Institute of Early American History and Culture; Chapel Hill: University of North Carolina Press, 1998), 229.

p. xvi   Only fifty years later: George Macartney, *An Account of Ireland in 1773 by a Late Chief Secretary of that Kingdom*, 55; cited in Kevin Kenny, *Ireland and the British Empire* (Oxford: Oxford University Press, 2006), 72 fn. 22.

p. xviii   "To the Hospitality and Assistance of these Friendly Indians": Catesby, *Natural History*, viii–ix.

Chapter 1: The Augustan Age

p. 1   only World War I: Matthew Parker, *The Sugar Barons: Family, Corruption, Empire, and War in the West Indies* (New York: Walker & Company, 2011), 47.

p. 2   "is said to have died": "Jekyll Family History." http://www.archerfamily.org.uk/family/jekyll.html. Accessed March 13, 2022.

p. 2   Captain Richard Catesby: *British Civil Wars, Commonwealth, and Protectorate 1638–1660*. http://wiki.bcw-project.org/royalist/dragoon-regiments/sir-robert-howard. Accessed April 5, 2022.

p. 2   a John Catesby was quartermaster: Ibid.

p. 2   A Captain Catesby: *British History Online*. https://www.british-history.ac.uk/commons-jrnl/vol2/pp891-892#h3-0008. Accessed April 5, 2022.

p. 2   the hearth-tax rolls: *British History Online*. https://www.british-history.ac.uk/london-hearth-tax/london-mddx/1666/st-dunstan-in-the-west-fleet-street. Accessed April 5, 2022.

p. 2   "Lord! How empty the streets are": Samuel Pepys, "Diary Entries from September 1666," *The Diary of Samuel Pepys*. https://www.pepysdiary.com/diary/1666/09/. Accessed April 6, 2022.

p. 3   "if any House be Infected": "Orders for the Prevention of the Plague, 1666," *The National Archives*. https://www.nationalarchives.gov.uk/education/resources/great-plague/source-2/. Accessed April 6, 2022.

p. 3   Seven months later: "Where the Great Fire of London Really Began," *Country Life* (February 12, 2016). https://www.countrylife.co.uk/country-life/where-the-great-fire-of-london-began-83288. Accessed March 16, 2022.

p. 3   Among those losing their homes: "Jekyll Family History." http://www.archerfamily.org.uk/family/jekyll.html. Accessed March 13, 2022.

p. 3 "the burning still rages": *The Diary of John Evelyn*, II, ed. William Bray (London: M. Walter Dunne, 1901). https://www .gutenberg.org/files/42081/42081-h/42081-h.htm. Accessed January 28, 2022.

p. 5 Even the medieval sport of cricket: Roy Porter, *English Society in the Eighteenth Century*, The Penguin Social History of Britain (London: Penguin Books, 1990), 236.

p. 5 "represented the temperate and tolerant society": Ibid., 235, 236.

p. 6 "danced in step to the phases of nature": Ibid., 11.

p. 7 "reached for a book in the evenings": W. G. Hoskins, *The Making of the English Landscape* (Dorset: Little Toller Books, 2013), 150.

p. 7 "the very touchstone": Thomas Mun, *A Discourse of Trade, from England unto the East Indies By T.M.*, London, 1621; quoted in William Dalrymple, *The Anarchy: The East India Company, Corporate Violence, and the Pillage of an Empire* (New York: Bloomsbury Publishing, 2019; Kindle edition), 21.

p. 7 "Some of the greatest and best": Daniel Defoe, *The Complete English Tradesman: In Familiar Letters; Directing Him in All the Several Parts and Progressions of Trade . . . Calculated for the Instruction of Our Inland Tradesmen; and Especially of Young Beginners* (London: Charles Rivington, 1726), 370, 371.

p. 8 "an informal empire of gentlemanly amateurs": Richard Drayton, "Knowledge and Empire," in *The Oxford History of the British Empire: Volume II: The Eighteenth Century*, ed. P. J. Marshall (Oxford: Oxford University Press, 1998), 237.

p. 9 Letters were also published: Ritchie Robertson, *The Enlightenment: The Pursuit of Happiness, 1680–1790* (New York: Harper, 2021), 375.

p. 10 "the courtly man of parts": James Delbourgo, *Collecting the World: Hans Sloane and the Origins of the British Museum* (Cambridge, MA: Belknap Press of Harvard University Press, 2017), 30.

p. 10 a virtuoso should ideally be: H. R. French, "'Ingenious & Learned Gentlemen': Social Perceptions and Self-Fashioning among Parish Elites in Essex, 1680–1740," *Social History* 25, no. 1 (January 2000), 60. https://www.jstor.org/stable/4286608. Accessed January 9, 2021.

p. 10 To be truly curious: Henrietta McBurney, *INH*, 14–15.

p. 10   "A telescope in the library": Amanda Vickery, *Behind Closed Doors: At Home in Georgian England* (New Haven, CT: Yale University Press, 2009), 243, 262.

p. 10   The Georgians were fascinated: Porter, *English Society in the Eighteenth Century*, 225.

p. 10   "Young aristocrats were expected": Roderick Floud, *England's Magnificent Gardens: How a Billion-Dollar Industry Transformed a Nation, from Charles II to Today* (New York: Pantheon Books, 2021), 60–61.

p. 11   What began in medieval times: Delbourgo, *Collecting the World*, 294.

p. 12   We have these details: Kim Todd, *Chrysalis: Maria Sibylla Merian and the Secrets of Metamorphosis* (Orlando: Harcourt, 2007), 122.

p. 13   The list of additions: David Brigham, "Mark Catesby and the Patronage of Natural History in the First Half of the Eighteenth Century," in Meyers and Beck Pritchard, *Empire's Nature*, 130.

p. 13   "You cannot err": Sloane to Sherard, September 2, 1698; quoted in Delbourgo, *Collecting the World*, 209.

p. 14   "gather yr speciments": Quoted in Charles E. Jarvis, "'Take with you a small Spudd or Trowell': James Petiver's Directions for Collecting Natural Curiosities," in *Naturalists in the Field: Collecting, Recording, and Preserving the Natural World from the Fifteenth to the Twenty-First Century*, ed. Arthur MacGregor (Leiden: Brill, 2018), 215.

p. 14   "In the Choice of these Things": Arthur MacGregor, Introduction, in MacGregor, *Naturalists in the Field*, 21.

p. 14   At this point in the Society's history: Delbourgo, *Collecting the World*, 161.

p. 15   "I earnestly intreat": MC to Collinson, January 5, 1723.

p. 15   Catesby and Bartram: Frick and Stearns, *Mark Catesby*, 90.

Chapter 2 Sudbury and Castle Hedingham 1683–1712

p. 17   The short interval: Frick and Stearns, *Mark Catesby*, 3.

p. 17   Five of those she delivered: McBurney, *INH*, 36.

p. 17   "I know nothing for which [Sudbury] is remarkable": Daniel Defoe, *Tour through the Eastern Counties of England, 1722*, Project Gutenberg eBook. https://www.gutenberg.org/files/983/983-h/983-h.htm. Accessed April 7, 2022.

p. 17   Defoe has been described: Robert McCrum, "The 100 Best Nonfiction Books: No 89—*A Tour Through the Whole Island of*

Great Britain by Daniel Defoe (1727)," *The Guardian*, October 16, 2017. https://www.theguardian.com/books/2017/oct/16/100 -best-nonfiction-books-no-89-a-tour-through-the-whole-island -of-great-britain-daniel-defoe-1727. Accessed April 8, 2022.

p. 18   His was an open landscape: Hoskins, *The Making of the English Landscape*, 170.

p. 18   "Mr. Catesby's House": Emma Brennan, "Trust Visit Highlighted Sudbury's Links to Renowned Artist Mark Catesby," *East Anglian Daily Times*, July 29, 2015. https://www .eadt.co.uk/news/trust-visit-highlighted-sudbury-s-links-to -renowned-artist-mark-2221170. Accessed May 5, 2022.

p. 19   He served as Sudbury's town clerk: Frick and Stearns, *Mark Catesby*, 5.

p. 19   "The professions flourished": Peter Ackroyd, *Revolution: The History of England: From the Battle of the Boyne to the Battle of Waterloo* (New York: Thomas Dunne Books, 2016), 102.

p. 19   In most cases: H. R. French, "'Ingenious & Learned Gentlemen,'" 48.

p. 19   These new professions: Porter, *English Society in the Eighteenth Century*, 41.

p. 19   In 1673 he was elected: Phillip Ludgrove, Beadle/Houseman of the Skinners' Company, email to the author, March 16, 2022.

p. 19   Known as the Skinners' Company. https://en.wikipedia.org /wiki/Livery_company. Accessed March 17, 2022.

p. 20   As warden, John Catesby: James Foster Wadmore, *Some Account of the Worshipful Company of Skinners of London: Being the Guild Or Fraternity of Corpus Christi* (London: Blades, East & Blades, 1902), 148.

p. 20   "John Catesby and William Cook Gentlemen": *House of Commons Journal* 12 (February 27, 1699): 528–531. https://www .british-history.ac.uk/commons-jrnl/vol12/pp528-531. Accessed July 15, 2022.

p. 20   "Since the mid-16th century": P. R. N. Carter, "Rich, Richard, First Baron Rich (1496/7–1567), Lord Chancellor," *Oxford Dictionary of National Biography*, September 23, 2004. https ://www.oxforddnb.com/view/10.1093/ref:odnb/9780198614128 .001.0001/odnb-9780198614128-e-23491. Accessed July 18, 2022.

p. 21   Two of Oliver Cromwell's sons: "Felsted School: History and Archives." https://www.felsted.org/about-felsted/history -and-archives. Accessed May 20, 2022.

p. 21   "the great schools of Eton": Daniel Defoe, *The Compleat English Gentleman*, ed. Karl D. Bulbring (London: David Nutt, 1890), 8.

p. 21   The next brother, Jekyll: McBurney, *INH*, 287 n. 22.

p. 21   Mark inherited houses in Sudbury: Frick and Stearns, *Mark Catesby*, 10.

p. 22   "a Father to [Mark]": Quoted in McBurney, *INH*, 287 n. 5.

p. 22   Most importantly for his nephew's future: Frick and Stearns, *Mark Catesby*, 6–8.

p. 23   After receiving his degree in 1648: Birkhead, *The Wonderful Mr Willughby* (London: Bloomsbury Publishing, 2018; Kindle edition), 34, 39.

p. 23   Scholars even today are unsure: Susan McMahon, *John Ray (1627–1705) and the Act of Uniformity 1662*, Notes and Records of the Royal Society of London (Royal Society, May 2000), 153. https://www.jstor.org/stable/531964. Accessed May 22, 2022.

p. 24   "a blockbuster": Birkhead, *The Wonderful Mr Willughby*, 238–239, 243.

p. 24   The *History of Insects*: Ibid., 268.

p. 25   Given these men's training and biases: Patrick Armstrong, *The English Parson-Naturalist: A Companionship between Science and Religion* (Leominster, UK: Gracewing, 2000), ix.

p. 25   "No work was more important in its propagation": Drayton, "Knowledge and Empire," 234.

p. 26   "Admitting the World to have been universally replenished": MC, *Natural History*, I, xv.

p. 26   "protected from the Cold": MC, *Natural History*, I, xvii.

p. 26   including his *Historia Plantarum*: Delbourgo, *Collecting the World*, 158.

p. 26   When Sloane was compiling his book: Sir Hans Sloane, *A voyage to the islands Madera, Barbados, Nieves, S. Christophers and Jamaica* . . . (London: Printed by B.M. for the Author, 1707), Preface, 4 (unpaginated). Ebook, Internet Archive. https://archive.org/details/mobot31753000820123.

p. 26   "when he was a small boy": Quoted in McBurney, *INH*, 39.

p. 27   "hapned to fall into the acquaintance": Quoted in Frick and Stearns, *Mark Catesby*, 9.

p. 27   "On the Coasts of America": MC to Sherard, May 5, 1722.

p. 27   "in all probability": Frick and Stearns, *Mark Catesby*, 10.

p. 28   the Republic of Letters was making regular deliveries: Armstrong, *The English Parson-Naturalist*, 15.

p. 28   "The early Inclination I had": MC, *Natural History*, I, v.

p. 30   It was a time when credentials and formal training were nonexistent: Porter, *English Society in the Eighteenth Century*, 76.

p. 30   "not bred a Painter": MC, *Natural History*, I, Preface, xi.

p. 31   By the time he departed: McBurney, *INH*, 103–104.

Chapter 3 The Temple Coffee House Club and the Royal Society

p. 33   "The Vertue of the COFFEE Drink": "The Vertue of the Coffee Drink." https://commons.wikimedia.org/wiki/File:The_Vertue _of_the_COFFEE_Drink.jpg. Accessed June 1, 2022.

p. 33   At their peak: Bonnie Calhoun, "Shaping the Public Sphere: EnglishCoffeehouses and French Salons and the Age of the Enlightenment," *Colgate Academic Review* 3, Article 7 (June 2012), 75.

p. 34   "a roaring fire guaranteed warmth": Ackroyd, *Revolution*, 37.

p. 34   most of London's coffeehouses: Liza Picard, *Dr. Johnson's London: Everyday Life in London 1724–1770* (London: Phoenix, 2000; Kindle edition), loc. 4286.

p. 34   Coffeehouses were so effective: Brian Cowan, *The Social Life of Coffee: The Emergence of the British Coffeehouse* (New Haven, CT: Yale University Press, 2005), 99.

p. 34   The coffeehouses were clustered: Nic Butler, "The Carolina Coffee House of London," *Charleston Time Machine*, January 30, 2020. https://www.ccpl.org/charleston-time-machine/carolina -coffee-house-london. Accessed January 6, 2022.

p. 34   traders to the Baltic: Picard, *Dr. Johnson's London*; Kindle edition, loc. 4286.

p. 35   the Grecian in Devereux Court: Delbourgo, *Collecting the World*, 154.

p. 35   the coffeehouse for naturalists: Margaret Riley, "The Club at Temple Coffee House," in *Studies in the History of Art, Volume 69: The Art of Natural History* (Washington, DC: National Gallery of Art, 2010), 253.

p. 35   "to pore over plant specimens": Riley, "The Club at Temple Coffee House," 253.

p. 35   Samuel Dale, apothecary-botanist: Ibid., 255.

p. 35   at the Temple you might encounter: Richard Drayton, *Nature's Government: Science, Imperial Britain, and the 'Improvement' of the World* (New Haven, CT: Yale University Press, 2000), 36.

p. 35   "tradesmen mingled easily with gentlemen": Frick and Stearns, *Mark Catesby*, 86.

p. 35   they were such a novelty: Cowan, *The Social Life of Coffee*, 228.

p. 35   "both a significant focal point": Riley, "The Club at Temple Coffee House," 257.

p. 35   "every member was obliged": McBurney, *INH*, 32.

p. 36   In 1662 the society received: "History of the Royal Society," Royal Society. https://royalsociety.org/about-us/history/. Accessed January 2, 2021.

p. 36   a lamp would be hung: Adrian Tinniswood, *The Royal Society and the Invention of Modern Science* (New York: Basic Books, 2019; Kindle edition), 58.

p. 37   science was being promulgated: John G. T. Anderson, *Deep Things Out of Darkness: A History of Natural History* (Berkeley: University of California Press, 2013), 52. https://www.jstor.org/stable/10.1525/j.ctt24hshw. Accessed January 5, 2022.

p. 38   the Society was careful to stress: Tinniswood, *The Royal Society*, 61.

p. 38   "for the use of travellers": Robert Boyle, "General heads for a natural history of a countrey, great or small, imparted likewise by Mr. Boyle," *Philosophical Transactions of the Royal Society* 1, no. 11 (April 12, 1666): 186, 188. https://royalsocietypublishing.org/doi/10.1098/rstl.1665.0082. Accessed January 5, 2022.

p. 38   "What Animals the Country has": Ibid., 188–189.

p. 38   "harnessed national commerce": Drayton, *Nature's Government*, 17.

p. 39   Merchants were recruited: Michael McKeon, *The Origins of the English Novel, 1600–1740* (Baltimore: Johns Hopkins University Press, 1987), 101.

p. 39   "array of Caribbean specimens": Christopher P. Iannini, *Fatal Revolutions: Natural History, West Indian Slavery, and the Routes of American Literature* (Williamsburg, VA: Omohundro Institute of Early American History and Culture; Chapel Hill: University of North Carolina Press, 2012; Kindle edition), 55.

p. 39   there were those exceptions: Porter, *English Society in the Eighteenth Century*, 23–24.

p. 39   The technology and knowledge needed: Hilary Rose, Foreword, in Lynette Hunter and Sarah Hutton, eds., *Women, Science, and Medicine 1500–1700: Mothers and Sisters of the Royal Society* (Phoenix Mill, UK: Sutton Publishing, 1997), xii.

p. 40   This experience had obvious applications: Lynette Hunter, "Women and Domestic Medicine: Lady Experimenters, 1570–1620," in Hunter and Hutton, *Women, Science, and Medicine*, 98.

p. 40   "emphasized the conversational benefits": Rob Iliffe and Frances Willmoth, "Astronomy and the Public Sphere: Margaret Flamsteed and Caroline Herschel as Assistant-Astronomers," in Hunter and Hutton, *Women, Science, and Medicine*, 241.

p. 41   "the epicenter for conversations about the colony": Nic Butler, "The Carolina Coffee House of London."

p. 42   "Discourse upon the usefulness of silk of spiders": *Philosophical Transactions* (January 1, 1710). https://royalsocietypublishing.org/doi/10.1098/rstl.1710.0001. Accessed February 1, 2022.

Chapter 4 Williamsburg, William Byrd, and the Frontier 1712–1717

p. 43   "where I arriv'd:" MC, *Natural History*, I, v.

p. 44   "supposed Husband": Frick and Stearns, *Mark Catesby*, 11.

p. 44   In Virginia, he became an ally: Ibid., 11–12.

p. 45   In Williamsburg, however: Brent Tarter, *Virginians and Their Histories* (Charlottesville: University of Virginia Press, 2020), 84.

p. 45   "live in the same neat manner": Quoted in Frick and Stearns, *Mark Catesby*, 12.

p. 45   "was not an impartial observer": Sarah Hand Meacham, "Mark Catesby's World: Virginia," in E. Charles Nelson and David J. Elliott, eds., *The Curious Mister Catesby: A "Truly Ingenious" Naturalist Explores New Worlds* (Athens: University of Georgia Press, 2015), 97.

p. 45   "criss-crossed the Atlantic": Delbourgo, *Collecting the World*, 239.

p. 46   "directed how I should mend my garden": William Byrd, *The Secret Diary of William Byrd of Westover, 1709–1712* (Richmond, VA: Dietz Press, 1941), Open Library. https://openlibrary.org/books/OL6423476MByrd.

p. 46   which typically took between four and nine hours: Meacham, "Mark Catesby's World: Virginia," 104.

p. 46   It was a sociable time: Frick and Stearns, *Mark Catesby*, 13.

p. 46   "were so merry": Byrd, *Secret Diary*, June 14, 1712.

p. 47   "I beat Jenny": Ibid., September 3, 1709.

p. 47   "found it in *his* Interest": MC, *Natural History*, I, xvii.

p. 48   "There is an Indian": Byrd, *Secret Diary*, September 23, 1709.

p. 48   "In the Year 1714": MC, *Natural History*, I, v.

p. 49   "in effect, one vast Indian orchard": Steve Nicholls, *Paradise Found: Nature in America at the Time of Discovery* (Chicago: University of Chicago Press, 2009), 120, 121.

p. 49 "an annual custom of the Indians": MC, *Natural History*, I, ii.

p. 49 "destroy'd in great Numbers": Ibid., xii.

p. 50 "I chiefly gratified my Inclination": Ibid., v.

p. 50 "on the opposite Shore": Ibid., ii–iii.

p. 51 "Sweet flowering Acacia": Quoted in Frick and Stearns, *Mark Catesby*, 14.

p. 51 "only [sent] from thence": Catesby, *Natural History*, I, v.

p. 52 "Checklist of Essential Material for Safely Shipping Plants": "Shipping Plants: Tips to Safely Ship Live Plants." https://www.easyship.com/blog/how-to-ship-plants. Accessed May 15, 2022.

p. 52 "a well-labeled herbarium specimen": Stephen A. Harris, "The Plant Collections of Mark Catesby in Oxford," in Nelson and Elliott, *The Curious Mister Catesby*, 173.

p. 52 around two thousand dried specimens: McBurney, *INH*, 221.

p. 52 Others were more interested: Ibid., 18.

p. 53 Mark may therefore have thought it necessary: E. Charles Nelson, "'The Truly Honest, Ingenious, and Modest Mr. Mark Catesby, F.R.S.': Documenting His Life (1682/83–1749)," in Nelson and Elliott, *The Curious Mister Catesby*, 9.

Chapter 5 Jamaica and the Caribbean 1717–1718

p. 55 "as they approached the South": Catesby, *Natural History*, I, xi.

p. 56 "At some leagues distance": James Knight, *The Natural, Moral, and Political History of Jamaica, and the Territories thereon Depending: From the First Discovery of the Island by Christopher Columbus to the Year 1746*, edited by Jack P. Greene and Taylor Stoermer (Charlottesville: University of Virginia Press, 2021), 387–388. https://www.jstor.org/stable/j.ctv1hhj104.19. Accessed June 12, 2022.

p. 57 "was extremely pleased with this Island": Sloane, *A voyage to the islands*, iii.

p. 58 "the Settlements and Plantations": Ibid., v.

p. 58 Jamaica by 1680: Parker, *The Sugar Barons*, 173.

p. 58 Morgan and his men fought their way: Ibid., 141.

p. 59 "When the Sand tumbled": Sloane, *A voyage to the islands*, lix.

p. 59 A yellow fever epidemic: Parker, *The Sugar Barons*, 196.

p. 60 "in one deft move": Marcus Rediker, *Between the Devil and the Deep Blue Sea: Merchant Seamen, Pirates and the Anglo-American Maritime World, 1700–1750* (Cambridge: Cambridge University Press, 1989), 57.

p. 61   The resulting boom in the slave trade: Marcus Rediker, *Villains of All Nations: Atlantic Pirates in the Golden Age* (Boston: Beacon Press, 2004), 143–145.

p. 61   One seventeenth-century English merchant seaman: Rediker, *Devil*, 80.

p. 61   there is some foundation: Arne Bialuschewski, "Daniel Defoe, Nathaniel Mist, and the 'General History of the Pyrates,'" *Papers of the Bibliographical Society of America* 98, no. 1 (March 2004): 21–38. https://www.jstor.org/stable/24295828. Accessed June 15, 2022.

p. 62   "the Truth of it can be no more contested": Capt. Charles Johnson, *A General History of the Robberies and Murders of the Most Notorious Pyrates* (London: 1724), 153.

p. 62   "consciously cultivated an image of himself": Rediker, *Villains*, 153.

p. 62   Other recurring Jolly Roger symbols: Rediker, *Devil*, 278.

p. 63   Willing buyers and sellers: Rediker, *Villains*, 29.

p. 63   Information flowed constantly: Rediker, *Devil*, 133–134.

p. 64   Jamaica's planters had to stay abreast: Trevor Burnard, "Those Other English Colonies: The Historiography of Jamaica in the Time of James Knight," in Greene and Stoermer, eds., *The Natural, Moral, and Political History of Jamaica*, 648.

p. 64   The mindless, soul-numbing drudgery: Parker, *The Sugar Barons*, 54.

p. 64   "When they begin to work": Knight, *The Natural, Moral, and Political History of Jamaica*, 552.

p. 65   The resulting development: Burnard, "Those Other English Colonies," 644 n. 4.

p. 65   made keener by short life expectancies: Philip D. Morgan, "Precocious Modernity: Environmental Change in the Early Caribbean," in Eva Sansavior and Richard Scholar, eds., *Caribbean Globalizations, 1492 to the Present Day* (Liverpool: Liverpool University Press, 2015), 83. https://www.jstor.org/stable/j.ctt1g0b8p8.8. Accessed January 20, 2021.

p. 65   "The risk of early death": Parker, *The Sugar Barons*, 46.

p. 65   "The West Indies had none of the things": Ibid., 294.

p. 65   One planter's main hall: Richard S. Dunn, *Sugar and Slaves: The Rise of the Planter Class in the English West Indies, 1624–1713* (Williamsburg, VA: Omohundro Institute of Early American History and Culture; Chapel Hill: University of North Carolina Press, 1972), 263, 264. https://www.jstor.org

/stable/10.5149/9780807899823_dunn.13. Accessed March 25, 2021.

p. 66 "The Houses of considerable Planters": Sir Hans Sloane, *A voyage to the islands*, xlvii.

p. 66 His collections were funded: Delbourgo, *Collecting the World*, 188.

p. 66 The Royal Society itself: Sam Kean, "Historians Expose Early Scientists' Debt to the Slave Trade," *Science,* April 4, 2019. https://www.sciencemag.org/news/2019/04/historians-expose-early-scientists-debt-slave-trade. Accessed January 29, 2021.

p. 67 "among the few Britons": Kathleen S. Murphy, "Collecting Slave Traders: James Petiver, Natural History, and the British Slave Trade," *William and Mary Quarterly* 70, no. 4 (October 2013), 650. https://www.jstor.org/stable/10.5309/willmaryquar.70.4.0637. Accessed January 30, 2021.

p. 67 "We do not often think": Murphy, "Collecting," 669.

p. 68 The surgeons' scientific training: Ibid., 650.

p. 68 "Slave ship surgeon Richard Planer": Ibid., 643

p. 68 "Informants ranged from field slaves": Iannini, *Fatal Revolutions*.

p. 69 "a famous Negro Dr": MC to Sherrard, February 7, 1722.

p. 69 because it was so commonplace to them: Murphy, "Collecting," 646.

p. 70 "our Sugar-islands": MC, *Natural History*, II, Appendix, 6.

p. 70 "two [quires] of Jamaica plants": Frick and Stearns, *Mark Catesby*, 15.

p. 70 "They are called in Jamaica": MC, *Natural History*, II, Appendix, 2.

p. 70 "Scolopendra": David J. Elliott, "Conclusions: Account, Appendix, *Hortus*, and other endings in Mark Catesby's Work," in Nelson and Elliott, *The Curious Mister Catesby*, 322.

p. 70 "The Alligator": MC, *Natural History*, II, 63.

p. 70 "The Green Lizard of Jamaica": Ibid., 66.

p. 71 "when in Bermudas distinguish any difference": MC to J. J. Dillenius, undated (postmarked February 3, 1736), McBurney, *INH*, 269.

p. 71 "many of which altered so much": MC to J. J. Dillenius, undated (postmarked February 3, 1736), Ibid., 269.

p. 71 "Tropick Bird": MC, *Natural History*, II, Appendix, 14.

p. 71 "They are good eating Fish": MC, *Natural History*, II, 8.

Chapter 6 London 1719–1722

p. 73   "Catesby is come from Virginia": Dale to Sherard, October 15, 1719; quoted in McBurney, *INH*, 46.

p. 74   "It's [a] pitty": Frick and Stearns, *Mark Catesby*, 17.

p. 74   "a Gentleman of a small fortune": Ibid., 19.

p. 74   "sent some observations": MC, *Natural History*, I, v–vi.

p. 75   "When a man is tired of London": James Boswell, *The Life of Samuel Johnson, LL.D.* (London: Printed by Henry Baldwin, 1791), II, 160. https://archive.org/details /lifesamueljohns00baldgoog/page/160/mode/2up?q=tired. Accessed June 19, 2022.

p. 75   "Almost every Body": Thomas Fairchild, *The city gardener. Containing the most experienced method of cultivating and ordering such ever-greens, fruit-trees, flowering shrubs, flowers, exotick plants, &c. as will be ornamental, and thrive best in the London gardens.* (London: Printed for T. Woodward, at the Half-Moon against St. Dunstans Church in Fleet-Street, and J. Peele, at Locke's Head in Pater-Noster Row, 1722), 8.

p. 76   "The common green Holly": Fairchild, *The city gardener*, 15–16.

p. 76   "The Virginian Accacia": Ibid., 17.

p. 76   "a fair Flower": Ibid., 23.

p. 76   "The Creeper of Virginia": Ibid., 54–55.

p. 77   "at nearly every house in the town": Quoted in Picard, *Dr. Johnson's London*; Kindle edition, loc. 5086.

p. 78   This was a convenient way: Zara Anishanslin, *Portrait of a Woman in Silk: Hidden Histories of the British Atlantic World* (New Haven, CT: Yale University Press, 2016), 191. https://www .jstor.org/stable/j.ctt1f5g60f.13.

p. 79   Sherard found nine additional sponsors: Frick and Stearns, *Mark Catesby*, 18–19.

p. 79   "But as Expences were necessary": Catesby, *Natural History*, I, vi.

p. 79   James Brydges, the Duke of Chandos: Matthew David Mitchell, "'Legitimate Commerce' in the Eighteenth Century: The Royal African Company of England under the Duke of Chandos, 1720–1726," *Enterprise and Society* 14, no. 3 (September 2013), 545–546.

p. 80   Chandos considered Catesby: Quoted in McBurney, *INH*, 28.

p. 80   "Mr Catesby goes next week": Ibid., 50.

NOTES

Chapter 7 Charleston 1722–1724

p. 81   Those aboard also watched: MC, *Natural History*, I, Preface, vii.

p. 82   "On the Coasts of America": MC to Sherard, May 5, 1722.

p. 83   "very commodious Harbour": John Lawson, *A New Voyage to Carolina; Containing the Exact Description and Natural History of That Country: Together with the Present State Thereof. And A Journal of a Thousand Miles, Travel'd Thro' Several Nations of Indians. Giving a Particular Account of Their Customs, Manners, &c.* (London: 1709; electronic edition), Documenting the American South, University of North Carolina at Chapel Hill. https://docsouth.unc.edu/nc/lawson/lawson.html. Accessed December 13, 2020.

p. 83   "As to the Buildings": Brian J. Enright, "An Account of Charles Town in 1725," *South Carolina Historical Magazine* (January 1960), 15. https://www.jstor.org/stable/27566266. Accessed November 12, 2021.

p. 83   At the wharves: Verner W. Crane, *The Southern Frontier 1670–1732* (Durham, NC: Duke University Press, 1929), 108.

p. 83   Catesby might have been dazzled: Peter H. Wood, *Black Majority: Negroes in South Carolina from 1670 through the Stono Rebellion* (New York: W. W. Norton, 1996), 170.

p. 84   Outside the fortifications: Nic Butler, "The 'Crisp Map' of 1711," *Rediscovering Charleston's Colonial Fortifications: A Weblog for the Mayor's 'Walled City' Task Force*, April 17, 2008. https://walledcitytaskforce.org/2008/04/17/crisp-map/. Accessed January 4, 2022.

p. 84   Smallpox epidemics: Walter J. Fraser Jr., *Charleston! Charleston! The History of a Southern City* (Columbia: University of South Carolina Press, 1989), 31, 38.

p. 85   "Charleston's golden age": George C. Rogers Jr., *Charleston in the Age of the Pinckneys* (Norman: University of Oklahoma Press, 1969), 3.

p. 85   Charleston also served: Jack Weatherford, *Indian Givers: How Native Americans Transformed the World* (New York: Broadway Books, 2010), 44–45.

p. 86   As usually happened: Lindley S. Butler, *A History of North Carolina in the Proprietary Era, 1629–1729* (Chapel Hill: University of North Carolina Press, 2021), 302. https://www.jstor.org/stable/10.5149/9781469667584_butler.20. Accessed June 14, 2022.

p. 86   In Boston: Rediker, *Villains*, 173.

p. 86   "I suppose ere this": MC to Sherard, November 13, 1723.

p. 87   "I dread the mischief": MC to William Sherard, June 26, 1723; in McBurney, *INH*, 248.

p. 87   "received me with much kindness": MC to Sherard, May 5, 1722.

p. 87   "The inhabited Parts": MC, *Natural History*, I, Preface, viii.

p. 88   "I am but now returned": MC to Sherard, June 20, 1722.

p. 88   "a few common Roots": Ibid.

p. 89   "This Tree I never saw": MC, *Natural History*, I, 43.

p. 89   "a very uncommon Plant": Ibid., I, 31.

p. 89   "particularly in the path": MC, *Hortus Britanno-Americanus*, 4.

p. 90   "Concealing useful things": MC, *Natural History*, I, xiv.

p. 91   With their versatility: Suzanne Linder Hurley, "Mark Catesby's Carolina Adventure," in Nelson and Elliott, *The Curious Mister Catesby*, 113–114.

p. 91   "I must confess": Lawson, *A New Voyage*, 80–81.

p. 91   "I distributed this seed": MC to Bartram, undated (April 1744).

p. 92   "had principally a Regard": MC, *Natural History*, I, ix.

p. 92   "Of Beasts": Ibid., x.

p. 93   "I always did them": Ibid., xi.

p. 93   Although he was aiming: Shepherd Krech III, "Catesby's Birds," in MacGregor, *Naturalists in the Field*, 314.

p. 94   "where it would admit of": MC, *Natural History*, I, xi.

p. 94   "Wherever you go ashoar": Quoted in Charles E. Jarvis, "'Take with you a small Spudd or Trowell': James Petiver's Directions for Collecting Natural Curiosities," in MacGregor, *Naturalists in the Field*, 215.

p. 94   "I thought of deferring": MC to Sherard, June 20, 1722.

p. 95   In these specimens: Krech, "Catesby's Birds," 284.

p. 95   Catesby placed snakes: Hurley, "Mark Catesby's Carolina Adventure," 122.

p. 95   "Sir, I desire": MC to Fairchild, date unknown but prior to 1724.

p. 95   At least one British botanist: McBurney, *INH*, 213.

p. 96   plant boxes were often sacrificed: Andrea Wulf, *The Brother Gardeners: Botany, Empire, and the Birth of an Obsession* (New York: Vintage Books, 2010), 22.

p. 96   "I very much believe": Christopher M. Parson and Kathleen S. Murphy, "Ecosystems under Sail: Specimen Transport in the Eighteenth-Century French and British Atlantics," *Early*

American Studies (Fall 2012): 509. https://www.jstor.org
/stable/23546692. Accessed January 30, 2021.

p. 96   they also performed natural history themselves: Murphy,
"Collecting," 641.

p. 96   Roaming from London to Calcutta: Ibid., 642.

p. 97   "They are many of them surly fellows": MC to Sherard,
October 30, 1724.

p. 97   "A packet of [letters] I have put": MC to Sherard, December 9,
1722.

p. 97   "The more specimens I collect": MC to Sherard, June 20, 1722.

p. 98   "I hope it is not expected": MC to Sherard, December 9, 1722.

p. 98   "Sloane supported Catesby's work": Delbourgo, *Collecting the
World*, 242.

p. 99   "My method": MC to Sherard, January 16, 1724.

p. 99   "seized with a swelling": MC to Sherard, December 10, 1722.

p. 99   "the greatest Floud": MC to Sherard, December 9, 1722.

p. 99   "I can plainly perceive": MC to Sherard, December 9, 1722.

Chapter 8 Slave Gardens and Medicines

p. 101   "but the Slaves of South Carolina": Lawson, *A New Voyage*, 5.

p. 101   Beginning around 1710: "The Sales of Incoming Africans on
the Wharves of Colonial Charleston," *Charleston Time Machine*,
podcast, August 30, 2019. Charleston Public Library. https
://www.ccpl.org/charleston-time-machine/sales-incoming
-africans-wharves-colonial-charleston#_edn1.

p. 102   by the early 1720s: Walter Edgar, *South Carolina: A History*
(Columbia: University of South Carolina Press, 1998),
144, 151.

p. 102   In the 1720s alone, almost nine thousand slaves: Ibid., 140.

p. 103   Seven of the early Carolina governors: Parker, *The Sugar Barons*,
n. 148–149.

p. 103   "to guide us over the Head": Wood, *Black Majority*, 118.

p. 103   And under the task system: Edgar, *South Carolina*, 79.

p. 103   "Carolina in the West Indies": Iannini, *Fatal Revolutions*, 91–92.

p. 104   The 1740 act would deny slaves: Wood, *Black Majority*, 212.

p. 105   The semitropical climate: "Origins of Inland Rice," *Forgotten
Fields: Inland Rice Plantations in the South Carolina Lowcountry*.
Lowcountry Digital History Initiative at the College of
Charleston. https://ldhi.library.cofc.edu/exhibits/show
/forgotten_fields/origins_of_inland_rice.

p. 105 The Carolina method of rice farming: "Slavery," *South Carolina Encyclopedia*. https://www.scencyclopedia.org/sce/entries/slavery/. Accessed July 12, 2022.

p. 105 "Charleston's planters": Jessica B. Harris, *High on the Hog: A Culinary Journey from Africa to America* (New York: Bloomsbury Publishing, 2011; Kindle edition), 70.

p. 106 this was an echo of conditions: Michael W. Twitty, *The Cooking Gene: A Journey Through African American Culinary History in the Old South* (New York: Amistad, 2018), 266.

p. 106 Sometimes they cultivated: Harris, *High on the Hog*, 96.

p. 106 "These spaces were little landscapes of resistance": Ibid., 269.

p. 107 all these were brought to America: Edgar, *South Carolina*, 192.

p. 107 "the Negro Slaves (who only dig it)": Krech, "Catesby's Birds," 292.

p. 107 "Where a vein or Artery": MC to Sherard, January 16, 1724.

p. 107 "I being at the house of Coll Blake": Ibid.

p. 108 "so called by way Eminence": MC to Sherard, February 7, 1723.

p. 108 "a Tropick Plant": MC, *Natural History*, II, 45.

p. 109 "They have likewise": William Bartram, *Travels and Other Writings*, ed. Thomas P. Slaughter (New York: Library of America, 1996), 377.

p. 109 "all Parts of the Tree": MC, *Natural History*, II, 85.

p. 109 "is called Mush": MC, *Natural History*, I, xvii.

p. 109 "The light-coloured [crabs]": MC, *Natural History*, II, 32.

p. 109 Okra probably was first introduced: Harris, *High on the Hog*, 17.

p. 109 The mucilaginous pod: Ibid., 247.

p. 109 Watermelon arrived: Ibid., 20.

p. 110 "At a place in Carolina": *Natural History*, I, vii.

p. 110 it is easily the earliest: Frick and Stearns, *Mark Catesby*, 74.

p. 111 "I hope my Brother": MC to Sherard, May 10, 1723.

Chapter 9 Fort Moore and the Frontier 1723–1725

p. 112 "I am now on my journey": MC to Sherard, March 19, 1723.

p. 112 "decaying leaves": Edgar, *South Carolina*, 6.

p. 112 Further inland rose the sandy hills: Christopher S. Swezey et al., "The Carolina Sandhills: Quaternary Eolian Sand Sheets and Dunes along the Updip Margin of the Atlantic Coastal Plain Province, Southeastern United States," *Quaternary Research* 86, no. 3 (2016): 280. doi:10.1016/j.yqres.2016.08.007.

p. 113 It was said: Edgar, *South Carolina*, 205.

p. 113   The conquistador Hernando de Soto: Ibid., 23.

p. 114   In return, Native Americans: Charles R. Cobb and Stephanie Sapp, "Imperial Anxiety and the Dissolution of Colonial Space and Practice at Fort Moore, South Carolina," in Neal Ferris, Rodney Harrison, and Michael Wilcox, eds., *Rethinking Colonial Pasts through Archaeology* (Oxford: Oxford University Press, 2015), 219.

p. 114   By 1712 about twenty-five percent: William L. Ramsey, "A Coat for 'Indian Cuffy': Mapping the Boundary between Freedom and Slavery in Colonial South Carolina," *South Carolina Historical Magazine* 103, no. 1 (January 2002), 48. http://www.jstor.org/stable/27570546. Accessed July 20, 2022.

p. 114   If Charleston is sometimes considered: Allan Gallay, *The Formation of a Planter Elite: Jonathan Bryan and the Southern Colonial Frontier* (Athens: University of Georgia Press, 1989), 299.

p. 114   The trade in enslaved Natives and pelts: Denise I. Bossy, "Godin & Co.: Charleston Merchants and the Indian Trade, 1674–1715," *South Carolina Historical Magazine* (April 2013), 97. https://www.jstor.org/stable/23645467. Accessed December 11, 2021.

p. 115   The colony had neither the population: Allan Gallay, *The Indian Slave Trade: The Rise of the English Empire in the American South, 1670–1717* (New Haven, CT: Yale University Press, 2002), 241.

p. 115   Authorities in Charleston were barraged: Edgar, *South Carolina*, 99.

p. 115   Of course Charleston was glad: Nicole Eustace, *Covered with Night: A Story of Murder and Indigenous Justice in Early America* (New York: Liveright Publishing Company, 2021), 9.

p. 115   In the wake of the war: Edgar, *South Carolina*, 102.

p. 115   Before the war: Philip M. Brown, "Early Indian Trade in the Development of South Carolina: Politics, Economics, and Social Mobility during the Proprietary Period, 1670–1719," *South Carolina Historical Magazine* 76, no. 3 (July 1975), 122. http://www.jstor.org/stable/27567318. Accessed July 20, 2022.

p. 116   "probably came closer": Cobb and Sapp, "Imperial Anxiety," In Ferris et al., eds., *Rethinking Colonial Pasts*, 212.

p. 117   As Europeans entered the area: Louis DeVorsey, "Indian Trails," *New Georgia Encyclopedia*, last modified September 29, 2020. https://www.georgiaencyclopedia.org/articles/history-archaeology/indian-trails. Accessed July 20, 2022.

p. 117   "Col. Moore, a Gentleman": MC, *Natural History*, I, 35.

p. 118 Often traders would assemble: Crane, *The Southern Frontier*, 126.

p. 118 To keep the path's minimal width: Moor, *On Trails: An Exploration* (New York: Simon & Schuster, 2016; Kindle edition), 164–165.

p. 118 Early observers frequently noted: Ibid., 169.

p. 118 The Cherokee regularly burned: Ibid.

p. 118 "Continuing some time": Bartram, *Travels*, 55.

p. 119 "on the Banks of these Rivers": MC, *Natural History,* I, iv.

p. 119 "The woods under the noble canopy": Suzanne Cameron Linder, *Anglican Churches in Colonial South Carolina: Their History and Architecture* (Charleston: Wyrick & Company, 2000), 74.

p. 120 "a stupendous bluff": Bartram, *Travels*, 261.

p. 120 "It is one of the sweetest Countrys": MC to Sherard, May 10, 1723.

p. 120 "by direction of the governor": Cobb and Sapp, "Imperial Anxiety," In Ferris et al., eds., *Rethinking Colonial Pasts*, 220.

p. 120 archaeologists have found: Ibid., 224, 225–226.

p. 120 Its isolation and supplies: Ibid., 227–228.

p. 121 "In early times": Bartam, *Travels*, 261.

p. 122 "I never saw any of these trees": MC, *Natural History*, II, Appendix, 20.

p. 122 A common tumblebug: Marcus Byrne and Helen Lunn, *Dance of the Dung Beetles: Their Role in Our Changing World* (Johannesburg: Wits University Press, 2019), 48. https://www .jstor.org/stable/10.18772/12019042347.6. Accessed July 9, 2021.

p. 122 "I was much delighted": MC, *Natural History*, I, viii–ix.

p. 123 "Indians are wholly ignorant": Ibid., xv.

p. 123 Nowhere did he cite: Susan Scott Parrish, *American Curiosity: Cultures of Natural History in the Colonial British Atlantic World* (Williamsburg, VA: Omohundro Institute of Early American History and Culture; Chapel Hill: University of North Carolina Press, 2006), 246.

p. 123 "To the Hospitality and Assistance": MC, *Natural History*, I, viii–ix.

p. 124 "Mary Robinson Widow": *South Carolina Gazette* (Charleston), August 17, 1738, 9. Thanks to Professor Suzanne Linder Hurley for providing this source.

p. 124 "My clothes consisted": Carl Linnaeus, *Lachesis Lapponica, or A Tour in Lapland*, trans. James Edward Smith (London: White & Cochrane, 1811), 1–2. https://archive.org/details /lachesislapponic01linn. Accessed January 9, 2022.

p. 125   "Mr. Lawson . . . has given": MC, *Natural History*, I, viii.

p. 126   "inhabiting the whole Extent of North America": Ibid., vii–viii.

p. 127   "generally tall, and well shap'd": Ibid., viii.

p. 128   "They are naturally": Ibid.

p. 128   "The Hind-part of their Belly": MC, *Natural History*, II, 63.

p. 128   "There are two obstructions": MC to Sherard, May 10, 1723.

p. 128   "tho' the Cherikees were also": *Natural History*, I, xii.

p. 128   "The Indians (as to this Life)": Ibid., viii; Whitney Barlow Robles, "The Rattlesnake and the Hibernaculum: Animals, Ignorance, and Extinction in the Early American Underworld," *William and Mary Quarterly* (January 2021), 21. https://www.jstor.org/stable/10.5309/willmaryquar.78.1.0003. Accessed March 25, 2021.

p. 129   "probably has occasioned": MC, *Natural History*, I, xv–xvi.

p. 130   "I now send you Sr": MC to Sloane, November 15, 1723.

p. 130   "these few Seeds and Acorns": Catesby to Collinson, January 5, 1723.

p. 131   "the ordinary thorowfare": Col. John Barnwell, quoted in Wood, *Black Majority*, 115.

p. 131   "their masterpieces in mechanicks": MC, *Natural History*, I, xi; MC to Sloane, November 27, 1724; MC to Sherard, November 13, 1723.

p. 132   "Here is a gentleman": MC to Sherard, August 16, 1724.

p. 132   "My sending Collections": MC to Sloane, August 15, 1724.

p. 133   "The discontent of Mr. DuBois": MC to Sherard, January 10, 1725.

p. 133   "I am Sr preparing to goe": MC to Sloane, January 5, 1725.

Chapter 10 Bahamas 1725–1726

p. 135   Because the Spanish in Florida: John Fitzhugh Miller, email conversation, July 29, 2022.

p. 135   "a Tract of small Islands": MC, *Natural History*, I, xviii.

p. 136   The Bahamas contained: Philip D. Morgan, J. R. McNeill, Matthew Mulcahy, and Stuart B. Schwartz, *Sea and Land: An Environmental History of the Caribbean* (New York: Oxford University Press, 2022), 28.

p. 136   "the unfathomable Abyss": MC, *Natural History*, I, xli.

p. 136   William Dampier's *A New Voyage*: William Dampier, *A New Voyage Round the World* (London: Penguin Books, 2020; Kindle edition), 74.

p. 136   Catesby echoed that claim: MC, *Natural History*, I, xviii.

NOTES

p. 137 Living off the largesse: Morgan et al., *Sea and Land*, 57.

p. 137 The Lucayans, the branch: Ibid., 59.

p. 137 They also had grown: Ibid., 79.

p. 137 The Lucayans knew their surroundings: Ibid., 50.

p. 138 He had been specifically tasked: Rediker, *Devil*, 56.

p. 138 "a tropical pleasure dome": Steven Johnson, *Enemy of All Mankind* (New York: Riverhead, 2020; Kindle edition), 193.

p. 138 This absentee authority: Devin Leigh, "Between Swamp and Sea: Bahamian Visitors in Southeast Florida before Miami," *Florida Historical Quarterly* (Spring 2015), 520. https://www.jstor.org/stable/43487711. Accessed November 7, 2021.

p. 138 But because it threatened the slave trade: Peter Linebaugh and Marcus Rediker, *The Many-Headed Hydra: Sailors, Slaves, Commoners, and the Hidden History of the Revolutionary*, Atlantic (Boston: Beacon Press, 2000), 328.

p. 139 On the other hand: Bialuschewski, *Daniel Defoe*, 31.

p. 139 In the end, when pirates disrupted: Rediker, *Villains*, 143–145.

p. 139 As many as 500 to 600 Anglo-American pirates: Rediker, *Devil*, 283.

p. 140 His debts forgiven: Anton Gill, *The Devil's Mariner: A Life of William Dampier, Pirate and Explorer, 1651–1715* (London: Sharpe Books, 2018; Kindle edition).

p. 140 "entertain'd by him": MC, *Natural History*, I, x.

p. 140 "blessed with a most serene Air": Ibid., xix.

p. 140 In the *Natural History* Catesby describes watching Governor Phenney: MC, *Natural History*, II, Appendix, 10.

p. 140 "it was two days so cold": MC, *Natural History*, I, xix.

p. 140 "particularly Ilathera": Ibid., x.

p. 141 He had seen sturgeon: Ibid., iii.

p. 141 "there being not any": Ibid., x.

p. 141 "collected many Submarine productions": Ibid., x.

p. 141 "so exceedingly clear": Ibid., xli–xlii.

p. 141 "I was surprised to find": Ibid., x.

p. 141 "Fish which do not retain their Colours": Ibid., xi.

p. 142 "Some kinds I saw not plenty of": Ibid.

p. 142 He also sent Sloane: McBurney, *INH*, 208.

p. 142 "the Barrenness of these rocky Islands": MC, *Natural History*, I, xviii.

p. 143 "made successive Collections": Ibid., x.

p. 143 "no good aspect": Ibid., xix.

p. 143   "descend the Hills in vast Numbers": MC, *Natural History*, II, 32.

p. 144   "in no less Esteem for Ship-building": Leigh, "Between Swamp and Sea," 525.

p. 144   "a Person of more than common Curiosity": MC, *Natural History*, II, 66.

p. 144   While governors and English merchants: Leigh, "Between Swamp and Sea," 535.

p. 145   "causes a general Fear": MC, *Natural History*, II, 95.

p. 145   He might merely have been: McBurney, *INH*, 54.

p. 145   "the Figures of the most remarkable Trees": MC, *Natural History*, I, xl.

p. 146   Mark Catesby's writings: W. Hardy Eshbaugh, "The Economic Botany and Ethnobotany of Mark Catesby," in *The Curious Mister Catesby*, 206.

p. 146   "Scarcity of it": Amy R. W. Meyers, "Picturing a World in Flux" in Meyers and Beck Pritchard, eds., *Empire's Nature*, 242 n. 16.

Chapter 11 Forerunners 1585–1709

p. 150   Increasing freedom of travel: Anderson, Deep Things out of Darkness, 52. https://www.jstor.org/stable/10.1525/j.ctt24hshw. Accessed January 5, 2022.

p. 150   Unlike Catesby, however: Paul Hulton, *America 1585: The Complete Drawings of John White* (Chapel Hill: University of North Carolina Press; London: British Museum Publications, 1984), 3.

p. 151   There is evidence: Kim Sloan, "Setting the Stage for John White, A Gentleman in Virginia," in *A New World: England's First View of America* (Chapel Hill: University of North Carolina Press, 2007), 11.

p. 151   However, he was already gentleman enough: Sloan, *A New World*, 26.

p. 151   From there the *Tiger* sailed: Hulton, *America 1585*, 9–10.

p. 152   Some, perhaps most, of White's work: Ibid., 12.

p. 153   "The first night we were on the island": Stefan Lorant, ed., *The New World: The First Pictures of America* (New York: Duell, Sloan & Pearce, 1946), 155.

p. 153   Thus began the legend: Hulton, *America 1585*, 14–15.

p. 153   It contained etched versions: Ibid., 17–18.

p. 154   "my fift & last voiage": Quoted in Sloan, *A New World*, 49.

p. 155   Whatever the reason: McBurney, *INH*, 224, 154–155.

p. 156   Dampier's adventurous and curious spirit: Nicholas Thomas, Introduction, in William Dampier, *A New Voyage Round the World* (London: Penguin Books, 2020; Kindle edition.), xvi.

p. 157   By September 1691: Ibid., xvii–xix.

p. 157   "Like Catesby, Dampier": Diana Preston and Michael Preston, *A Pirate of Exquisite Mind: The Life of William Dampier* (London: Transworld, 2010), 63.

p. 157   "I dined with Mr. Pepys": *Diary of John Evelyn*, II, August 25, 1698.

p. 157   "After all, considering that the main of this Voyage": Dampier, *A New Voyage*, 3–4.

p. 158   These artifacts still exist: Thomas, Introduction, in Dampier, *A New Voyage*, i, xx.

p. 158   It inspired Jonathan Swift's: Ibid., viii.

p. 158   "About one thousand entries": Preston and Preston, *A Pirate of Exquisite Mind*, 69.

p. 159   among Sloane's collections: Thomas, Introduction, in Dampier, *A New Voyage*, i.

p. 159   "They frequent the Bahama Islands": MC, *Natural History*, I, 87.

p. 159   Catesby also quoted: MC, *Natural History*, II, Appendix, 6.

p. 159   "Dampier says the Wood": MC, *Natural History*, II, 96.

p. 160   "of exquisite mind": Samuel Taylor Coleridge, *Table Talk of Samuel Taylor Coleridge and The Rime of the Ancient Mariner, Christabel, &c.* (London: George Routledge and Sons, 1884), 145. https://archive.org/details/tabletalksamuel01morlgoog /page/n150/mode/2up. Accessed August 28, 2022.

p. 161   That same year: René Sigrist, "On Some Social Characteristics of the Eighteenth-Century Botanists," in André Holenstein et al., eds., *Scholars in Action: The Practice of Knowledge and the Figure of the Savant in the 18th Century* (Leiden: Brill, 2013), 213.

p. 161   "For I, by His benign favor": Charles Plumier, in Preface to *American Sea, Land, and Sky (Solum, Salam, Caelum Americanum)*, c. 1693–1696. Quoted in Theodore Wells Pietsch, *Charles Plumier, (1646–1704) and His Drawings of French and Caribbean Fishes* (Paris: Publications Scientifiques du Muséum, 2017), 17. https://books.openedition.org/mnhn/5055?lang=en. Accessed August 28, 2022.

p. 161   Most of them were plants: William D. Anderson Jr., review of *Charles Plumier,* by Theodore W. Pietsch, *Copeia* 106 (2018), 399. https://www.jstor.org/stable/10.2307/26872548. Accessed August 13, 2022.

p. 161 Plumier also named the magnolia: Stephen B. Heard, *Charles Darwin's Barnacle and David Bowie's Spider: How Scientific Names Celebrate Adventurers, Heroes, and Even a Few Scoundrels* (New Haven, CT: Yale University Press, 2020), 26.

p. 161 His images of fishes: François J. Meunier, Foreword, in Wells Pietsch, *Charles Plumier*.

p. 162 For the scientific names of plants: Ibid., 196.

p. 163 "The insects' origin and propagation": Todd, *Chrysalis*, 129.

p. 163 "launched herself to a place": Ibid., 146.

p. 163 "experience shows that such Worms": Heard, *Charles Darwin's Barnacle*, 41.

p. 164 "as an abortifacient": Maria Sibylla Merian, *Insects of Surinam* (Los Angeles: Taschen America, 2009), 158; Todd, *Chrysalis*, 180.

p. 164 And also like Catesby: Heard, *Charles Darwin's Barnacle*, 47–48.

p. 164 Merian utilized African and Amerindian collectors: Morgan et al., *Sea and Land*, 123.

p. 165 "before then": Todd, *Chrysalis*, 173.

p. 165 Merian and Catesby both chose: Katharina Schmidt-Loske, "Maria Sibylla Merian's 'extremely costly' journey to nature's treasure house," Introduction to Merian, *Insects of Surinam*, 17.

p. 166 the composition of the Heliconias is uncrowded: Merian, *Insects of Surinam*, 78, 160, 176.

p. 166 This notable addition: Delbourgo, *Collecting the World*, 203–204.

p. 166 "Merian has described them": MC, *Natural History*, II, ix, 9.

p. 167 When reviewing another work: McBurney, *INH*, 217.

p. 167 he spent fifteen months: Delbourgo, *Collecting the World*, 10.

p. 168 "the Royal Society secretary's indispensable guide": Ibid., 168–169.

p. 168 "a Gentleman, who had been abroad": Lawson, *A New Voyage*.

p. 169 *A New Voyage to Carolina* was published: Ibid.

p. 169 Yet another role of Lawson's: M. B. Simpson Jr., "John Lawson's *A New Voyage to Carolina* and His 'Compleat History': The Mark Catesby Connection," in Nelson and Elliott, *The Curious Mister Catesby*, 82.

p. 169 "& such Ingenious Gentlemen": Simpson, 80.

p. 170 A modern scholar has written: Ibid., 75.

p. 170 In his book, Catesby gave Lawson: E. Charles Nelson and Alison A. Petretti, "Mark Catesby's Copy of John Lawson's *The History of Carolina* (London 1714)," *Archives of Natural History*, April 2021, pp. 185–187. https://www.euppublishing.com/doi/full/10.3366/anh.2021.0699. Accessed September 4, 2022.

Chapter 12 London and the *Natural History* 1726–1731

p. 174   But that meant expensive paper: Leslie K. Overstreet, "The Publication of Mark Catesby's *The Natural History of Carolina, Florida, and the Bahama Islands*," in Nelson and Elliott, *The Curious Mister Catesby*, 155.

p. 175   "Gentlemen, most skill'd": MC, *Natural History*, I, xi.

p. 175   for a time he lived on Bond Street: Ellen T. Harris, "Joseph Goupy and George Frideric Handel: From Professional Triumphs to Personal Estrangement," *Huntington Library Quarterly* 71, no. 3 (September 2008): 398. https://www.jstor .org/stable/10.1525/hlq.2008.71.3.397. Accessed July 19, 2022.

p. 175   Goupy was popular: Bruce Robertson and Robert Dance, "Joseph Goupy and the Art of the Copy," *Bulletin of the Cleveland Museum of Art*, 75, no. 10 (December 1988), 360. https://www .jstor.org/stable/25160054. Accessed August 3, 2022.

p. 176   He painted sets: Harris, 405.

p. 176   "beautiful in their own right": Ibid., 370.

p. 176   "At length": MC, *Natural History*, I, xi.

p. 176   He borrowed small elements: McBurney, *INH*, 142–143.

p. 176   Other artists' depictions: McBurney in Nelson and Elliott, *The Curious Mister Catesby*, 150–151; MC, *Natural History*, II, 76.

p. 177   *Proposals, for printing an essay*: Overstreet, in Nelson and Elliott, *The Curious Mister Catesby*, 157.

p. 179   Counting the purchasers: Ibid., 160.

p. 179   a third of those 155 subscribers: Mark Laird and Margaret Riley, "The Congenial Climate of Coffeehouse Horticulture: The Historia plantarum rariorum and the Catalogue plantarum," in National Gallery of Art, *Studies in the History of Art* 69 (2008): 226–259, 234.

p. 179   "an example of subscription publishing": Ibid.

p. 179   They positioned themselves: David Brigham, "Mark Catesby and the Patronage of Natural History in the First Half of the Eighteenth Century," in Meyers and Beck Pritchard, *Empire's Nature*, 139.

p. 179   "at great loss how to introduce": Manuscript statement by Peter Collinson in his copy of *Natural History*, quoted in Frick and Stearns, *Mark Catesby*, 50–51.

p. 180   "he lived more in the broad sunshine": "Richard Mead," *Oxford Dictionary of National Biography* (Oxford: Oxford University Press, 2004), 37: 641.

p. 180   "To this new Genus": MC, *Natural History*, II, Appendix, 1.

p. 181   Catesby apparently lived and worked: Overstreet, in Nelson and Elliott, *The Curious Mister Catesby*, 157.

p. 181   One indication of Catesby's closeness: Quoted in Nelson and Elliott, *The Curious Mister Catesby*, 15.

p. 181   "your uncle Mr. Mark Catesby": George Rutherford to Elizabeth Jones, June 27, 1728. McBurney, *INH*, 278.

p. 182   "I can at present but ill spare": MC to Elizabeth Jones, March 1, 1730.

p. 183   "As I was not bred a Painter": MC, *Natural History*, I, xi.

p. 183   "to follow the humour of the Feathers": Ibid., xi.

p. 183   "I have been less prolix": Ibid., xi–xii.

p. 183   "the Paints, particularly Greens": Ibid., xii.

p. 184   "The whole was done": MC, *Natural History*, II, 20.

p. 184   It is possible that the colorists worked: McBurney, *INH*, 80–81, 88–89.

p. 184   "As to the French Translation": MC, *Natural History*, I, xii.

p. 185   Notably, Catesby was one of the first: Judith Magee, "Following in the Footsteps of Mark Catesby," in *The Curious Mister Catesby,* caption, 285.

p. 186   "was once among the most familiar": Noel F. R. Snyder, *The Carolina Parakeet: Glimpses of a Vanished Bird* (Princeton, NJ: Princeton University Press, 2004), 1.

p. 186   "their guts are certain": MC, *Natural History,* I, 11.

p. 186   This may have been because: J. Drew Lanham, "Forever Gone: How Bird Lives and Black Lives Intertwine under the Long Shadow of History," *Orion Magazine.* https://orionmagazine.org/article/forever-gone. Accessed July 20, 2022.

p. 186   "are destroyed in great numbers": John J. Audubon, *Ornithological Biography*, quoted in Snyder, *The Carolina Parakeet*, 110.

p. 187   "the most abundant bird": Joel Greenberg, *A Feathered River across the Sky: The Passenger Pigeon's Flight to Extinction* (New York: Bloomsbury USA, 2014), 1.

p. 187   "about the size of our English wood-pigeon": MC, *Natural History,* I, 23.

p. 187   "This comes of settling a country!": James Fenimore Cooper, *Leatherstocking Tales, Volume I* (New York: Library of America, 1985), 248.

p. 188   Less than a century: Greenberg, *A Feathered River*, 170.

p. 188   "drooping wings atremble": Ibid., 187–188.

p. 188   Those familiar with the pileated woodpecker: Jerome A. Jackson, *In Search of the Ivory-Billed Woodpecker* (Washington, DC: Smithsonian Books, 2004), 3.

p. 188   "Seeing an ivory-bill": Ibid., 2.

p. 188   "seeks the most towering trees": Alexander Wilson, *American Ornithology*, quoted in Jackson, *In Search*, 43.

p. 189   "The bills of these birds": MC, *Natural History*, I, 16.

p. 189   However, in April 2022: Steven Latta et al., "Multiple Lines of Evidence Indicate Survival of the Ivory-Billed Woodpecker in Louisiana." https://www.biorxiv.org/content/10.1101/2022.04.0 6.487399v1.full.pdf. Accessed April 17, 2022.

p. 189   "They don't want people": Oliver Milman, "Back from the Dead? Elusive Ivory-Billed Woodpecker Not Extinct, Researchers Say," *The Guardian*, April 13, 2022. https://www .theguardian.com/environment/2022/apr/13/ivory-bill-wood pecker-not-extinct-researchers-say. Accessed June 14, 2022.

p. 190   "Very few of the Birds": MC, *Natural History*, I, xii.

p. 191   "I have sent you a continuation": MC to Elizabeth Jones, December 30, 1731; McBurney, *INH*, 268.

p. 192   "There being a Frontice-Piece": Overstreet in Nelson and Elliott, *The Curious Mister Catesby*, 163.

p. 192   At least some: Ibid., 165.

p. 192   "thus happily situated in a Climate": MC, *Natural History*, I, i.

p. 192   "there has been various Conjectures": Ibid., vii.

p. 194   "I confess it is now time": MC, *Natural History*, II, Appendix, 20.

p. 194   "Catesby's noble work": Frick and Stearns, *Mark Catesby*, 42.

Chapter 13 The "Curious and Magnificent Work" 1731–1746

p. 197   "LONDON—The last week": *Newcastle Courant*, May 31, 1729, 3.

p. 198   "The illustrations were so unique": Andrea Wulf, *The Brother Gardeners*, 27.

p. 198   Twenty guineas was a little more: B. R. Mitchell, *British Historical Statistics* (New York: Cambridge University Press, 1988), 153.

p. 198   A standard novel: Porter, *English Society in the Eighteenth Century*, 235.

p. 199   "I esteem it a singular Happiness": MC, *Natural History*, I, dedication, unpaginated.

p. 199   "The women of the Hanoverian court": Edward Dolnick, *The Clockwork Universe: Isaac Newton, the Royal Society, and the Birth of the Modern World* (New York: HarperCollins, 2011), 263.

p. 199   Caroline was probably more savvy: Ackroyd, *Revolution*, 93.

p. 199   Her youth had been spent: Wolf Burchard and Kathryn Jones,
          "The German Princesses as British Patrons," in Joanna Marschner,
          David Bindman, and Lisa L. Ford, eds. *Enlightened Princesses:
          Caroline, Augusta, Charlotte, and the Shaping of the Modern World*
          (New Haven, CT: Yale University Press, 2017), 109.

p. 199   "You may have more wit": Brian Young, "Caroline of Ansbach:
          The Brainpower behind the Throne of George II," *The Telegraph*,
          November 19, 2017. https://www.telegraph.co.uk/books/what
          -to-read/caroline-ansbach-brainpower-behind-throne-george-ii/.
          Accessed October 1, 2022.

p. 200   "play[ed] an important part": Marschner, Bindman, and Ford,
          Enlightened Princesses, ix.

p. 200   "charms of her person": William Coxe, *Memoirs of the Life and
          Administration of Sir Robert Walpole, Earl of Orford* (London:
          Longman, Hurst, Rees, Orme, & Brown, 1816), 271.

p. 200   "a stuffed hummingbird": Burchard and Jones, 125.

p. 200   Caroline also took her children: Clarissa Campbell Orr,
          "Conversations, Knowledge, and Influence," in Marschner,
          Bindman, and Ford, *Enlightened Princesses*, 280.

p. 200   "if pervasive influence is taken as the criterion": Joseph Roach,
          "Public and Private Stages," in Marschner, Bindman, and Ford,
          Enlightened Princesses, 164.

p. 201   Together with Frederick: Joanna Marschner, "Becoming British:
          The Role of the Hanoverian Queen Consort," in Anke Gilleir
          and Aude Defurne, eds., *Strategic Imaginations: Women and the
          Gender of Sovereignty in European Culture* (Leuven, Belgium:
          Leuven University Press, 2020), 244.

p. 201   Augusta also developed another interest: Mark Laird, "An August
          Domain: Gardening and Collecting in the Princesses' Kew," in
          Marschner, Bindman, and Ford, *Enlightened Princesses*, 139.

p. 201   "Our Author proposes": Cromwell Mortimer, "An Account of
          Mark Catesby's Essay . . . ," *Philosophical Transactions* (October
          31, 1730), 425.

p. 202   "Mark Catesby a Gentleman well Skill'd": Quoted in Frick and
          Stearns, *Mark Catesby*, 38.

p. 202   a missive from William Byrd in Virginia: Ibid., 40–41.

p. 202   Catesby added to the society's store: Ibid., 41.

p. 203   Catesby continued to mine his knowledge: McBurney, *INH*, 216.

p. 203   It's easy to imagine Catesby: Ibid., 62.

p. 204 "when Carl Linnaeus": Birkhead, *The Wonderful Mr Willughby*, 235–236.

p. 204 But the power of Linnaeus's ideas: McBurney, *INH*, 218.

p. 204 Nor, in the absence of clear and concise illustrations: Andrea Wulf, *The Brother Gardeners*, 116.

p. 205 Linnaeus bestowed the names: C. E. Jarvis, "Carl Linnaeus and the Influence of Mark Catesby's Botanical Work," in Nelson and Elliott, *The Curious Mister Catesby*, 201.

p. 205 Through his work cataloguing the royal libraries: Jarvis, "Carl Linnaeus and the Influence of Mark Catesby's Botanical Work," 194–195.

p. 205 "if but a few of them be acceptable": MC to Linnaeus, March 26, 1745; McBurney, *INH*, 275.

p. 206 "I am told of an animal": MC to Bartram, undated but probably 1742.

p. 206 "The reading of thy acceptable letter": Bartram to MC, undated but c. 1741.

p. 207 "I infer from this": MC to Dillenius, postmarked February 3, 1736.

p. 208 "Lying on the Deck of a Sloop": MC, "Of Birds of Passage, by Mr. Mark Catesby, F.R.S. Read at a Meeting of the Royal Society, March 5. 1746–7," *Philosophical Transactions of the Royal Society* (March–May 1747), 438.

p. 208 "when, by the Approach of our Winter": Ibid., 435.

p. 208 "found out, and coveted": Ibid., 443–444.

p. 209 "These authors have done very little": Bartam, *Travels*, 236.

p. 209 "so impoverished himself": Frick and Stearns, *Mark Catesby*, 86.

p. 210 "He had faults": Krech, "Catesby's Birds," 290.

p. 210 "A number of Catesby's images": Ibid., 289.

p. 210 "is very well known": Frick and Stearns, *Mark Catesby*, 47.

Chapter 14: Nurseryman and Experimental Horticulturalist 1731–1749

p. 212 "turn the rare exotics": Laird and Riley, "The Congenial Climate," 241.

p. 213 The craze for North American plants: Mark Laird, "From Callicarpa to Catalpa: The Impact of Mark Catesby's Plant Introductions on English Gardens of the Eighteenth Century," in Meyers and Beck Pritchard, eds., *Empire's Nature*, 184.

p. 213 "a vast network of intellectual and material exchange": Therese O'Malley, "The Culture of Gardens," in *Empire's Nature*, 149.

p. 213   When Stephen Bacon died: Elliott, in *The Curious Mister Catesby*, 327.

p. 213   Gray had been born: Kathleen Clark, "What the Nurserymen Did for Us: The Roles and Influence of the Nursery Trade on the Landscapes and Gardens of the Eighteenth Century," *Garden History* 40, no. 1 (Summer 2012): 28–29. https://www .jstor.org/stable/41719885. Accessed January 30, 2021.

p. 213   Peter Kalm in 1748: Quoted in McBurney, *INH*, 157–158.

p. 214   Although the broadside is undated: McBurney, *INH*, 96, 98.

p. 214   thirty-five of the seventy-two plants: Ibid., 96.

p. 214   "This stately Tree": MC, *Natural History*, II, 61.

p. 215   though not legal under Church law: "Fleet Marriages." https ://www.familyhistory.co.uk/parish-records/fleet-marriages. Accessed October 13, 2022.

p. 215   "May Fair stands": John Southerden Burn, *The Fleet Registers: Comprising the History of Fleet Marriages, and Some Account of the Parsons and Marriage-House Keepers . . .* (London: Rivingtons et al., 1833), 96.

p. 215   "porch at the door": Burn, 98.

p. 215   There Catesby and Elizabeth were married: https://www.find mypast.co.uk/transcript?id=TNA%2FRG7%2FMAR%2F00305 595%2F1. Accessed October 10, 2022.

p. 216   They created or modified: David Jacques, *Gardens of Court and Country: English Design, 1630–1730* (New Haven, CT: Yale University Press, 2017); quoted in Floud, *England's Magnificent Gardens*, 61.

p. 216   Firs, pines, and plane trees: Floud, *England's Magnificent Gardens*, 62–63.

p. 216   This colonial expansion: Ibid., 348.

p. 217   "To consider how many authors": Batty Langley, *New principles of gardening: or, The laying out and planting parterres, groves, wildernesses, labyrinths, avenues, parks, &c . . .* (1728), iii, Eighteenth Century Collections Online, link.gale.com/apps /doc/CW0108660926/ECCO?u=tel_a_uots&sid=bookmark -ECCO&xid=b3d47876&pg=18. Accessed March 26, 2022.

p. 217   "grand and elegant Taste": Ibid., iv.

p. 217   "when we come to copy, or imitate Nature": Ibid., vi, vii.

p. 217   "associated with patriotism and rustic virtue": Todd Longstaffe -Gowan, "Hankering after Horticulture," in Marschner, Bindman, and Ford, *Enlightened Princesses*, 353.

p. 218 In 1734 Frederick, Prince of Wales: Floud, *England's Magnificent Gardens*, 64.

p. 218 "yet we find the Taste at that Time": Philip Miller, *The Gardeners Dictionary*, 2nd ed. (1733), ix.

p. 218 "on every aspect of horticulture": Wulf, *The Brother Gardeners*, 34.

p. 218 Mark Catesby, who had sent Miller seeds: Ibid., 46.

p. 219 The very name: Ibid., 37.

p. 219 By 1731, Miller had transformed: Ibid., 38, 39.

p. 219 "the seeds of this Plant": Philip Miller, *Figures of the Most Beautiful, Useful and Uncommon Plants Described in the Gardeners Dictionary* (London, 1755), 18; quoted in Anishanslin, *Portrait of a Woman in Silk*, 93.

p. 219 "The Trees & Shrubs": Peter Collinson to John Bartram, December 3, 1741; quoted in Anishanslin, *Portrait of a Woman in Silk*, 93.

p. 220 "Catalpah called so by the Indians": British Natural History Museum, London; quoted in McBurney, *INH*, 100–101.

p. 220 "was unknown to the inhabited parts of Carolina": MC, *Natural History*, I, 49.

p. 220 "it is since become naturalized": MC, *Hortus Britanno-americanus*, 25.

p. 221 In the decade and a half: Laird and Riley, "The Congenial Climate," 227, 243.

p. 221 The eighty-five "Curious Trees and Shrubs": David J. Elliott, "Conclusions: Account, Appendix, *Hortus*, and Other Endings in Mark Catesby's Work," in Nelson and Elliott, *The Curious Mister Catesby*, 328.

p. 222 "this monument, this self-composed epitaph": Frick and Stearns, *Mark Catesby*, 69.

p. 222 "many kinds of American plants": MC, *Hortus britanno-americanus*, i.

p. 222 Catesby was elected an honorary member: McBurney, *INH*, 14, 63.

p. 223 "tall, meagre, hard favoured": Quoted in Frick and Stearns, *Mark Catesby*, 46.

p. 223 "I will not vindicate my silence": MC to Bartram, November 17, 1748; see McBurney, *INH*, 277, first n2.

p. 223 "poor Mr. Catesby's Legs": E. Charles Nelson, "'The Truly Honest, Ingenious, and Modest Mr. Mark Catesby, F.R.S.':

Documenting His Life (1682/83–1749)," in Nelson and Elliott, *The Curious Mister Catesby*, 17.

p. 224 "Crossing the way in holbore": Edwards to Thomas Pennant, December 5, 1761; quoted in McBurney, *INH*, 19.

p. 224 "On Saturday morning": *Gentleman's Magazine*, XX (1750), 30–31.

p. 225 "He was in his behaver": Edwards to Thomas Pennant, December 5, 1761; quoted in McBurney, *INH*, 65.

Epilogue

p. 227 "to my loving cousin": Quoted in McBurney, *INH*, 1.

p. 227 "whole fortune": Edwards to Pennant, December 5, 1761; quoted in McBurney, *INH*, 65.

p. 228 "Catesby was always more erratic": Frick and Stearns, *Mark Catesby*, 100.

p. 228 In 1771, four decades after the first printing: Ibid.

p. 228 as late as 1818: Ibid., 105.

p. 230 "the Largest White-Bill Woodpecker": MC, *Natural History*, I, 16.

p. 230 Linnaeus later consulted the *Natural History*: Alan Feduccia, ed. *Catesby's Birds of Colonial America*. The Fred W. Morrison Series in Southern Studies (Chapel Hill, NC: University of North Carolina Press, 1985), xi.

p. 231 Illustrations of plants and animals began appearing without backgrounds: Judith Magee, "Following in the Footsteps of Catesby," in Nelson and Elliott, *The Curious Mister Catesby*, 286.

p. 231 "In Linnaeus's wake": Todd, *Chrysalis*, 201–202.

p. 231 Universities and laboratories: Ibid., 246.

p. 231 Their ways of cataloguing and presenting information: Iannini, *Fatal Revolutions*, 125.

p. 232 "founder of American ornithology": Frick and Stearns, *Mark Catesby*, 56.

p. 233 "Among amphibian and reptile species": Aaron M. Bauer, "Catesby's Animals (Other Than Birds) in *The Natural History of Carolina, Florida and the Bahama Islands*," in Nelson and Elliott, *The Curious Mister Catesby*, 264.

p. 233 In 1920: Frick and Stearns, *Mark Catesby*, 67.

p. 233 "Mark Catesby, whose [work] marks the beginning": Quoted in David Yih, "Mark Catesby: Pioneering Naturalist, Artist, and Horticulturist," *Arnoldia: The Magazine of the Arnold Arboretum* (February 2013), 36. http://arnoldia.arboretum.harvard.edu

/pdf/articles/2013-70-3-mark-catesby-pioneering-naturalist
-artist-and-horticulturist.pdf. Accessed January 16, 2022.

p. 234 Over nine hundred of his dried plants: McBurney, *INH*, 210,
221–222.

p. 234 Cabinet ministers being driven: Laird, "From Callicarpa to
Catalpa," in Meyers and Beck Pritchard, *Empire's Nature*, 224;
author email from Paul Wood, October 26, 2022.

p. 234 "embodied a fusion of empire and information": Delbourgo,
Collecting the World, 341.

p. 235 Recently, researchers with Britain's National Trust: Sam Knight,
"Britain's Idyllic Country Houses Reveal a Darker History,"
New Yorker, August 23, 2021.

p. 235 "Scratch almost any institution": Maya Jasanoff, "Operation
Legacy: How the British Remember Their Empire—or Fail To,"
New Yorker, November 2, 2020, 81.

INDEX